IN THE COMPANY OF PATRIOTS

VIRGINIA BRACKETT

Virginia Brackett

To Anne-Marie - a sister of words

SUNBURY PRESS
Mechanicsburg, PA USA

Published by Sunbury Press, Inc.
Mechanicsburg, Pennsylvania

www.sunburypress.com

ISBN: 978-1-62006-344-6 (Trade paperback)

Library of Congress Control Number: 2019951545

FIRST SUNBURY PRESS EDITION: October 2019

Product of the United States of America
0 1 1 2 3 5 8 13 21 34 55

Set in Adobe Garamond
Designed by Crystal Devine
Cover by Lawrence Knorr
Edited by Andrianna Dowell

Continue the Enlightenment!

To my Grands:

Masyn, Katherine, Rory, Presli, Sam, Tom, and Bo:

my seven points of light.

- CONTENTS -

INTRODUCTION

I have no memory of my father, Captain Ed Roberts, who was killed by a sniper in Korea when I was eight months old. Now, over a span of more than a half century, I seek to know him. In-depth knowledge remains unlikely at such distance of both space and time. Still, I want to share anything I may learn of his life and of my own process of discovery. If I succeed, others may benefit. They might also know more of a worthy life, knowledge that generally adds value to our own lives. As to how success can be measured, that will be revealed over time. In addition, I hope readers may comprehend the grace of enlightenment that I received during my journey. I understand the term "grace" via the Protestant fold in which I matured as "undeserved merit."

The little knowledge of Ed Roberts that supported the early steps of my journey came from rare stories told by my mother, Helen. I call them stories, rather than history, because the concept of history suggests facts. Stories, on the other hand, allow for perspective and the addition of new voices in their retelling. Across time's chasm, the clearest shouts become echoes. Details are muted, and sense emerges. Facts remain important but are not all-crucial to human understanding.

Helen didn't talk often about Ed because, before I became old enough to ask the inevitable questions, I had another father. My stepfather, a fine, quiet man, loved me as well as my sister and brother without question. Our strong family unit, crafted with care and precision, later welcomed the birth of a new member, his daughter and our half-sister.

Helen likely felt little need to introduce a possibly troubling ghost to our table. Naturally, she and my aunt and uncle referred to Ed from time to time, often with humor and always with respect. When the day came that I asked for information, Helen hid nothing. She had buried Ed physically but had never intended to bury her memories. Like all memories, however, they were tempered by loss, softened by age. Our one extended conversation grew into an article, the first of my published writing. But I never returned to ask more, to learn more, to write more. Then she was gone.

When I think of symbolic acts I've seen in movies or read about in literature that relate to accessing the memories or the thoughts of another, my favorite is the donning of that Other's glasses. The act suggests that one might gain access to another's vision. The other day, I pulled my mother's glasses from the drawer where they've been for the many years following her death. I put them on, but far from sharpening my vision, they blurred it. In that manner, I created my own symbolism, understanding that we can never adopt another's vision as our own. Where my mother's vision sharpened her perceptions, it could not sharpen mine. I would need much more than her input to eventually form my own vision of my father. That realization somewhat eases my frustration, and, in a sense, my guilt over having waited so long to pursue my elusive goal.

I decided that I would also seek to celebrate the journey that coming to know my father represents. Honestly, I began this search not only for my father, but for what my clearer vision of him will mean to my sense of self and to that of my children and grandchildren. That new vision will surely be revealed during the journey. Boxes of family artifacts existed, waiting to be opened by new fingers. I knew that any discovery I made might open the gate to a new path on my journey to understand. The family depends upon me to tell the story, which will naturally extend beyond my own field of sight. I felt some trepidation over what I might discover; details that may not support the label "hero," often applied to one who dies in service to country. And so, I set to work with a mixed set of skills at hand—those of exploration and adventure, but also of self-defense.

A few months into the project, I discovered that I needn't have been concerned with disappointment, disillusionment, or my ability to complete the task. As so often happens with initiatives of this sort, once in process, they in no way resemble the form first envisioned. My project has been supported by perspectives that have transformed its shape, size and significance. Matters I had not imagined loom large, relegating many of my basic concerns to the shadows. All emerge into light and take focus through their relationship to input from the many voices that contribute to this narrative. Some speak of sympathy and faith to my mother in letters of condolence; voices of a different timbre ring from official government correspondence; the radio voice of Cedric Foster reads a letter from my mother, her voice on the air. I find a different focus from poetry written by Korean War veterans and their families; from my own correspondence with veterans quick to respond to my request for assistance; from the chauvinistic journalism of wartime; and from my conversations with colleagues. I began the project seeking to understand my father only through what I perceived as a personal loss, a piece missing from my life. But I came to see that the localized understanding with which I began could not shed any true light on my self-conflict or vision of my father. That fallacy revealed itself through the remembrance and reflection of others, voices in wavelengths that bend, deflect and emerge anew, like white light through a prism. The resultant color replaces shadows in the room that is my father's life and my own.

I dedicate this project of discovery and knowing to that multitude who first embraced, and then overpowered, my own mission. They also helped me understand that such an initiative rarely finds a natural end. It evolves into the future, further than my limited vision can see, growing with stories from new generations. A few years before beginning my research, I asked my younger daughter to transcribe the words of her grandfather from his Korean War letters. Her reaction to interacting with him in that manner proved profound, producing the thoughts at the book's conclusion.

Speaking voices of World War II and the Korean War, like those that assisted me, continue to rapidly fade. Happily, technology allows them to bequeath a certain treasure of writing and recordings, a rich inheritance that offers opportunity, as well as responsibility. By preserving many stories through endless journeys of discovery like my own, we move beyond a simple self-focused desire for knowledge. A restructured project becomes one of remembrance and honor. In the book *Poems of the Korean War: the Hermit Kingdom*, Maureen Hurley may best express this thought as she writes,

> When I wear the clothing of the dead,
> they see glimpses of light again ("Sixth of August").

- CHAPTER ONE -

"SUCH FINE MEN"

September 27, 2006

My name is Virginia Brackett, and I am searching for information about my father, who you would have known as Lieutenant Edmund C. Roberts of the DO Company 422nd. I never knew my father, as he died fighting as a Captain in Korea when I was eight months old. This many years later, I am researching his involvement in two wars and hoping to come to know him a little better . . . If you have even the slightest memory of my father that you would not mind sharing, I would be immensely grateful.

Personal Correspondence – Virginia Brackett

I never knew my father. And when I began what I thought of as a search to find that knowledge, a number of questions stood poised for the asking, one of the most important being "What part of me is like him?" That seemed a healthy question that almost anyone would judge "normal." When I decided to seek that knowledge, I began my journey searching for those with whom he shared a relationship perhaps even more intimate than that shared with family—the military men he trained with, lived with, and accompanied into battle. Their assessment, even at this distance of several decades, might be revealed in something other than the golden aura that seems today to hover over all who die in military service. Newspaper articles and personal correspondence to my mother often describe my father as a "hero." One might expect such reference to a soldier at various times missing in action, a prisoner of war, and, finally, killed by a Korean sniper's bullet, fighting at a time when America's position as a world leader was clear and accepted.

Yet, I bear a cautious cynicism regarding the word "hero." As with many such reductive terms, the word "hero" has been overused, rendering it almost a cliché, and one might argue misapplied when measured against the classical definition of the term. The change over time, if not agreeable, may yet be understandable, as ours is a culture in love with labels; we crave compartmentalization. That craving for the larger-than-life human depiction of those sometimes sadly victimized, or simply in the wrong place at the wrong time, betrays a rejection of our own humanity, a rejection I view as unhealthy. It represents denial and stymies the result we seek, which is an understanding of the motivations behind our actions, heroic or not. Multiple sources labeled my father as not only a hero but also a soldier's soldier, the finest man several of my mother's correspondents had ever known. The realist in me longed for the smallest hint of negativity. The cardboard cutout I visualized badly needed dimension, a literal edge, added through a realistic approach to the development of his character. How could I know my father without some hint of his weaknesses, the character warts we all seek to conceal?

My brother Bruce knows more of him than I and has a more balanced view, but even his knowledge remains shrouded in the veil of half-truth. He was only eight years old when Captain Ed Roberts died. What if in my pursuit of others who knew Ed and who might offer some insight that none of our remaining family members possessed, we learn things we do not want to know? Should I open the family mythology to the balance that any negative comments about him might offer? My project would focus on the personalization of the effect of war, rather than on the historic events of the wars in which he participated. That public history would naturally prove crucial, providing context for my more personal history. But the most important context would be the individual input by strange voices, those foreign to our comfortable circle.

Yet another question encroached my comfort zone. As I learn more about my father's dedication to the military, will I better accept an ideology that contradicts my own? I don't understand war, other than on the simplest level of comprehending the meaning of terms such as power, control, killing, and more recently, terrorism. In an early attempt to gain insight, I talked to my husband, an authority by virtue of participation, about his Vietnam service. A lefty peacenik from way back, he openly states he would have "dodged" the draft had the opportunity presented itself. However, he surprises me by explaining that even so, he values his military time. He served six months in-country as a medic and doesn't emphasize the waste and brutality. Rather, he appreciates the unique situational immediacy and resultant bonding between servicemen as positive aspects of a regrettable situation. That thought reminds me of a Studs Terkel interview in his book, *The Good War.* One interviewee states, "The reason you storm the beaches is not patriotism or bravery . . . It's that sense of not wanting to fail your buddies. There's . . . a special sense of kinship" (Rasmus).

My father may have felt that kinship strongly enough to "re-up," a term I've learned means a re-enlistment in the military following the fulfillment of one's initial contract or inscription. It's one of many new words I'm learning, as I consider my father's choices. I appreciate that lack of common language often challenges communication and understanding. I experienced that challenge as I began formal research for this book. I mistakenly e-mailed an organization representing the 17th Artillery, rather than the 17th Infantry, of which my father was a part. I received a gently corrective response:

> Virginia,
> If no one has directed you yet, I suggest this site for your
> search: www.17thinfantry.com/korea.asp
> i got your message from our site, 17th ARTILLERY which
> is not the same as 17th INFANTRY.
> Good luck, Doug

Thank you, Doug.

But more importantly, I remind myself that true communication between individuals may also be challenged by a lack of common experience. I observe this constantly in the classroom, where a large number of international students not only enrich classroom interaction for me, but also for the students born and raised in the United States. Early in my career, I chose a textbook that emphasized American pop culture and its effect on marketing. The first assignment instructed students to write about packaging in the common supermarket and their experience in selecting items for purchase. As one Kenyan student explained, "In Africa we rarely or never think of packaging as we buy things in the market and they are not packaged. With this [assignment], we can't participate in any discussion." I tried to visualize myself, like this student, in a foreign environment, such as that my father experienced in Korea. I can't truly visualize the physical landscape, but I can imagine his frustration and, more specifically, his fear. Fear always relates to things unknown, just as familiarity generally brings some sense of comfort and diminishes threat. The army structure and personnel offered my father that familiarity through structure, ritual, and that language, which I may misunderstand. My saving grace is that one needn't completely understand in order to learn.

I began this journey armed mainly with knowledge about my father that grew from family comments and my often over-active imagination. I assume such power of invention may have led me to simply make up what I wanted to believe about my absent father, as it had in other areas. I once wrote a detailed description of my first dog, a cocker spaniel mix named Junior. My story came complete with the image of my opening the front door on my sixth birthday to find my cousin holding a black puppy, a large red bow around its neck. Years later as I related this story to my mother, I noticed her forehead wrinkling. "I remember the dog," she told me, "but I don't think it was a birthday present." In an indignant phone call made to elicit support from my sister Kay, I asked what details she remembered regarding my acquisition of Junior. "I remember the dog," she said, "but I don't remember a red bow. Was he really a birthday gift?"

Puzzled and slightly insulted by their responses, I resolved to mentally catalog additional details that completed my specific memory. They included distinct sensory recollections of that puppy, complete with smell and touch. Junior would come in from the brisk outside air smelling elemental and salty, like blood or perspiration. He did not just wag his tail, which my Uncle Don had not docked to the familiar cocker stub, but instead employed it to produce a full-body wiggle, a festival of jubilation, as only puppies can. My memory featured his tongue's pink warmth everywhere at once, as I took him from my cousin's arms—up my nostril, sweeping across an eyelid, flicking an earlobe, then an elbow. I later shared with my class that in that specific instance of the birthday present dog, I preferred, and elected to keep, my own (perhaps) enriched story in lieu of sketchy family details. However, as I prepared these years later to ask questions regarding my father, I wondered whether I stood emotionally equipped to watch far more important mythology challenged, whether I could accept the sharper and perhaps less appealing image that might emerge. For now, that image of my father had no specific shape. An amorphous cloud, it swirled around my head and settled like a mantle on my shoulders, light and undemanding. Who knew what it might later become, as it grew corners and peaks, a narrative form reshaping its once-soft folds into sharp points of realization.

The choice of narrative form provokes yet another question. How might I frame this journey so as to interest others? Some might label it a self-indulgent intellectual exercise, a pretentious attempt to hijack my father's life and shape it to my will. I find painful that others could judge my study soulless, but how to imbue it with a soul? More importantly, how could I lend this narrative what now seemed an elusive air of truth?

While putting in time on our elliptical rider, I often listen to National Public Radio. One day I realized that what draws me to NPR is not only its many voices but more specifically, their varied concepts of truth. Commentators on "human interest" shows introduce common topics, then allow everyday people to tell their stories. As if by magic, what may appear quite ordinary or mundane when stated as a general topic, becomes through this specific framing of storytelling and personalization extraordinary, or even mystical.

For instance, one woman received an odd, but still seemingly unexciting charge; she was to collect human hair in an Atlantic state for an art project taking shape a world away in China. At first repelled at the thought of having to "handle" hair from unknown origins, she set about gathering ounces that soon equaled pounds of curls, top knots, dreadlocks, and split ends, all to become, in the hands of another, art. It was that promise that moved her, the dream that cast-offs from our bodies might shape medium with the potential to move our souls. The Chinese artist wove hair gathered from around the world into a braid many feet long, dyed multiple colors in its final rendering. The artist sought to suggest unity in the braid's blending of millions of strands, a representation of the fact that we are all players in the drama labeled the human condition.

The artist contributed the fewest words to the report, while the reporter shaped the largest number. The observations of the worker, the at-first-repelled woman, swept away in the end by the shape her efforts took, framed the actions with color and passion and verve. Each narrator perceived the project differently, but each proved necessary to the story. Like those participating in that initiative, I must examine so-called "facts" from many perspectives and try to identify a commonality. As I would discover, some of those perspectives did not agree. One person cautioned me not to trust the report of another. He wrote that he had "discovered that his recollection of Korea and mine were 180 degrees apart." For me, the distance between now and then would not be measured by a narrative straight line or even the rigidity of "truth." Rather, my charge would be to represent narrative waves that ebbed, flowed, and at times crashed against one another. My job was not to interrogate contrasting truths that I could never resolve, but rather to listen, read, and hopefully find a pattern in the weaving of those narratives from which I could draw some sense of my father's life.

The pattern pieces do emerge clearly from my many sources. I read of one centuries-old on a typed page from my mother's, Helen's, genealogy search that emphasizes the irony and chance inherent to all life experience. The particular discovery would remain unknown to Ed, of course, and would not even have existed as a realized connection had he not died in Korea. Helen detects a bloodline connection between Ed and her second husband, my step-father Bob, which amazed her.

> 26 December 1986
>
> On 21 June 1919 in Galesburg, Illinois, Edmund Condon Roberts, Jr was born to Edmund C. and Winifred (Aylesbury) Roberts. Less than 30 days later Helen W. [her middle name was WinoJeanne, which she detested and rarely referenced] was born in Galesburg, Ill. To John Clinton and Elsie Maud (Copeland) Kost. Helen and Ed were married in Galesburg on 18 December 1941. Ed was killed in Korea on 3 January 1951, leaving Helen and three children: Bruce Ingram Roberts, Linda Kay Roberts and Mary Virginia 'Ginger' Roberts.
>
> On 13 December 1953 Helen met Robert Francis 'Bob' Ferranti, and they were married 6 May 1954 in Pine Bluff, Ark., and on 13 August 1955, Nancy Lillys Ferranti was born in Pine Bluff.
>
> After working on their individual genealogies for about ten or twelve years, Helen had exhausted her line and started working on Ed's lines. In October of this year, an amazing discovery was made in New Hampshire. Ed and Bob had a common ancestor, Nicholas Gaylord, born in Normandy, France, in 1525, and died in Pitminster, Somerset, England. Nicholas was the father of John, born in Pitminster about 1558, a direct ancestor of Ed, and the father of Hugh, born about 1553 in Pitminster, and a direct ancestor of Bob. The attached ancestor charts shows this relationship.

I do find the shared ancestry of my father and step-father of interest, but I find more interesting the summary approach common to family histories. Lives tidily contained in a sentence, or in some instances, a few phrases map themselves in facts about birth, marriage, offspring, and death. The flow charts that result from a genealogy study contain vital bits of information that allow those who come later to know those who came before. It is history to satisfy the minimalist and yields much wealth.

I find in one storage container an ancient scrapbook, brimming with yellowed newspaper clippings dating to the 19th century. The first page bears a label in all upper-case letters: ROBERTS. Beneath it appears a lovely hand-written inscription: "This Book is for Jesse I. Roberts—a gift from his Mother." "His Mother" signs beneath her statement, "Cornelia Roberts. June 24th 1889." The last half of the scrapbook maintains a family history that focuses on the forbearers of Ed Roberts. In addition to the many articles from Missouri, there are also newspapers from Kentucky. I find a page of ancestor summaries in my mother's handwriting that begins, "Jesse C. Ingram and Cornelia Ingram went to St. Joe by steamboat from Dover, Tenn. in 1851. Dover was known as Ft. Donelson during [the] Civil War." One relation about whom I find multiple articles is H. Clay Roberts from Nashville, Tennessee who died in 1880 at age 46. He had served in the Tennessee House of Representatives and the Senate and was a candidate for Congress at the time of his sudden death. The full text of multiple addresses he made while serving in Tennessee is printed in the paper.

Family correspondence reveals members moving from Tennessee and bringing slaves along. Because I matured in Arkansas, the legacy of slavery is familiar, if uncomfortable. While I'm slightly dismayed by this information, I am hardly surprised. In the spring of 1852, for instance, James Kay (this family line is the source of my older sister's middle name), along with the J. C. Ingram mentioned above, father of Mrs. James C. Roberts, left Dover, Tennessee. The families took forty-five slaves and traveled by "steam packet" down the Cumberland and Ohio Rivers and up the Mississippi and Missouri Rivers to St. Joe. Mrs. Roberts, my mother writes, "is quoted in 1906, 'colored people were very scarce in this part of the country at that time, and the clerks used to come out of the stores to look at the slaves that we brought along.'" A clipping from the 1830s reads, "James C. Roberts, Esqr., a former member of the Legislature from this county, yesterday sent off upwards of 20,000 dollars worth [*sic*] of Negroes belonging to himself and his father-in-law, Jesse C. Ingram. They were sent into Kansas via Platte County Railroad to Atchison, taking a large amount of furniture and clothing." I lived in Platte County, Missouri when I began this project about 50 miles south of St. Joseph, Missouri, the St. Joe the family references. The family's southern sensibilities become evident as I turn the pages, which contain many items focusing on the Civil War, including an obituary for Mrs. Robert E. Lee and a program from the Seventh Annual Reunion of United Confederate Veterans from Nashville, Tennessee, June 22–24, 1897.

In addition to the family history, I find a full manuscript of poems titled "The Grocery Garden," written by my great-grandmother, Mrs. Jessie I. (Eva Donovan) Roberts. I find many additional poems, among them one titled "I Am Not Dead," its voice that of one who had died, "called . . . to come home" to God, and I wonder whether Eva Roberts wrote that after losing her child.

I began multiple conversations in the first stages of my investigation. They arise from a colleague also writing of war and its participants; with vets from my father's World War II Battalion (one, who as a prisoner, shared the Stalag made infamous by Kurt Vonnegut in *Slaughterhouse Five*); with vets from my father's Korean War Regiment (one will tell me he was among the last to speak with my father); with the Korean War vet and his son who founded and staffed the local Center for the Study of the Korean War; with a librarian from the University of Chicago about the politician, author and member of Eisenhower's cabinet, Robert E. Merriam, (one of several) with whom my father corresponded. I also held one-way conversations with silent sources, including yellowed wartime newspaper clippings; a 1951 radio broadcast from Boston by Cedric Foster reading a letter from my mother about my father's death; the stack of my mother's personal wartime correspondence with friends and family; the stack of her formal wartime correspondence, mostly following Ed's death, from governors, senators, college presidents, a secretary of war, commanding General Van Fleet and the faceless U.S. Government; a book of poetry written by Korean War veterans. Will I discover the truth about war and my father from these many narratives? I do not know.

The slightest remark adds knowledge. I would meet with my father's dear friend, Dean Lindstrom, 70 years later in the Lindstrom's T.V. and Appliance Store, a fixture in Galesburg, Illinois since 1925. At that point, three generations of Dean's family had run the business. After I introduce myself, he cries as he speaks softly about my father and shares memories of their childhood and college days. I listen, admiring his sharp remembrances and the still-acute feeling of loss that permeates his statements. I ask a question I had long wanted to ask of someone who knew my father as a young man. Because no one else I knew of in Ed's family had served in the military, I wonder why service held such attraction. "I don't know," Dean tells me. "I do know that we called him 'Sarge,' even as kids, but I don't know how or why that began. He always wanted to be a soldier." This related fact—a boy nicknamed Sarge—lacked the element of motivation for my father's actions I hoped to find. Such motivation is seldom identified by children to support childhood fantasy; they have no need to explain their actions. But it also relieved me of the burden of seeking an answer that likely remains unavailable. In 2011, I will read Dean's obituary in the online version of Galesburg's newspaper, *The Register-Mail.* He was hailed by all as a personable man who liked people and enjoyed his job, typical of those of his generation and too-rare in today's impersonal business climate.

The aspect of this search that leaves me most humbled and grateful is my interaction with those like Dean, but especially the military veterans who knew Ed and those who did not. A troublesome aspect of that connection is the fact that we lose them daily. In an issue of *The Cub of the Golden Lion*, published for decades by and for the veterans of my father's 106th Infantry Division, the Adjutant asked, in light of its dwindling membership, "Should the 106th Association be retired or continue for life?" Only ten percent of the present membership can attend reunions and finding members willing to serve on the board becomes increasingly difficult. The Association's Second Vice President had to enter the hospital, the Adjutant explained, and when released, entered a nursing home for recovery. Fortunately, the Vice President returned home, but many will never return from such institutions. This incident remains a portent of the future. As the Chaplain's message in *The Cub* notes, he often asks himself when listening to those speaking of their POW experience, "What produced such fine men? Why didn't their horrendous experiences embitter them and debase their lives?" (Trueman). We will soon lack this invaluable resource. Too few of those in succeeding generations understand until they spend time with the WWII veterans how that war defined many of those men's lives, especially in the case of the enlisted men. Thankfully, many projects for remembrance of this remarkable group, along with the veterans of the Korean War, are in process.

Through my correspondence, a veteran directs me to one such project. This website focuses on Korean War veterans, a less-celebrated group than those of WWII. At his urging, I visit a link to that site, staring in amazement at what I discover. The first line reads, "Korean War Project Casualty Entry For," the second line had my father's name, and the third line "Hostile, Died (KIA)." I clicked on a "further remembrances" link and read with a mixture of anxiety, delight, and disbelief remarks posted by a man named John C. He wrote:

> Captain Ed R. commanded Co A, 17th Infantry, Seventh Division from approximately September 1950 until his death . . . He was an excellent commander. I do not recall any time when he played the martinet role, lost his temper or expressed anything but the most even-handed leadership. On the morning of his death, he and his driver [drove] north on the mountain road from our position in Tanyang Pass to investigate possible guerrilla activity. He had put me in charge . . . during his absence. Full story of Roberts' death is in my article, entitled, His Last Command, which was published in the January 1995 edition of ARMY Magazine (AUSA) (Carrig).

An article? Published about my father? The message was posted in 2004. Not only did an article exist, but also an individual who had served with my father, an individual so strongly affected by the events of that service that he wrote an article about it 45 years later.

I paused in my excitement to reflect upon the devotion of these men to one another. I was both dumbfounded and intrigued by such memories that refuse to shake themselves from heart and mind. The following day I read in a poem titled "Repository" of just such a memory—a ". . . college quarterback / named Adam / died / in the Korean War"—and of this speaker's wonder in discovering that Adam's alma mater has no record of this life. He also wonders at the power of his heart and mind, the power of certain memory. He echoes his fallen comrade's surname as if to assure himself of its existence.

> "Vanesca!"
> (Do I spell his name correctly?)
> "Vanesca!"
> (I say it again, so someone will remember.)
> "Vanesca!"
> (What is this repository that keeps the names,
> The souls of men!) (Magner)

He asks the question that I had put to the universe, a question represented now by one lieutenant who somehow carried my father's face and words with him, surely a burden, likely a privilege. What is the source of power for this repository?

In a small cedar chest, which I have moved about for years, there are various objects related to my father, some of which he carried with him, others of which he wore. I decide to catalog them in anticipation of this project. As I carefully lift each out, I discover a strange object shaped like a giant guitar pick. The smooth curvature contains surface swirls, causing it to resemble the Arkansas agate rocks I once collected during my fifth-grade geology craze phase. I flip it over several times in my hands, studying the swirled pattern. Deeper inside the chest, I find an ancient pair of goggles containing two of the giant guitar picks. So, they are lenses, I think, with some puzzlement. I won't realize until later in my investigation that my father rather famously drove a tank, and these are likely what he wore. Once he peered through these same lenses, with a clear view of his objective. I hold them to my eyes, the swirls from decomposition of the material clouding my view. Another fine symbol, I determine, for my attempt to view a past I can in no way ever accurately envision. As I add the artifacts to my list, I also mentally catalog this symbol along with my mother's glasses.

I decide to read more about tanks and their uses during WWII. I find the statements below in a report by the General Board, United States Forces, European Theater, filed shortly after WWII. Its mission is noted as follows: "Prepare a report and recommendations on the tactical employment, technique, organization and equipment of separate tank battalions." On the topic of the operation of separate tank battalions in the European Theater, the report comments,

> The separate tank battalions were organized as GHQ Reserve Battalions, and were assigned to armies. However, in actual practice and operation, a tank battalion was attached to an infantry division and usually operated with it throughout the European campaign. But, because there were only 28 medium and two light separate tank battalions for 42 infantry divisions in the Theater, there were few that, for short periods, did not operate with two or more different divisions. So close was the tank battalion integrated with the combat echelons of the division to which it was attached, the narrative of operations of them is usually that of the division to which it was attached.

I find of most interest the following statement of the importance of military teams:

> Combat Teams. In modern warfare the combat team has become the keystone of all successful operations. The complexity of new weapons and the limitations of each gives [*sic*] a complete interdependence of them on others to attain efficiency. Nothing is more helpless than a lone tank without artillery or infantry support. Its inherent blindness, its weight and size make it the natural target of all enemy fires. If friendly artillery is not coordinated, a hidden group of anti-tank guns will soon get it, or if there is no infantry near, as soon as the tank slows down it becomes easy pray [*sic*] to an enemy infantryman with an anti-tank rocket gun ("Organization").

I find these statements particularly applicable to the concept of groups of men who become entirely dependent upon one another in war. Perhaps the strength my father found in this web of interdependency was the factor that enticed him to return to the military after first separating from it following his WWII service.

As I look in the mirror for traces of my mother in my own face, I suspect Captain Edmund Condon Roberts, Jr., is also there. Because I was eight months old when he died—only two months old when he left his family with my mother's sister and husband to wait out the time until we could join him—I obviously have no memories of this man. I've seen many photographs and know his face well, but no photographs exist of him with me. He mentioned me once in a letter from Korea: at least I think he did, writing what seemed to be a response to Mother's description of my smile:

> 1 September 1950
> My Dearest,
> I received two letters from you today one of them with the swell pictures in it and the clippings. You are sure right when you say she is cute. She sure has the big grin hasn't

> she. Sure wish I could see her. The other pictures are good too. Everybody still looks the same.

In addition to the tank goggles, I find a baby cup, its battered silver shape reflecting my enthusiasm for banging it while in my highchair, engraved with my name and "The Officers & Ladies 25th FA BN." I pull out the horse tooth Ed discovered in his German POW camp soup; it remained a perennial favorite in my grade school show-and-tell days. I find his war medals, insignia and various war patches, the Golden Lion of the 106th Division and the Buffalo of the 17th Infantry Regiment Association decorating many. The flag that draped his coffin before burial in 1951, his remains finally returned from Korea for burial, is on display in my house. These are my physical connections to my father. My siblings may hold family photographs in their hands; photos of myself with him I hold in my imagination.

I remain in preparation. I collect facts supportive of my journey as if packing a suitcase for a long trip. The packing represents an important ritual of physical, mental and emotional organization, the contents selected carefully from many possible items. Those items are sanitized, folded in neat thirds, compartmentalized, counted and inventoried, a cheerful, if flawed, attempt to control the future, a confident plan to meet and champion whatever awaits. Blues, blacks, and browns are matched; soaps, gels, and powders placed in containers; new items packed along the way to replace exhausted resources. When the journey is completed, containers will be empty, perhaps discarded; clothing once attentively folded, rumpled and smashed; soiled items stuffed into a bag; and regrets logged over items forgotten and left behind. I decide to not invest much time contemplating the possible appearance of my suitcase upon completion of my journey. Should I bring home things I did not necessarily want and discard things I treasure along the way, so be it. I will not be the same person with the same needs that began the journey, and that matters greatly.

I return to Ed's September 1st letter. In its conclusion I read of both my father's fear and his confidence:

> We just got in from another big maneuver . . . and for once it didn't rain . . . The boys are working pretty well and I think we will do well . . . I'm a little bit worried about being able to do the job but I feel better about it than I did. I was mighty scared at first but with the training we have had I have gained quite a bit of confidence.

I pause to consider his final phrase. I know that he helped give his "boys" confidence, but who helped him? As I study his face in a photo, I see nothing suggesting a warrior. All I can see, in truth, is a reflection of my brother's eyes and nose. More than one person who served with Ed has written of his soft voice. That description doesn't suggest the speaker of the next words:

> If people in the US could only see how hard [the men] are working. They are a pretty rough lot . . . but they will make good soldiers . . . We are killers and are going to get an opportunity very soon to do a lot of just that. That just isn't part of my makeup but then if it [*sic*] them or you I guess you get used to it.

So he did not feel himself an instinctive killer. This statement seems odd coming from a man who willingly served in the infantry, had been captured in the previous war, had managed a challenging escape from a prison of war camp and received a decoration from General Patton. But then, he had been part of an entire battalion captured during the Battle of the Bulge, an untried group, placed supposedly out of harm's way. A German General had other ideas and swept across their exact position, taking my father and many other prisoners of war. I suspect he felt like the speaker in William Wantling's poem, who explains,

> We found a certain inner logic to
> our violence
> A game in which each player and

> his mate
> understood all rules ("Korea 1953")

Just as suddenly as Ed's tone altered to consider his duty to kill, it shifted again, lightening. He describes the Koreans that accompanied him and a sergeant of whom he was obviously quite fond:

> You would get a kick out of my two Korean bodyguards. they [*sic*] stick to me like glue. Pretty sharp boys . . . My 1st Sgt left today to get made a warrant officer . . . He is a dandy. He really has got the company jumping when he says jump. Guess that is all for now. Will write more the 1st chance I get. All my love, Ed

"Guess that is all for now." How strange to detach one's self in such a manner. I recently heard a physician who served in Iraq describe the last two weeks before a recruit is deployed as a time during which he must distance himself from everything. Otherwise, he won't be able to separate emotionally, as well as physically, from his present life to begin a new one in a strange place. Earlier in this letter, my father has told my mother she needn't send him "sports clippings," as "We get good sport news in the Stars and Stripes which we see every day." He mentions he has told her this before. Although he doesn't write this in a mean way, but rather quite matter-of-factly, I think if I were the recipient, such a remark might hurt my feelings. And I think that in his place I would value the clippings simply because they came from "home," however he envisioned that. His practical attitude annoys me, for the sake of my mother, in the States on her own with three children for whom to care. His remark seems even colder in light of the fact that he had mentioned early on,

> You were wondering about no letters for awhile. You have received some by now I'm sure. However by the time you read this I think you will know that from now on letters will be few and far between.

Still, he writes, "Guess that is all for now."

One story about war I remember with special clarity. It stays with me not only because I have discussed it with students in literature courses, but because I had the opportunity in Chicago to hear the author; it is "The Things They Carried" by Tim O'Brien, now a widely-anthologized and familiar story to many. I had read the novel by the same name long before I read the short story. Mr. O'Brien applies "Carried" both literally and metaphysically, allowing readers insight into the contents of various men's backpacks while in-country in Vietnam. Readers also come to understand the emotional burdens each bore. I remember during my initial reading thinking about the private nature of what O'Brien's details reveal of each man. In his address to the large Chicago audience, he made clear that such sharing did not prove a simple matter, nor did he take the responsibility lightly. In his fiction, one man carries extra food rations, another pounds of extra ammunition, another a large knife, another a bible, others chocolate and assorted provisions, and their lieutenant a photograph and letter. The photograph and letter eventually undergo ritualistic burial when the lieutenant realizes that he cannot let thoughts of those at home distract him from the demands of the duties at hand.

I strike metaphorical pay dirt a few months into my investigation when the author of the note placed on the Korean War Project internet site in remembrance of my father writes to me. He read of my search in a notice posted on another website and in a corresponding publication. His first line proved tentative in tone, as he questioned whether I was indeed Captain Roberts' daughter. I quickly respond, supplying various details about my father in order to confirm. Within 24 hours, I receive his second note, and I can hardly digest what I read. I remain famished at this point for real details, and my eyes race across his message.

> 11-25-06 4:05PM
> Virginia Brackett,
> In several cases in the past I have responded to requests such as yours only to be disappointed when I heard nothing

> further from the 'searcher'. Therefore, your quick and appreciative response was more than welcome.
>
> Now that we are in contact, I have much to share with you. During the first six months or so of the Korean War I served under your father; he commanded Company A, 17th Infantry, Seventh Division and I had the 1st Platoon of Company A. We were short an Executive Officer and, as the ranking first lieutenant, Captain Roberts turned the company over to me on that fateful day, 3 January 1951.

He tells me about the 1995 article, and I again marvel that his words had existed out there in print for more than ten years without my knowledge. Within months of beginning my odyssey, I have located a guide, a turn-key to help unlock my mystery. I anxiously await a copy of the article, which he has promised to mail. A few days later, I hear through e-mail from another correspondent who mentions Major Carrig:

> Subject: about your dad
> Date: Thu, 30 Nov 2006 20:05:07 -0500
> VIRGINIA
> I was there at the same time as you father, unfortunately i had just returned from the hospital in Japan the day that he died. Maj. John T. Carrig may be able to give you some information, he served under your father as a 1st Lt in the 1st plt. of A co John had wrote about your dad in 1995, It was called His last command. I have a copy of his text if you would like to have it. I don't have Johns e-mail address but i think Stewart Rothman may have it. Ill give you Stu's e-address and also i think stu was in your dad's outfit too.
> J. N.

I tell my new e-mail correspondent that I am in contact with Major Carrig who has agreed to mail me a copy of his article; I'm more than anxious to receive it. Within moments, this correspondent responds, his e-mail bearing an attachment that is the article in electronic form; he had scanned it some time ago for his own records. I devour it, again and again, crying at its conclusion. And again, I feel the press of time, the weight of the impending passing of these voices of war. I do correspond with the Stu Rothman mentioned in the e-mail, receiving twice the most gracious replies and offers to help. Mr. Rothman would pass away in February of 2007, about a year following the beginning of my research.

As I repeatedly take in Major Carrig's story of my father's final hours, I again marvel over the resonance of memories decades old. I am especially captivated by the final order my father sent to then-Lieutenant Carrig, frightened by his own admission, left in charge of the company when my father had departed to investigate gunfire. "Come in Strength." The one survivor from my father's small investigative party passed on the message to Lieutenant Carrig after he staggered into camp. As far as anyone knows, these were Captain Edmund Roberts' final words ("His Last Command").

I practice the phrase aloud, at first whispering, then with more confidence. I speculate on its meaning, words likely familiar to the military ear, but mysterious to me. I imagine that phrase to mean that one should bring all one has to the fight or challenge, to spare no exertion in response. I also imagine the effort that speaking such words required as my father lay dying, understanding the gravity of the situation, and understanding that he would never see his family again. I wonder whether for the slightest moment he might have tried to imagine his wife receiving the news, tried to imagine her life without him, tried to understand why fate determined that he would die here and now after having survived a WWII POW camp, after having tried unsuccessfully to re-adjust to civilian life, after momentously deciding to join the military again. These things I can never know. I can only take his command to heart and begin my journey.

- CHAPTER TWO -

"A THOUSAND DELIGHTS"

Tell all the truth but tell it slant—
Success in Circuit lies
Too bright for our infirm Delight
The Truth's superb surprise

As Lightning to the Children eased
With explanation kind
The Truth must dazzle gradually
Or every man be blind—

Emily Dickinson (1830–1886)

Investigating my parents' past brings both joys and challenges. Certainly, I discover no scandalous revelations to make readers blush. I delight in my discovery of two young people that I might have wanted to hang out with. I feel like a spy, but a happy and surely privileged one, as I leaf through their scrapbooks.

I'm amused to discover that Helen Kost and Ed Roberts dated off and on—usually on—during their four years at Knox College in Galesburg, Illinois. If someone told me this before I read it, I would have correctly guessed that my mother was the one initiating several break-ups. She would base the brief separations on matters trivial to the mature onlooker, but of utmost import to one caught up in the terrifying thrill of first love, as was her right. I see this as I carefully turn the crumbling pages of her scrapbook.

Textured grey veins and a still-vibrant red sailboat decorate the front of this intimate collection. Inside at the top of the cover, I see my mother's handwriting: "Helen Kost owner. Memory Book of Knox College life from 1937–." I pause to consider the missing end date, wondering whether my mother, ever-so-attentive to such matters, forgot to add the date, or simply didn't recognize the endpoint to that stage in her life. And who could blame her? It was a heady, invigorating time. In a way, she never truly left it behind. She remained dedicated to her Knox legacy, attending reunions and sustaining a robust correspondence with classmates until her death from cancer shortly before what would have been her 76th birthday. Had Ed survived, he would have done the same. His experience at Knox proved so positive that he accepted an offer to manage its new student center following his WWII service. I will later find a comment by Mother that the position "didn't work out," with no further explanation. By the end of my research, none was required, as I knew it was because he could never completely detach himself from service. At this distance, one can see clearly that both Helen and Ed found a group of shared friends early on to which they clung, and by which they were embraced. Those communities became, without a plan or particular notice, a support system in both joy and grief.

Beneath my mother's inscription, her writing flows around the printed name (in the computer age, we achieve the effect by selecting "wrap text" from our page layout menu) on a small formal card commonly in use in their day; she has secured it to the inside cover with glue. Her script reads: "This book was given to me by Miss Marian Louise Rose for graduation, June, 1937. Galesburg, IL." The reference is to her high school graduation, which provided a springboard into college life, a life that she knew she would want to recall. Scrapbooks, by nature and name, offer concrete bits of paper and fabric through which memory may flow.

Like many Midwestern American families, ours has always celebrated important dates, representing the accomplishments of others or our own.

Even across the distance of a world war, Ed would write through V-Mail from Germany in November 1944, "We had a swell Thanksgiving Dinner with turkey and all the trimmings. Sure was good. Hope you had a nice one too. I'm waiting to hear about Bruce's birthday party." In later decades our newly re-constituted family of four kids would be supported on a modest income that dictated that we had to rotate years for each to hold formal birthday parties. However, intimate family observations marked each. My Aunt Ginny, Uncle Don, and cousin Jim (the Sperrys), along with my Grandma Kost in later years, became part of the group that shared our graduations, concerts, all the various passages to maturity. Those were in addition, of course, to the major annual holiday gatherings. Ginny and Helen rotated the Christmas and Thanksgiving events at their respective houses, with Grandma Kost always contributing treats of her own. In other words, we enjoyed typical family holidays.

Our house sat across from our church, convenient for the religious holidays. Every other year, we gathered at our house prior to Christmas Eve services and then returned after to open modest gifts and enjoy a "cold" dinner. After a few years, my practical mother opted for one of the first artificial trees in our neighborhood, white and decorated with all-pink Christmas balls. I remember agreeing with my younger sister Nan that it was like having a rubber turkey for Thanksgiving, a sentiment with which I can't help but believe my father would agree. Christmas Day dinner at the Sperry house, with their decorated pungent white pine, was my favorite. The Sperrys lived on a few acres, "the farm," that lay beyond the town's boundary for its first decade or so. In the years before the city limits crept close and eventually ensnared it, its isolated acreage suggested secrets and mystery. It offered the perfect stage for my imagination.

My sisters and I always preferred gatherings at the farm where Don raised Hereford cattle. More important for us was his long line of mostly Quarter horses, one Tennessee Walker, and one stubborn Shetland pony. Lady, Little Red, Buddy, Little Champ, Big Champ, and Duchess all at some point remained in residence and available for enthusiastic riding, although they did not usually share our enthusiasm. We enjoyed the nearby Saddle Club, riding in parades, and driving the pony-pulled covered wagon despite the infamous incident in which the ponies ignored my commands, rounded a corner too quickly, and turned over the wagon, sending the kids aboard flying. But most of all, we lived to gallop up and down the fence most visible to the nearby country road.

We reveled in full portrayal of the three Cartwright brothers from the television show "Bonanza." Everything about the farm delighted and intrigued us, from the cattle prods and "cattle gaps" in the roads, to haylofts, and feral cats. We watched spell-bound as newborn calves dropped to the ground magically cushioned by huge bubbles protruding from heifer bottoms, and we loved the tack room, made yummy with the pungent smell of leather and contents of oat bins. My aunt and uncle, lynchpins in that protective community that surrounded my parents in their youth, continued to play a crucial role following my father's death for all of us, but perhaps most strongly for my older brother.

My brother Bruce had little interest in riding or horses, but one summer Don determined to teach him to "be a man" by putting him in charge of a haying crew on the farm. The all African-American crew was composed of men older and far more experienced than Bruce would ever be with such work, and they took full good-natured advantage of his naiveté. That was one example of Don's interaction with Bruce that differed from his interaction with us girls. While we all loved and appreciated our step-father Bob, Don stepped into the breach created by Ed's absence, assisting Bruce to learn much about sweat, harvest, and human nature. My brother wrote Don and Ginny a letter much later expressing his gratitude for all they had meant to him. He told them that he felt supremely fortunate to have had three fathers to guide him: Ed, Don, and Bob. Ginny later shared with him that they were moved to tears by that statement.

Below my mother's note in the scrapbook, she had glued an invitation from the Pi Beta Phi sorority during Greek "rush" week to attend an informal tea. She "pledged" that group and remained a dedicated member for life; her necklace bearing its crest dangles from the frame of a photo that features my grandparents in my room, like a tiny shield. Decades later, she would urge me to consider pledging Pi Phi as a "legacy"; my grandmother, mother, and aunt had all belonged. I would pledge a different sorority, Alpha Chi Omega, although I received a bid from Pi Phi. On my campus, the Pi Phis majored in social activity; of a different style than fit my personality. I later learned that the Alpha Chi president had called all of the "sisters" to the door of their house to watch pledge hopefuls during rush. They observed the small group of freshmen of which I was a part trudge up a steep hill to attend a party for prospective pledges at the Pi Phi house. One of my future sisters commented, "The pledges destined to raise the Pi Phi grade average are on the move." On that campus, the Pi Phis were considered high-status and high-maintenance, and my instincts whispered that neither image suited me. I would select a different community, one that on the surface offered appeal.

Many of my decisions over the years have been made based on such "gut feelings." I recently discussed with my eldest the fact that research continues to reveal more about intestinal bacteria and their importance to our day-to-day functioning, far beyond the contribution to simple digestion. The bacteria, microbial communities, may be responsible when their environment is right, for countering conditions varying from mood disorders to various inflammations. They can also, under unfavorable conditions, contribute to the success of auto-immune diseases and allergic disorders. My daughter and I wonder together about the origin of the phrase "gut feeling" and are both open to the idea that our ancestors may have intuited what science in the post-post-modern age is just now discovering. Because we both hold medical technology degrees, which partly explains why the topic appeals, we have gained a healthy respect through lab work for such organisms invisible to the unaided eye. We've personally recorded in the lab growth patterns of bacteria "streaked" onto the proper agar environment by special metal loops and studied smears from the resultant colonies on slides under microscopes. The close perspective tells us much about the subject of study, but without knowledge of environmental factors (context), we see only a small segment of what we need to know.

I turn again to the scrapbook, the context for my parents' early relationship. At this stage, I don't engage the microscopic view. I pull back instead, scanning a broad historical horizon for clues as to their identities and, ultimately, my own. I'm naturally most interested in learning about my father, having never met him. I also investigate his scrapbook with a collection gathered for him by another hand; I later discover that hand is his mother's, not a surprise. My paternal grandmother, Winifred "Muzz" Aylesbury Roberts was a major force in her son's life. I recall my mother laughing—although without much humor—about the fact that after Ed's capture and internment in a German prison camp, he wrote to Muzz before he wrote to her.

Ed's scrapbook has a far more masculine appearance than Helen's, with spiral metal bindings holding together plain black leather covers. The front cover contains a small inset of a watercolor landscape in its lower right corner. Occasional hand-written explanations appear with the artifacts, but more often, they simply supply a date or identify an occasion. Information about Ed's own Greek rush experience covers the first page, and much information about his ROTC experience appears later. As I look through his collection, a number of articles and artifacts from his high school and college years are identical to those that Helen saved.

The proof that my parents' lives ran on parallel tracks, even in their earliest years, comforts my romantic notions of destiny. I feel more strongly drawn to Helen's book, due to her innocent, wide-eyed and frankly emotional commentary. Even though I lived with my mother Helen Kost Roberts Ferranti for many years, I feel certain that following Ed's death, she became a person who greatly differed from the Helen Kost that I will find in the scrapbook. Wouldn't anyone? And so I also anticipate learning more about this "before" Helen, one not yet tried by reality, each page that I turn contributing to the profile.

Helen's journey into adulthood begins on the first scrapbook page, its path bordered by bright mementos. They provide the setting and the cast for scenes from her late teens. She includes the first of many Chicago remembrances that I will discover. This one is the signature of a musician named Freddy Martin on a piece of paper from the Aragon Ballroom. Its printed description reads "Ballroom of a Thousand Delights." I learn the Aragon still exists, although it has experienced many changes since its heyday in the 1940s when crowds of more than 15,000 might dance there on any given evening. Helen contributes her own judgment with a single word: "Beautiful." The big-band era offered a soundtrack for my mother's youth, as evidenced by the many enthusiastic references to the bands and to dancing that I find throughout her collection.

For example, a March 29, 1940 handbill for the "Firemen's Annual Ball" notes that it will feature music by Art Kassel and his "Kassels in the Air" orchestra. Many years later Helen will complain that she can find only a single radio station in our home of Pine Bluff Arkansas that still offered the music she loved. Eventually, she would find none. Below the Aragon memento is a bill, beneath which she writes, "Hotel Morrison in Chicago. 1st Hotel I'd ever stayed in. Loved it. Right down in Loop." That she would enjoy such trips as a high school senior isn't too surprising. I learned early about her status as the spoiled youngest, and by my Aunt Ginny's account, a bonus child in a prosperous family, a charge Helen never denied.

I find a letter informing Helen that based on her scholastic achievements she has "been appointed an Honor Scholar" for her freshman year at Knox. The letter lists five benefits of membership, including that she will be allowed to engage in independent Honors studies, may enroll as a freshman in sophomore classes, and will receive "Sophomore social privileges." She notes beneath the letter, "Didn't mean much—teachers just expected us to get better grades." As a one-time director of an Honors Academy at a four-year private university north of Kansas City, I know that expectation well. Then I encounter the first reference to Ed Roberts. It is a card with the note, "I hope I shall see you again now that you are 'of age'! Oodles of Love, Ed." She writes beneath it, "with my birthday present from Ed Roberts – 1937. 18 yrs. old." I have seen photos of Ed at that stage, wearing a high school letter sweater. I try to imagine him writing the note, full of confidence that he would soon jockey into a favored position with this pretty high school girl. Family mythology likens Ed to Helen, a spoiled favorite indulged by his family, always surrounded by friends, and, while not wealthy, never lacking funds. Ed and Helen would make the proverbial perfect match, approved and blessed by all by the time they married four and a half years later.

In the early stages of my research into Ed's military service with my first e-mail contacts in 2006, I encounter incredibly helpful individuals. I discover that family members in search of information about servicemen abound. Their requests for assistance, asking those who knew anything about their father, uncle, or grandfather to contact them, are evident on many military websites. I am blessed to almost immediately locate a man named John Kline who I discover through the publication *The Cub* of the 106th Division, the group with which my father served in WWII. My continuing education into the military reveals that as of WWII, 28 troops (non-officers) constitute an infantry platoon; four platoons make up a company; four companies comprise a battalion; four battalions equal a regiment; and four regiments are in one division, with some variance. I calculate that more than 7,000 men, to which one must add officers, administrators, cooks, and others, including a rare female administrative figure, would constitute a Division. Understandably, Mr. Kline tells me I will need to identify my father's company and supply details in addition to his Division, which I do. I do not yet know these many numbers by heart and have to find them in my records. I eventually make a cheat sheet listing Ed's many military assignments, like the ones I made in high school to keep straight characters in Russian novels.

After some inquiries, John (he has invited me to stop addressing him as Mr. Kline) sends me a list of individuals who served in my father's company. He writes in September, "GINGER—We struck Gold!! Here is a list of his buddies in 'D' Company, 422nd Combat Infantry Regiment. Good Hunting—I hope that some of these current members of the Association will remember him." Below his message appears a separate email message from an individual with whom John had communicated, reading, "Yeah, I remember him. He was the Exec Officer of Co D, 422, while at Atterbury. I believe he went overseas in that position, although by then I was up in Co C myself. I heard that he was also in Nam and that he was killed there. Thats [*sic*] about all I ever knew about him." That man must have assumed that Ed became career military because he placed him in another war several decades following their shared experience. The assumption, if not the fact, was correct, as that was Ed's intention before a Korean sniper intervened on January 3, 1951.

I pause to read about Camp Atterbury, located in Indiana. I learn that my father's 106th "Golden Lion" (I have Ed's military patches that bear a distinct lion's head decoration) Division was the last big unit to be trained at Atterbury during World War II. The Division members spent about eight months at the camp before departing for England in October 1944. With brief additional training and spare arms, the troops were positioned in France on December 11. Although the "green" troops were supposed to be out of harm's way, within a few days, General Von Rundstedt led his Germans directly through that territory in what would be known as the Battle of the Bulge, a reference by reporters to the distinctive inward bulge in the line of armaments of war maps. The German name, *Unternehmen Wacht am Rhein*, Operation Watch on the Rhine, the French *Bataille des Ardennes*, Battle of the Ardennes, or the formal dubbing by the Allies of the battle as The Ardennes Counteroffensive, never trumped the name by which the common reader knew it best. The Golden Lions suffered 8,663 casualties in a period of less than a month. I recall reading a similar statistic in an unattributed newspaper clipping published immediately after the battle among my mother's documents. The next paragraph in that article noted that several men were said to have been captured and imprisoned. She had circled the paragraph in blue ink and written a single word beside it— "Hopeful."

John continues to assist in my search. He replies to one veteran who responds to the call for information, "Here is the daughter seeking info. She must know where he [Ed Roberts] is buried. Feel free to contact her." And then to me, "Ginger this is going to a friend in Holland that inquired about this." I do know where Ed is buried. He is in a military cemetery in Little Rock, Arkansas, about 45 minutes from where I grew up. My brother at about age eight was handed the flag that covered his father's casket during his military funeral; a black and white photo captures that moment. Due to a delay in the arrival of Ed's remains, the funeral was held during the summer of 1951. At some point, I got the flag, and after some years, I pulled it from the box in which I had carried it as I moved about. Planning to display the flag in some way, I looked it over with my children and we counted the 48 stars, discussing the increase in states and stars since its day. I took it to a dry cleaner where I lived at the time in Joplin, Missouri. When I returned to pick it up and pulled out my wallet, the owner looked down at the counter and said, "I don't charge for American flags." The flag is now folded into the traditional three-cornered shape inside a display case in my living room. I was 56 years old when I began this project. I had never visited Ed's grave.

Another correspondent wrote about Ed that:

> Once he called me in his office just to ask me about my life. We spent about ten minutes. That meant a lot to me, Captain had a rough job. Almost all of his men had been in the stock aid or in serious trouble with the army at one time or another. He stood to any one of us and never backed down. He was very mentally strong, he was also very strong, he was fair. It seemed easy for him.

I keep in mind this idea of strength, and how it might be defined. I believe that I understand it in the sense in which this veteran applies it. I want to also understand it in application to Ed's relationship with Helen, which seems to have had strength, even in its earliest days.

As a freshman in her first few weeks of school, Helen is thrilled to be invited to pledge with the Pi Phis and has snipped the ends from a bow that she writes was "pinned on me," adding them to her scrapbook. She describes the pinning ceremony, common to most sororities, as "one of the biggest thrills I ever had." She adds that she "went to the Custer to eat," referring to a Galesburg hotel, following the ceremony where she "wore white." The date is September 23, 1937. Ed would pledge Phi Delta Theta fraternity, and the two would enjoy Greek life together. Helen later describes a party where she served as hostess and brought Ed on a double date. Her script borders his name card, and she writes, "Everyone says it's the keenest party they've ever been to." As one who appreciates lively descriptors, I enjoy my mother's use of terms like "keen," "swell," and "peachy," the latter used to later describe a young musician she had known since 7th grade who left Knox to seek a professional career. She also comments on an article announcing, "Alma Archer's Lectures Here Treat For Knox." Archer was a hometown success story, although she would not impress my mother. The article reads, in part:

> The series of lectures to be presented by Alma Archer and her personally trained assistants in the theatre next week is an opportunity exceedingly unusual for college girls. Wealthy women in New York and other style centers are regular patrons of Alma Archer's School of Smartness, and countless American women follow her syndicated column in the important newspapers of the country . . . Modern women and especially modern college women realize the need of being charming, dressed in style, well groomed, and mentally and physically attractive . . . Archer has by virtue of study and application made this recognized need into a practical science . . .

In her freshman wisdom, Helen labels the presentation "kinda screwy" in one place and in another writes, "Sorta goofy. Alma Archer is nuts. The whole town just laughed at her."

Despite my mother's dismissive attitude, I learn from Archer's March 1988 obituary that she was a syndicated columnist for the *New York Mirror*:

> Highlights of her career included interviewing Adolf Hitler, drinking with Ernest Hemingway in Paris and sailing south

> of France with James Joyce. In 1937 she was featured in a full-page ad in the Saturday Evening Post promoting Chrysler automobiles and proclaiming her 'one of the world's great authorities on style and smartness' ("Alma Archer").

She died in a Galesburg nursing home.

My 21st-century perspective finds fascinating the many names and greeting cards, invitations, programs, and dance cards that my mother saved to include in her collection. I think about framing some of the treasures that I have discovered, rescuing them from the crumbling scrapbook pages. Note-worthies include a card featuring some of Snow White's dwarfs with a 1938 Walt Disney Enterprises copyright date sent from Ed to Helen. It marks the celebration of her 19th birthday. Members of the *Antiques Roadshow* crowd, of which I am one, would no doubt love that card.

The formal invitations are adorned with beautifully stylized covers, each resembling a tiny booklet measuring about three inches in length and two in width. Some contain a few sheets of paper with details about the event and/or lines on which young women can write the names of their dance partners upon arriving at the party. Purple felt material covers one invitation; it sports a gold ribbon "spine," a tassel hanging from its end. A second invitation's cover is composed of heavy black paper with a diamond cut-out. Behind the cut-out lurks an elongated dragon on a diamond-shaped crest iconic of Helen's sorority. Another resembles a silver bookmark, the front piece a chevron-shaped purple ribbon with icon embossed in silver. The Christmas Prom dance card has a blue leather cover bearing an embossed top hat and cane. The invitation to a Scabbard and Blade (an ROTC fraternity) celebration has a multi-color cover with a plastic overlay on which appear three figures, the first a military eagle. A second human figure wears a stylized uniform that makes me think of illustrations I've seen of the Foreign Legion. A third and the largest figure is the head of a demure woman, eyes cast downward as she appears to look over her shoulder, her form depicted in bold, curved lines. However, plucked arched brows and perfectly-shaped dark lips suggest something other than modesty, reminiscent of an *arts nouveau* design.

My favorite is the invitation to the 1937 Christmas prom. Its plastic cover depicts a formally-attired couple, frozen in a graceful dance turn, sophisticated and elegant. With no floor or ceiling as a frame, they float effortlessly in air. My mother never worked to emphasize her femininity, practical to a fault when I knew her. Still, I like to imagine her pre-mother stage, among a group that swirled around a ballroom, dancers lost in the music and their youth. Who knows, perhaps prior to the challenges of the next decade, she was indeed the perfect participant for these events, following the lead of her male escorts. I do recall her telling me that when married to Ed, she had depended on him to do everything. At the time, I suffered dissonance in applying that image to the fiercely independent woman with whom I lived. My older sister and I both inherited her take-charge nature, which we've passed on to our own daughters. The sole invitation that I discover in Ed's scrapbook is suitably male, shaped like a beer bottle, fashioned from dull orange paper and unadorned, other than by letters. It invites him to the "Bowery Party" to take place on December 3, 1938.

By November of their freshman year, Helen and Ed had become a couple. Beneath yet another party favor she writes "Went with Ed Roberts. Simply a perfect party." Ed's name card and florist cards in his handwriting frequently appear. Underneath a later item, she writes, "Went with Ed but had a fight. (I got mad cause he drank beer)." This remark fits well the opinionated woman I knew. Although by that time alcohol was no longer an object of her disdain, the disapproved actions of others resulted in one of her most oft-spoken remarks, meant to curb our own tendencies: "People just don't *do* things like that." On the same page beneath another party favor, I'm amused to read "Went with Bob," and a card tucked on another page indicates that the afore-mentioned Bob sent her flowers and signed the card "Love." Then I see my father's handwriting on another card: "Helen: I hope you haven't regretted any of the 3 years. Lots of

Love Ed." No matter the source of distraction, Helen was not pulled off their romance for long. She obligingly explains beneath: "got this cute card with 3 red roses, Jan 19, 1938 from Ed cause we call this date our 'anniversary.' (3 years ago tonite) we really started liking each other." She has taped a small student newspaper blurb lower on the page that reads:

> "CONGRATULATIONS"
> To one of the swellest couples at Knox this year (even though they are just freshies) . . .
> HELEN KOST and ED ROBERTS.
> They celebrated their third "anniversary." Here's to many more.
> P.S. Note the bracelet being worn lately.
> MUST BE!

This came from a column titled "Knocks Student" that appeared in a campus publication. The wordplay on the college name suggests that the writers adopted as their mission the criticism, or dissing, of their peers. Helen writes, "We were awful surprised cause they hardly ever say anything nice in it." When I later leaf through Ed's scrapbook, I find copies of the complete columns in which they are mentioned.

Ed and Helen would continue to attract attention while at Knox among not only students, but also administrators and instructors. I find a hand-written note inviting Helen to tea with one Grace Smythe that suggests exclusivity in its first words: "I'm asking a few girls . . ." Helen has written below the note, "Miss Smythe was new Dean of girls – 1938. Youngest girls' Dean in America. A peach." Later in the scrapbook, I discover a copy of a letter sent to faculty from Grace Smythe with her correct title, Dean of Women. The letter details Smythe's receipt of "A number of requests for some kind of a wage-standard" that have "come from those employing girls to take care of their children and from the girls employed." The rate suggested during the "Evening (children asleep)" is 50 cents for a minimum of 4 hours duty, plus transportation. Dean Smythe adds that "For a period less than four hours – 15 cents an hour" would be reasonable. When the children are awake during the day "requiring full-time attention" the rate she suggests is "35 cents per hour." She then requests the faculty members' "reaction." I choose to think of Dean Smythe as a proto-feminist. Although Helen could never be labeled a feminist, her interest in social justice and gender and racial equality that provided a model for my own ideals may have been influenced by what appears to be the progressive attitudes of her faculty and Dean. Later circumstances of widowhood that led her to barter secretarial services at a pediatrician's office in exchange for the treatment of her three children may also have contributed to such awareness.

I find Helen listed among the Cast of Characters in the Knox Theater production of "Patience or Bunthorne's Bride" a musical comedy by Gilbert and Sullivan. Her part: one of the "Other Rapturous Maidens." In another program, she is listed as portraying a "Village Girl," and Ed is listed as property master; he fulfills those same duties in additional productions, evidenced by the many copies of programs in his own scrapbook. I feel confident that he served mainly to be close to Helen. I find a second hand-written invitation for Helen to tea with Grace Smythe in October 1939 as one of "A few girls . . . having tea with me . . ." While I'm pleased to find so many positive indications about the reception and involvement of my parents on campus, I search for any artifact that will offer a more balanced, realistic view. I'm relieved, for reality's sake, to find much further along in the collection a note, typed anonymously on water-marked paper. It reads "Helen Kost: Don't see enough of you. Cool in your attitude towars [*sic*] the pledges. Some people really do like you so drop that inferiority complex." While not written in a purely negative tone, its objective seems to be prompting an attitude correction on Helen's part. I am pleased and not terribly surprised that she saved and included it. She was a firm believer in the power of constructive criticism.

Later, a notice appears in a publication titled "The Student," for which Helen became a reporter. It reads "HELEN KOST IS NOW THE PROUD POSSESSOR OF A PHI DELT PIN DONATED BY ONE Ed Roberts," and her note explains that she "took it Xmas Eve – 1938."

Young women commonly wore the fraternity pin of their "steady." Soon after is a newspaper note: "SOMETHING HAS GONE awry with the Helen Kost-Ed Roberts combination. She gave him back his pin. Rumor has it that several other Phi Delt pins are only hanging by a thread." She writes beneath the blurb, "I gave it back February 25. Took it back again March 20th, 1938," making me wonder whether she confused the original December date, or simply did not include the printed notice in chronological order. In any event, she clearly was no pushover, and Ed was occasionally put on notice not to take her for granted.

Later she wrote a brief history of their relationship in her Bride's Book:

> Attended Hitchcock Junior High School, Galesburg High School, and Knox College together. In same crowd from eighth grade on. Dated from sophomore year on—never steadily until sophomore year in college. In high school he as a member of the Lincoln Debating Club, I, of the Elizabethan Literary Society. I wore his Lincoln pin in between fights.

The Elizabethan Literary Society! I begin to list the attributes and inclinations that I apparently inherited from my parents. Can a love of literature—Renaissance literature, to be exact—be genetic? If so, I inherited that gene.

Two cards from "Bud," the nickname given to Ed by his half-brother Mike Thompson, appear. As far as we know, Helen never called Ed by that name, but his family members did. The first card reads, "Darling, Let's have a swell time in spite of your hurt foot. Love Bud." Helen explains beside the note in her clear script that her ankle was swollen, which prevented her from dancing. I can feel her frustration, as dancing was a passion at that age. Another card reads, "I hope this fits well with that purty [*sic*] dress. Also the escort (Ahem). Love, Bud." Ed as Bud shows his sense of humor and disarming ability to be silly. So, apparently does Ed as Ed, evidenced by a florist card reading, "Est-ce-que je veres aime beaucoup. Ugh. (two languages) Ed." I suspect Helen may have teased Ed about the fact that she became adept at multiple languages, while he did not. His message may prove that to be true. I request a colleague's help with translation, and learn it "loosely" reads, "I would come to see you loved to do that."

I see on his report cards that Ed completed three rounds of courses in French, scoring "C" grades each time. Among the various report cards saved by his mother, I find no "A" grade and one "D" grade in math. I suspect he may have been what I call a reluctant student, one fully capable but not invested in education. His energies showed results in Military Science, in leading the golf team to victory, and in leadership roles in his fraternity, as well as in college-related, but non-academic activities. By 1939, he received a letter from the Knox College Business Office, confirming his appointment as "Student Employment Manager" for the following year, which might extend to the next year as well "if the arrangement is mutually satisfactory." In the summer, he will receive $90 and during the school term the "equivalent of full tuition," quite a nice non-academic scholarship. As a manager, he was charged with finding employment for any student who desired it, and conditions of his employment include that he "give up the job of lifeguard at the Soangetaha Club," Galesburg's country club, although he may continue as Property Manager for Knox's theater. However, "it is further understood that you will not take on any major offices or chairmanships in your fraternity." The letter writer, Auditor J. Wilson Pennington, appears well-acquainted with Ed's many and varied interests. As manager, Ed would write ads such as the following:

> FIRST CALL!
> FOR WHOM –
> Business men and housewives in Galesburg!
> FOR WHAT –
> A chance to use a Knox College boy or girl to help in your
> business or in your home with whatever duties they might

> perform. Fifty students will need help this year in order that they may complete their education successfully. They are willing and able. They will render any service of which they are capable to earn their board and room or money to defray the expenses of an education.
> CALL US NOW!

Ed also wrote full-length articles describing the services and status of the Employment Bureau. In one he emphasizes the importance of employment to students who must have it in order to finance their education, encouraging those for whom work "is not essential" to "leave it off your schedule" in deference to those in need. His penchant for organization and his ability to convince others to follow his lead surfaces in such activities. It will prove crucial during his military career.

I find a small newspaper blurb that Muzz has included, noting that Ed won a radio as "a winner in the General Mills radio contest conducted last spring." Later I find an enthusiastic award letter from General Mills, Inc. in Minneapolis. It reads, in part,

> Congratulations to the winner! The judge tells us it was a close race—the Nomination Sweepstakes contest—with a large field running neck and neck down the home stretch. But your entry was one of those brought up to the judge's stand to receive the cup. Only instead of a cup, there's a Fairbanks Morse radio coming to you . . . On this splendid radio we know Gold Medal [the name of the popular baking flour] Feature Time will come in bright and clear five mornings a week, and you won't miss a word of it. With Betty Crocker's daily helpful suggestions and Gold Medal products, your home-making problems should be much simplified!

I wonder in which of Ed's domestic problems the Morse radio might have assisted.

Another clipping reports that as a singer in his church choir, that of the First Presbyterian where Helen is also recognized, Ed was entrusted with the "Block Choir Medal" with instructions to wear it every Sunday on his coat for a year when "he must return it to be awarded to some other boy." I reflect on the fact that my brother has a lovely singing voice that he has contributed to his church choir for decades and my own, while not so strong as his, has been adequate for choir singing. My older sister as a professional organist has participated as a musician in church services for many years. In an earlier clipping from 1937, I read that both of our parents took part in "Young People's Sunday" presentations at the First Universalist Church, Ed making an address titled "The Challenge to Youth," and Helen serving as an usher.

They obviously shared many activities, another clipping reporting that both made the "Second Period" Honor Roll at Hitchcock Junior High. I now begin to see names that I'll see again repeatedly in both scrapbooks of those in their inner circle. Later I'll find them in newspaper clippings that detail war activities of the local boys. They include Dean Lindstrom and Robert (Bob) Mariner, perhaps the Bob from the party invitations in Helen's scrapbook. In addition, Ed had been quite active as a Boy Scout, earning the Order of the Arrow. He also attended Camp Highlands for Boys as a child and taught swimming there during a college summer, as I see in a newspaper photo. No doubt, Ed would have been proud of his own Eagle Scout son.

I review a printed booklet from Camp Highlands and find several interesting facts about its founder and the director and counselors; I pause to read the camp's history online. As I suspected from its description, it was a Laboratory School founded in 1904 by Harry O. Gillet, Elementary School Principal at the Chicago Laboratory School. Located on Plum Lake in Wisconsin, accessible only by water or rail, its purpose was athletic, leadership, and character training for boys. All three were well suited for Ed Roberts. The private Camp's director and later owner at the time Ed worked there was William James Monilaw, M.D., who answered Ed's letter of inquiry about serving as a summer counselor. The booklet details Monilaw's activities before becoming the director. He was "coach of Athletics, Drake University, Des Moines, Iowa. Manager and Coach of Football and Track Athletics, University of Missouri. Medical Examiner and Head of Department of Physical Education, Elementary and High Schools, University of Chicago." The camp had "Midget," "Junior," and "Senior" accommodations, and all of the Counselors held advanced degrees. Also featured was "J. Jay Berwanger, student, University of Chicago, Star Football Player and Athlete. A Gentleman and a Leader."

I'm shocked when I discover at another website that Berwanger was the first winner of the Downtown Athletic Club Trophy in 1935, which one year later was renamed the Heisman Trophy. He was also the first player ever drafted by the National Football League but proved too expensive for the Philadelphia Eagles who traded negotiation rights to the Chicago Bears. Berwanger never played for the Bears due to a salary dispute and became a manufacturer of car parts, using his trophy as a doorstop. Historic connections continue, as I learn that Berwanger, described as a modest man, had a rough encounter on the field with future president Gerald Ford as he played the position of center for the University of Michigan. The encounter resulted in what is described as a later "distinctive scar" for the President. I try to find the scar in photographs of Ford without success. I later visit the camp's website, and after contacting its webmaster, I locate my father's youthful face in photos from the Camp's Gallery ("Camp Highlands"). I watch Ed's leadership traits develop page by page through his activities and exposure to such mentors.

One of my earliest correspondents named Wesley passed away in 2007 before he was able to send to me a copy of a letter that he told me he had sent to my mother after he learned of Ed's death. He was in his eighties and ill, and I greatly appreciated the effort that he did make on my behalf. Perhaps his summing up the gist of the letter that he had written was enough after all: "The [main point] of my initial comment to your family was that your father was the finest American Army

Officer ever." That was the type of high praise I would read repeatedly from those who served with my father. After his death, Wesley's wife sent me a brief message, and I was touched to understand that her husband had shared details of my own mission with her: "I'm very, very sorry you never [knew your] father. Wesley said, 'He was a fierce man, a good soldier, and a proud American'."

As part of Ed's and Helen's see-saw romance, she refused several of his marriage proposals following graduation in order to pursue her goal to become a teacher. I smile to see another newspaper blurb reading "'My man ROBERTS', says HELEN KOST. That's pretty good HELEN, but that ain't the way we heerd it!" As I turn more pages in her book, I feel nostalgic for a time I never knew. Maybe it's more for the girl I come to know during this project, the type of girl that I could have been friends with in my own college experience, regardless of our likely different social circles.

Then I see the first mention of the military in an invitation and an article titled "Knox Military Gala on Friday is Gay Event":

> One hundred and fifty couples comfortably crowded the flag-bedecked Roof Garden Friday night at the annual Knox college military ball. Tiny Hill, three-hundred-pound orchestra leader, and his entertaining band were musical hosts to the annual formal affair. The dance, sponsored by the senior men of the Knox R.O.T.C. unit was featured by the full dress of the battalion officers, the presentation of the five co-ed sponsors, and the pledging of eleven new boys to the honorary military fraternity, Scabbard and Blade.

I knew that Ed had participated at Knox in ROTC, an activity that led to military service upon graduation as a Second Lieutenant. When I turn to his scrapbook, I find many articles that relate to his college military preparation. During one summer, "ROTC Men Get Taste of Camp Life at Custer," where "Amid sand, heat, and cries of 'Why do we have to get up so early?' the Knox contingent of the ROTC spent a very full and exciting six weeks at Camp Custer near Battle Creek, Michigan." I also see several Reserve Officer Training Certificates noting his accomplishments, and his leadership in ROTC is evident.

Ed's activities in addition to those of his fraternity, where he served on many social event committees, are also on display. He became captain of the golf team and was elected by the athletic board of control to be the manager of the basketball team, according to a school paper blurb. I have long kept on display a photo of my future parents sitting together during their college years, Helen staring at Ed with clear admiration. Her legs stretched out in front of her, she wears the quintessential bobby sox and oxford shoes of the era, while Ed wears his letter sweater and holds a pipe. They obviously relish their upperclassmen status in this posed photo. Another newspaper blurb reads "Someone Should Tell KOST AND ROBERTS THAT IT ISN'T CUTE to call Zeman 'BABY' EVEN THOUGH HE IS Ed's pledge son. Give him a chance to grow up—he sure needs it." Like my mother, Ed remained fiercely dedicated to his alma mater and is mentioned often in its alumni newsletters. Following his death, his photo would appear on the newsletter cover as the first Knox alum killed in Korea.

Helen's second semester course schedule indicates that she enrolled in English, Latin, French, Math, Phys. Ed., and Psychology. I later find a check voucher on which is typed, "1st prize Lawrence Prize in Freshman Latin Composition." She writes a note beside a newspaper article focusing on student achievement that identifies her prize—$30.

I'm curious as to its value in terms of today's dollars. I soon learn that such calculations are complicated. The federal minimum wage in 1939 was 25 cents an hour. If equated to the federal minimum wage in 2018, that 25 cents would be valued at $7.25. However, 25 cents in 1939 may have had more power to purchase than in 2018. For example, Helen could ride the bus or streetcar five times for a quarter. Following that approach, 25 cents in 1939 compares to about $15 in the second decade of the 21st century. Way to go with that prize, Mom.

I recall that when one of my children's accomplishments was noted in a local paper many years later, Helen told me that hardly a month went by while I was growing up that either my siblings or I would not be mentioned in our town paper. We did become a bunch of high achievers. All of us, including my half-sister Nancy, would earn multiple college degrees and Ed's three offspring would end up with PhD's in completely different fields: organic chemistry, music, and English. Helen majored in those languages for which she had a passion and later taught Latin and French. I smile to see a report card that bears a "C" in English, with As and Bs in all other subjects. Below it is a letter informing Helen that she ranks in the top 10% of the class and will remain in Honors. I smile because of what might be considered a "low" GPA today, until one considers the grade inflation that most American students enjoy in the 21st century.

I treasure this image of my mother—young, in or out of love, depending upon the moment, busy with classes and college activities. I don't have to try hard to conjure this picture, because in one of her several photo albums, the black and white photos are in front of me, complete with explanatory labels, like those I had seen in her scrapbook. This respect for history that leads to a careful captioning of events and people in scrapbooks and on the back of photos is something that I inherited from my mother, a habit for which I am grateful. While some of my friends lament their inheritance of shoe boxes filled with photographs of unidentified people and times, my family will always have those details. Not only do such labels supply facts, but they also get at the truth of those pictured. Helen adds to her version of that "truth" by providing commentary with some photos.

In one photo, she is turned to the right, standing in front of some bushes, her head cocked slightly. She has written a one-word question beneath the photo. It is written in white ink that jumps from the black background of the scrapbook page: "Coy?" Was that a descriptor to which she aspired? As I recall my ever-practical mother, it seems unlikely, but, again, this was long before she was anyone's mother with no thoughts about war and loss yet in mind. She used to tell me of those days, attempting to inspire me to stop reading for a while and go outside during the summer to "get some exercise." She said more than once, "We used to play tennis all morning, swim all afternoon, and dance all night." The "we" included her sister, Ginny, older by several years whose namesake I am, and Ginny's future husband and my future uncle, Don Sperry. They had both also graduated from Knox where Don participated in ROTC in 1935. Following their 1936 graduation, he completed his obligation, serving as a lieutenant. When WWII broke out, he would be called back to service and become a Captain but was never shipped overseas. I learn through the family artifacts that he joined the National Guard and would be a Lieutenant Colonel at the conclusion of his service. He and Ginny would, within a matter of a few years, assume a crucial role in Helen's and her children's lives.

I recall something unusual about Ginny and Don's marriage but am unsure of facts. The marriage had been kept secret for a time, but I don't know why. I don't know whether Ginny wanted to hide it from friends and/or family, or if it remained secret because married women could not hold a number of jobs, including that of teacher. My older sister Kay reminds me that Don's background was far more challenging than that of the Kosts or the Roberts, and his and Ginny's first years were not spent comfortably. She theorizes that Ginny may have wanted to flirt with rebellion in her choice of a partner.

As I continue working my way through Helen's scrapbook, the contents are not so well-organized. Helen likely became too busy to give the various items the necessary attention. I find her hand-written note with the self-instruction to "Start here" that divides the organized first half of the scrapbook from the second, in which stacks of documents and mementos have been placed between several pages. So, she had intended to complete the scrapbook. As I examine each artifact in each stack, I watch her move toward graduation, a path illustrated with additional invitations, grade cards, letters and many more Chicago souvenirs. In another collection, I discover a delightful collection of postcards from the 1934 Chicago's World Fair, along with "A Century of Progress" Railway Tourist Combination Book that includes an unused 25 cent ticket for the Lagoon Boats. Tickets that had been used indicate that she took the Sky Ride and visited the Sky Ride Tower. A separate bill notes that "Four States are visible from these soaring towers." She also enjoyed "Frank Buck's Jungle Camp" and a visit to "Merrie England." How she loved Chicago.

In 1999, I moved to Chicago from Oklahoma where I had taught at the University level for three years. I began teaching at a two-year college, where I also directed a Scholars (Honors) Program. I recalled my mother's fondness for Chicago that I see now in her mementos through her comments when I was a child. The Southern town that she selected to raise my siblings and me, Pine Bluff, Arkansas could not offer a greater contrast to Chicago. I will only fully understand many years later her sacrifice for us when she chose not to return to Illinois. I loved the city from the moment that we arrived. Family and friends found curious my immediate affinity for what they viewed as a large and impersonal community. Most of them questioned our moving from small-town, cordial Oklahoma to a (stereotypical) "dirty" and "rude" city when my husband found employment with DePaul University. Long a creative writer, I continued my writing after our move, intersecting my academic studies with my creative interests when possible. As theater buffs, my husband and I attended many performances and decided to subscribe to the Steppenwolf Theater. One of our joys was riding the elevated train, the "el," from our first house in Oak Park to the performances downtown, close to Lincoln Park. A few years after we arrived, Steppenwolf sent out a call to subscribers and others, asking for the submission of writing samples for consideration to participate in a creative writing project. I submitted a piece and shortly thereafter received an invitation to take part in a days-long creative workshop in the spring of 2002.

As a member of a startlingly eclectic group in terms of all demographic criteria—age, race, height, weight, political and social attitudes—I wrote in the mornings along with the others. The almost automatic development of relationships based on our creative urges thrilled me. A good number of the group members were theater professionals, but they quickly eased any alienation I felt, and I became fascinated as I learned many details about life on the stage. Even now, years later, I delight in following the careers of several of my fellow writer-performers, they the professionals, I the one-and-done novice.

We rehearsed structured scenes based on the previous day's writing in the afternoons, which would be processed overnight by the workshop director, Jessica Thebus, and Resident Artist Kimberly Senior, both of whom later became award-winning directors. The pieces that we developed that spring would become a script, presented as "No Place Like Home" in Steppenwolf's downstairs theater space in January 2003 ("No Place"). Invited to take part in the production as part of a chorus (in the classical sense—not a singing group), I enthusiastically accepted and finally realized a lifelong fantasy to appear on a notable performance stage. I ended my brief run with a new-found respect for stage performers and the endless hours they are willing to devote to preparation for a show that typically runs for a few weeks. The veteran cast members graciously rescued me on occasion from my own ignorance—"No, you can't take the costumes home to show your husband."

In an early version of the script, as characters speak of their backgrounds and their homes, the wonderful actor Cedric Young's character says in *Moment 17*, "My dad died in the Pacific—World War Two. Never got to, you know, meet him. Pictures, I got pictures. I know what he looked like. But as far as human contact, no" ("No Place"). I could relate to the gap in that fictional character's home, a home that represented the thousands of early baby-boomer American children who matured with missing fathers. I think again of the lack of photos in which I appear with my father. He had to leave when I was two months old, and they simply never guessed they would have no future opportunity for family pictures. In a letter that I received from a veteran in November 2007, he describes Ed: "I remember his face well. He was a very nice looking man, soft-spoken and kind to all of us." I found Chicago a comfort, learning from my brother-in-law that he remembered Helen mentioning that she and Ed had spent time on Navy Pier, then a functional naval establishment, now a tourist draw. When I walked there, I imagined myself in their shadow.

The final lines of the script spoken by Cedric, ones that I wrote based on my reaction to Chicago as home, would later be cut from the script and never heard during the performances. I recall Cedric telling me of his fondness for the lines and his disappointment that he wouldn't get to speak them. They read, "My home has been my home for only three years. But it became mine the first time I walked through the door. I had been looking for my home my whole life. I had only marked time elsewhere for the past 48 years. I knew I was home right away because I felt I belonged. Its spaces, its corners, its arched doorways, its shadows, its sunlight patches. Even the smell of the old walls. It slipped around my body like time riding a second hand. We belong together, and I said, 'Hello'" ("No Place").

A 1937 letter in the scrapbook informs Helen that she has been voted "the opportunity to earn $45.00 on our N.Y.A. program during the current semester," some type of a service honor, I'm guessing, with an assignment to the library. Her employment would prove crucial when she applied for a teaching position following graduation. Many unattributed newspaper articles mark her junior and senior years at Knox. Several tout the making of a film titled "Those Were the Days" on the Knox campus based on a book written by Knox alum George Fitch. I learn that after graduating from Knox in 1897, Fitch became "the foremost of the American humorists and was listed in 'Who's Who' . . . eventually serving in the Illinois House of Representatives for the Conservative Party and as the president of American Press Humorists' Club." According to one article, he based the fictional college in his "Siwash Stories" on Knox, and thus created the phrase "Old Siwash," a nickname later widely adopted to apply to any small college. I quickly dash away for more research that confirms that statement. Another article details Galesburg's embrace and celebration of the opportunity:

> Walk into a cigar store and the clerk who leaps to wait on you is wearing a Van Dyke; drive into a filling station and the attendant greets you thru handlebar mustaches; an ancient horseless carriage putts protestingly down the street: on the sidewalks girls in high necked shirtwaists and

> ankle length skirts are pretty and try to be prim. This is Galesburg, 1940, transforming itself into Galesburg, 1904.

I'm pleased to see Dean Smythe make another appearance in an article by a woman student writer in the campus paper dated October 6, 1939. It describes the campus frenzy in preparation for filming:

> Such a sight as did meet my eyes—Scotch half-sox and rats in the hair dos, Tommy Archer informing people to get out of her hair, Natalie Bell in the process of putting on a corset for the benefit of the still publicity man, Miss Smythe trying to maintain her dignity in the face of all these indignities . . .

I remember hearing that Mom and friends had been extras in the movie and find photos in her other book and in Ed's of several in costume, although neither she nor Ed are among them. I do find a five by seven photo of Helen in full costume at age thirteen as part of a group of four young women, in a synchronized dance step. Her outfit reminds me of what I saw Haley Mills wear as she portrayed the early 20th-century character Pollyanna in Disney's 1960 film version of Eleanor Porter's novel *Pollyanna* (1913). I read the novel twice as a child, pleased to identify another optimist like myself—one description of the character notes that she is "radically optimistic" ("Pollyanna"). I like the paradox. I inserted myself at age ten in the novel, and later the movie scenes, as I would those of Scarlett O'Hara from another novel when a teenager. At this late age, I'm finally realizing the source of my sometimes dramatic bent, oftentimes lamented by my long-suffering husband. Thanks, Mom, for yet another gift.

I turn over a small newspaper photo of an actress to see the headline "Problems Today Like Lincoln's Says La Follette. 'We Should Worry About the United States, Not Europe.'" Most of the article is cut away, but it begins, "Saturday last, the college celebrated the eighty-first anniversary of the Galesburg Lincoln-Douglas debate. Former Governor

Philip F. La Follette of Wisconsin addressed a large audience in which the number of Knox students was noticeably small." I am aware, of course, of the United States' non-involvement during the first years of World War II, and the headline makes clear that La Follette's voice would have joined the many supporting a domestic focus. At that time perhaps Helen, as one of the students contributing to the "noticeably small" size of the crowd remained oblivious to, or able to ignore, the encroaching threat posed by Hitler and his gathering of forces overseas, with the help of such politicians. That she may have been a part of that crowd seems doubtful, due to the absence of any evidence indicating an interest in politics on hers or Ed's part. However, his involvement in ROTC and their knowledge that he would enter service just after graduation had to make the business of war, however seemingly remote, a focus.

A later clipping, pushed into the back of the scrapbook, made clear that she did not remain oblivious. No date appears on the clipping, but the headline "Hitler Spurns British Warning of War" includes in its banner four photos that depict Hitler, Stalin, Von Ribbentrop and Molotov. I pause to confirm what seems an obvious link between the Soviet foreign minister Molotov and the Molotov cocktail, a poor man's incendiary bomb with which I am familiar. A bit of quick research tells me that the bomb is indeed the Soviet minister's namesake. "Molotov cocktail" was coined by the Finns following the invasion of Finland by Russian forces in 1939, a few months after the beginning of World War II. The Finns used this simple but ingenious and effective "grenade," as did later urban guerillas, due to its inexpensive nature and easy assembly. If it at first seemed to lack true destructive power, it well satisfied the objective to damage and even destroy objects. It proved particularly effective when pitted against tanks, as the cocktail would set the tank fuel afire. I looked again at Molotov's face and thought about the forever effect that some individuals have on civilization.

Helen did not include the entire article, but the brief explanation below the photos labels the four "European scene-shifters: men who figure most prominent in drafting a non-aggression pact between Germany and Soviet Russia and who probably will sign the final version." Because the pact between those two countries was signed on August 23, 1939, I don't need to research the date of publication. Hitler's reasoning that Germany could protect itself from fighting on two fronts through the pact was based on a lesson learned from World War I when dual fronts sapped German resources. Von Ribbentrop of Germany and Molotov of Russia would first sign an economic agreement. The agreed-upon Soviet supply of food and munitions later prevented a British blockade from harming the Germans. The non-aggression pact meant that Germany could push through Poland, and the Soviets would not defend Poland, a former ally. Within days, the Second World War began in Europe. Two years later, Hitler broke the treaty and attacked the Soviet Union, which eventually suffered military and civilian causalities of more than 24,000,000, according to the World War II Museum in New Orleans website. I cannot know how much attention Ed paid to such events, but I will venture to guess that he did. He certainly did later.

As a writer, I remain fascinated by the strategic use of rhetoric and its power. Over centuries, those individuals who may not want to call attention to themselves as aggressive have tempered their action with rhetoric. When I teach writing, I use the same word used by those who convince others of the necessity of war: strategy. Those persuading others to accept aggression often use a skilled rhetorical brush that paints their position as one of protection, defense, and rarely as an offense. I search for articles about the events that led to the involvement of the United States military forces in World War II and see on the front page of *The New York Times* on Sunday June 22, 1941, a number of headlines, all relating to the war in Europe. One, written by C. Brookes Peters and provided via telephone bears the main headline "BAD FAITH CHARGED." Other titles appear below it in list format: "Goebbels Reads Attack on Soviet—Ribbentrop Announces War"; "BALTIC MADE ISSUE"; "Finns and Rumanians Are Called Allies in Plans of Assault." The article begins with the information that Germany had broken the treaty: "Germany began their long rumored invasion" of Communist Soviet Russia, "the non-aggression and amity pact . . . signed in August, 1939 forgotten." Troops of Finland and

Romania joined them. "Propaganda minister" Joseph Goebbels, who read the Fuhrer's proclamation over a "national hookup," called the action "necessary . . . because, in spite of his [Hitler's] unceasing efforts to preserve peace in this area" it became clear that Russia, in coalition with England, targeted Germany for ruin "by prolonging the war." An internal headline reads "Designed 'to Save Reich'." Hitler noted the action is "designed to save the Reich and with it all Europe from the machinations of the Jewish Anglo-Saxon war mongers." German forces will oppose "this menace with all the might at their disposal . . . the German people are fully aware that they are called upon not only to defend their native land, but to save the entire civilized world from the deadly dangers of Bolshevism and clear the way for true social progress in Europe." The Fuhrer reiterates, "The task is to safeguard Europe and thus save all." He adds, deflecting responsibility for his own actions, "I have therefore decided today to give the fate of the German people and the Reich and of Europe again into the hands of our soldiers" ("New York Times"). The power of rhetoric. Strong political leaders know and apply it well, deflecting accusations of aggression by relabeling, by repackaging, by construing their position as a heroic and sacrificial one designed to preserve, rather than destroy. Marketing at its best.

Despite, or perhaps because of, its insidious design, that rhetorical approach is one with which the Western world remains familiar after centuries of application. I pause to consider how the approach to the "new" war labeled terrorism with its lack of veiled rhetoric worked in this century to knock the Western world off balance. The new terrorist enemies of the United States do not follow traditional rules. They declare and demonstrate their aggression openly with no concern for tact. They speak a different language unrelated to classical Greek philosophy that unites much of the Western world. Their language varies from our own not only in sense, but in sensibility as well. In a "normal" war, enemies may communicate and establish "rules" of deportment—an amazing notion to begin with—but without shared values, even such structured, arbitrary discussion becomes difficult.

When I return to the scrapbook contents, I am reminded of the controlled gender interaction on campus during my parents' era. I find a Student Council petition of the administration "to open the Common Room for the use of the students . . . The Council pledges itself to see that" certain "rules are enforced." As I scan through the rules, I see that students tend to behave the same regardless of the time period, thus giving the rules a familiar tone. The rules indict the "carving of initials on furniture and woodwork" and make clear that "the Common Room shall be used for relaxation but not as a convenient place in which to nap." The rule that catches my eye, written in all caps reads: "THE COMMON ROOM SHALL NOT BE USED AS A ROMANTIC RENDEZVOUS." My own dorms when I attended college were gender-segregated, and we had an evening curfew, although such rules would be modified shortly thereafter. I recall as a freshman that after dinner and a movie, my friend and I were convinced by our upperclassmen dates that the time was 30 minutes later than we thought. If true, if we arrived at the dorm after curfew, we would find the doors locked. We were less than entertained by the joke on the uninitiated after racing up the steps to our front door to discover the truth. When my own children later enrolled in University classes, I found my momentary shock upon learning that dorms at that point housed both genders without curfews amusing as an indication of my age. Now I observe the few gender barriers on campuses and celebrate most of the freedoms but know that others have led to extreme physical threats against young women. Were our three generations' attitudes toward gender-interaction on America's college campuses graphed, they would result in a slow but relentless slope upward, in the name of progress.

Among the other items in mother's scrapbook I find a card with the name "Mrs. Edmund Condon Roberts," formally embossed, and it clicks that that is Ed's mother, later my grandmother, Muzz. I turn to Ed's scrapbook, and I recall a photo of Muzz and pause to think of her. After Ed's death, my mother did her best to keep us three children in touch with Muzz and her husband, our grandfather, "Dee." Following Helen's marriage to my stepfather Bob, four years after Ed's death, the whole group of us traveled to Illinois for visits. I return to the scrapbook to smile at the formality of Mrs. Roberts' message to her future daughter-in-law. Muzz has written on the card "Congratulations—for the Three A's and Two B's." The social dictates of the day make distinguishing the attitudes among the players who determined my future difficult. Muzz always seemed to address Helen formally, but that doesn't necessarily indicate a lack of affection or pride in her accomplishments. Although my mother never receives 100% A grades, she will graduate in 1941 cum laude, another testimony to the difference in the judgment of the quality of student work during her era and my own.

Graduation parties are announced via more ornate invitations. One indicates that Helen and Ed attend a Military Ball. Among the final of the many florist cards, one reads "Helen, This is the last one of these, lets [*sic*] make it the best. 0000 [I interpret these zeroes as "hugs" symbols] Ed." I'm reminded of the icons and emojis used to express such feelings via modern electronic communication. I like that Ed was always so affectionate to her on paper. In each of his many letters from Korea that I have, he rarely fails to let her know that he loves her.

I find a list written in Helen's hand, presumably of graduation gifts. I am confident that she wrote thank you notes for each, a social convention that I learned and have been sorry to observe dissipate in the age of informal communications via social media. The list includes:

> Mom & dad – $10
> Grandfather – 5.00
> Mrs. R – traveling kit
> Mrs. Custer – Ronson lighter
> Margie – cig case
> Ed – hope chest [I suspect he looked forward to a swift engagement following graduation]

From others she received: pins, hankies, compacts, a wallet, a slip, and dessert dishes.

I find a bulletin from "Headquaretes [*sic*], Military Department, Knox College, Galesburg, Illinois" dated May 22, 1941 announcing the Memorial parade in which the ROTC Battalion and Band will take part. Helen includes several copies of the Commencement Ceremony program that listed her as one of a very few cum laude students in her small class, and Ed's name appears on the list of graduates that follows.

I read the final artifact more than once. It is a hand bill, printed on orange paper in bold black type, the letters in various colors. It reads:

American Cotton
WASTED
American Workers
STARVING

Japanese Silk Supports
Japanese Soldiers
Japanese Soldiers Are
RAPING
Chinese Girls

The contrast between the handbill's raw call to action and the joyful activities represented by the lovely invitations that I viewed earlier in the scrapbook gives me pause. The unadorned rhetoric of its stark message, meant to evoke terror and outrage, proves effective. Then an image flashes into mind, as I recall having seen a souvenir from the 1934 World's Fair Japanese exhibit, and I search for it in a separate box. I locate a postcard with pictures of "Tea Girls in Native Costumes." The young women stand in a semi-circle outside the "Japan Tea Hall at A Century of Progress." I carefully unfold some plastic wrap, its contents the proof that my mother had visited that Hall and was likely enthralled by its sights, so different from those familiar to her. Nestled inside the plastic are two delicately decorated handkerchiefs with the phrase, "1933 Japanese Silk." Each bears a round red stamp on which appears a snow-capped mountain, perhaps

Mount Fuji. Decades before cyberspace could offer international virtual experiences with a mere finger stroke, the handkerchief art no doubt inspired my young mother to dream of the beauty of an exotic land. Print circles the mountain, reading, "The Central Raw Silk Association of Japan." The two representations of Japan, produced about nine years apart, could not stand in much greater contrast. Which artifact, I wonder, best represents the "real" world of my mother's youth, its "truth"?

The answer may be that the scrapbook, with its carefully archived and narrated artifacts and memories from positive experiences, such as a world fair, represents fantasy, an escape from challenges of the real world, and by contrast, the handbill, included almost as an after-thought, grim reality. However, I could also argue that my mother's mementos and photos more clearly represent reality, because they are the story of *her* true existence at the time the artifacts were assembled. There again arises that slippery topic of truth. The handbill represents many things—the rapid change in the socio-political climate, the constant struggle for world dominance, the power of rhetoric to stereotype and brand. Indeed, that chilling handbill represented a rhetorically-constructed reality, but for individuals far from the safety of the Kost home. Of course, everything has its time. One day Ed Roberts would be intimately involved with an Asian conflict that would claim his life, its seeds visible in the content of my mother's keepsake. And at that moment, no truth would be more glaring than the reality that we build through our choices.

But the couple had much to enjoy before that happened, all understood through the context of their youth and education. My mother's existence would become the marathon that most lives represent—a long distance traveled along a common road with many stops and starts in the steady move forward. For her, obstacles would be encountered and negotiated, respite found in regular joy, concluding with the gradual diminishing of a steady light. My father's life, bright and brief, would represent the limited time granted a sprinter, consumed by speed and permitted no change in course. For him, minutes would glide past riding a second hand, relentless and steady, his landscape dotted by momentary grace.

- CHAPTER THREE -

AN APPRECIATION OF PARTICULARS

Homer's *Odyssey* offers, in addition to the seminal version of the hero's journey, a powerful statement about the effects of war. The *Odyssey* is often viewed as a "sequel" to Homer's *Iliad*, a work which, in the opinion of many, neither indicts nor encourages those who make war, but rather clarifies its universal nature, dependent upon shared attributes of human nature. Those universalities, Homer suggests, will extend into perpetuity, as intrinsic elements usually do. However, all writers understand that the *Odyssey* also provides the most basic primer for telling a good story. The bard of Homer's day and centuries thereafter would repeat aloud Homer's epic tome and preserve general rules of story-telling, also intrinsic to human nature. The first rule: A good story provides sustenance for the spirit. Homer's exhausted and starving adventurer storyteller would be granted shelter and physical sustenance from a stranger-host upon request, but only in exchange for the promise that he later shares his tale. The second rule: Few stories worth telling are not altered following the first rendition. They are reduced again to their basic elements to be reshaped, refashioned, and re-invigorated by the bard's energy and creativity. Such is the process of revision in story-telling. Writers who followed Homer notice that the activities of Odysseus' wife, Penelope, well symbolize that process.

Accused by turns of cunning, manipulation, strategy and value of her title (attributes which would have been applauded in a male), Queen Penelope comes under attack early in *The Odyssey* for withholding her natural and worldly gifts from suitors, who declare her available, due to her husband's twenty-year absence. Loyal to Odysseus, she is desperate to hold off suitors and preserve her son's inheritance. In the final few years, she develops a strategy—she spends entire days weaving and nights dismantling a death shroud, supposedly intended for her father-in-law, Laertes, still very much alive. She will not commit herself and her husband's property to any of the suitors until she completes the shroud. The suitors, temporarily none the wiser to the rather transparent ruse, begrudgingly accept her excuse to delay choosing one of them as Odysseus' successor. She repeats this nocturnal unraveling of her daylight creation several hundred times during the final three years of her husband's twenty-year absence. Her weaving, unraveling and re-weaving can be compared to the story-telling process. That comparison becomes an obvious one when we say that humans *weave* tales. We also revise our stories, unraveling parts of them to begin again, adding this bit and that until, perhaps not completely satisfied with the results, but knowing we must at some point end our efforts, we reach a resolution. The French label that conclusion the *denoument*, which means an unraveling.

Penelope's lineage may be that of the mythical Arachne; both are mentored by Athena, but to different ends. Arachne spins thread in the morning and in the afternoon uses it to weave the most beautiful of fabrics. Her pride caused her to claim to her teacher that her own weaving would prove superior to that of her mentor. In the contest that followed between student and instructor, Arachne's threads were so thin they floated, yet so strong that when interlocked through patterns, could trap a mighty beast. We discovered later its simple science—strands of protein lock into fiber. But in the weaving contest, Athena bested her student's "over-reaching" efforts. The judgment against Arachne by Athena's fellow mythic royals was that she could no longer weave. Arachne accepted that pride defeated her, but she grieved the punishment, as weaving provided her spiritual sustenance. Athena took pity on Arachne and transformed her into a spider so that she could forever pursue the activity that brought her joy. Arachne again proved that single strands develop into patterns that gain great strength at the web's completion, as do the varied strands and patterns in storytelling.

The complicated rules of a spider's web-weaving dictate that the common web consists of threads that are anchors and spirals, bridges and radials. The orb web may appear during creation to go off track for a time, but the spider's efforts culminate in perfect symmetric design. Spiders mesmerize when observed at work for long periods, as might the writer of the well-crafted tale, were his or her technique as easily observed. The story, like the web, appears not from single lines with an immediate connection of two points, but from repeated patterns, perhaps at first not obvious to the viewer. In a breath-taking final *denouement*, the spider runs the spiral thread from the middle of the web to its outer points, guaranteeing it will not be caught in its own design. Storytellers must do the same, staging a timely escape from their patiently crafted narrative and ensnaring readers in their skillful design.

When I open my mother's photograph album, pictures loosed from years-old sticky corner tabs tumble into my lap in a happy pile, reflecting the youthful fun that each capture. Every page is dated at the top; on the first, I read "1928." I'm grateful again to find many identifying labels, products of my mother's organizational penchant.

Some photos capture large groups of girls, their names dutifully recorded on the reverse sides. Many names are familiar because I heard them often in my youth. Through my research, I have now also seen the names in my parents' scrapbooks. They include Helen's best friend, Florence "Flossie" Dexter, later Edwards—I will spend part of a summer vacation at age eleven at the Pontiac, Illinois home of Flossie and Bill Edwards. I recall the thrill and terror of riding the train alone from Arkansas for my visit. Flossie appears in the earliest photos from 1929 as a part of Helen's tenth birthday party.

I linger over a photo of my mother in 1939 with two other children, her hair cut short with a row of straight bangs. I recall finding in a storage box a small plastic bag labeled "Helen's curls from her first haircut, age 3," its silky contents both appealing and repellent, as is true of most relics.

With her dark straight cropped hair, overalls—one strap askew—and a short-sleeve shirt, she reminds me of the Jean Louise "Scout" Finch that I envisioned as in the seventh grade I read *To Kill a Mockingbird* for the first of many times. I find humorous that one pant leg is rolled up with the awareness of the symbolism that particular fashion statement would bear in later decades as a sign of gang membership. Both pant legs had no-doubt been rolled up earlier that day, one later freeing itself from constraint, as she remained oblivious. That is another trait I inherited from Helen; the only fashion statements we reflect are of the accidental variety.

I see another familiar name—Dean Lindstrom—on pages dated 1936. In the first of several photos, he stands alone, a young man bundled in a long coat against the cold. The black and white hues intensify the cold effect on the viewer of the wintery scene. I turn the page to see him again, this time dressed in trousers with suspenders and a long-sleeved white shirt, his hands thrust perhaps self-consciously into his pockets. Dean stands in a group of four boys, to the left of a teen-aged Ed Roberts who is dressed in a "G" high school letter sweater. My father's right arm hangs across the shoulder of a boy labeled by name as Bob Mariner, evoking the name "Bob" that I have by now encountered several times in my parents' scrapbooks. I assume this must be him, and I'm pleased to formally meet Bob. My brother Bruce would attend Knox College during his freshman year where he met and spoke with many of Ed's boyhood acquaintances. Bruce remarked on the fact that each of the group claimed to be not just Ed's friend, but Ed's "best friend."

I have vague memories of the train ride I took with Helen, my Aunt Ginny, and Ginny's adopted son, my cousin Jim from Pine Bluff, or perhaps Little Rock, Arkansas, to Galesburg for my Grandfather John's funeral. As a child of about four years, I was most impressed with the stacked beds, or berths, separated from the public hallway by a flimsy curtain, and wary of the attendants who moved about the train watching everyone, especially us children, closely. Jim encountered snow for the first time in Galesburg. I encountered a claw-foot tub and held my mother's hand tightly at the bathing hour, reluctant to climb into the belly of that beast.

I return to the photo album and peer closely at a 1937 photo of Carl Sandburg, a native of Galesburg, speaking at the re-dedication of Old Main on the Knox campus. I wonder whether Mom took the photo. She seems to have, as she has recorded the date of the speech on the back of the photo where I also see the developer's stamp. The stamp proves it was developed in a local establishment on the day following Sandburg's speech. I have introduced students to Sandburg's Hog Butcher and cat's feet in the classroom and respect his work. I have read that he felt cheated out of his proper status as a poet by his contemporary, Robert Frost. Helen—always a good storyteller—recounted with dramatic indignity how Sandburg's nephew sat behind her in grade school and dipped the ends of her braids into his desk inkwell. She did not appreciate his attention at the time but did appreciate ours, as she told the tale many years later.

Dozens of photos show young people at play in broad yards with their pets, posing on car hoods, in jaunty hats, swimsuits, slacks, dresses, formal wear, ties, fur coats, top hats, at picnics, at church, on Scouting ventures, on boats, on parade floats, raucous, shy, mugging, posed in formal and informal groups, at ease and in discomfort. They tell stories familiar to us all. For a moment, I want to play Cassandra, to yell "watch out!", to warn them. But I know they would not listen, nor would I have at their age. With so little behind them, so very much of value must lie ahead. Their confidence in that fact is apparent. Helen and Ed would lose touch with very few of the members of their gang, thanks to their parents who shared news when they lived away, and to the voluminous letter-writing in which my mother engaged. They dealt with the distance without Facebook or the ease of today's social media. Helen liked nothing better than to receive "first-class mail," a rarity now.

I locate another photograph album that begins with a page dated 1941, and I move back and forth between the two collections. On the page dated June 1941, I find photos of a car named "Blondie." In one, Ed leans casually against the passenger door, and in another he is driving, the background a blur of grass and trees. My husband tracks down the model in the photo to find this information: "The 1941 Plymouth Special

Deluxe Convertible had a longer wheelbase than Ford and Chevy—but also had a higher price tag."

Helen began teaching upon graduation, a position that thrilled her. I find two letters of reference written by those who supervised her in the library position that she held during her last two years at Knox. A Mrs. C. H. Hanson, Knox College Teacher Placement Bureau, types, in part that she has found Helen Kost;

> to be quite intelligent, industrious, and thoroughly reliable. She has a most pleasant personality, yet also is so capable and self-possessed that she obtains the cooperation and respect of others easily. Her calm and self-possessed competence should make her an excellent teacher. Her personality and appearance are of the best, and her sincere interest in others would be valuable to her as a teacher . . . In fact, I might say this of Miss Kost: of all the student assistants I have had in the last two years, in my opinion Miss Kost would make the most successful teacher.

And Arthur McNally, Assistant Librarian writes, "I do not believe you could find a more capable individual, nor one with so excellent a personality and character. I have the greatest confidence in her and in her ability." Ed proposed marriage immediately following their graduation from Knox, before he left for his first military assignment. Helen knew, however, that women teachers could not marry. Thus, she refused Ed's first proposals, intent upon striking out on her own in this new world to which those who knew her felt her well-suited. Their efforts on her behalf proved successful, and she moved into her next chapter with anticipation.

A newspaper blurb titled "Teacher Resigns" notes that the English and Latin teacher at Rushville High School will retire. It reads in part "At the meeting of the committee held this morning Miss Helen Kost of Galesburg was employed to fill the vacancy . . . Miss Kost is a graduate of Knox College and she comes here with excellent recommendations. She is a sister of John Kost, a former member of the local high school faculty." The retiring teacher, Miss Logan has served as "a faithful teacher" and "now decides to devote more attention to her domestic interests." Although I'm well aware of the era's attitude toward working women, my feminist hackles rise at the personal reality that my mother and others were deemed unfit to work due to "domestic interests." Ironically, a world war was required to change that attitude, as women stepped into a workforce diminished by the absence of men, one that gladly embraced women to fill its many gaps and shore up the crippled economy. Another newspaper blurb lets readers know that "Helen Kost of Galesburg, Ill, was in Rushville Tuesday conferring with Supt. R G. Smith about her school work for the coming year." I later find a photo of "Sup. Smith" standing before what must be an entrance to a school building, dressed in a suit with a bow tie. In addition to teaching, she assumed duties that I find listed on a mimeographed sheet:

Kost
Ch. H.S. Publicity Staff
Assist in Girls Ath Activities
Make up Ch. Senior and Jr. Class Plays – H.S. Operetta
Co-Ch. Junior Senior Banquet and Prom Junior Adviser

Next to her own assignments, she includes those of a teacher that I discover upon consulting the newspaper blurb as the new biology teacher:

Masocco
Ch. Social Com. Council
Charm School Ch.
Girls Athletic Activities
Girls P.E. Demonstration Senior Adviser

Helen's journalism, theater, and social activities in high school and college will stand her in good stead as she assists with activities unrelated to her language courses. One hopes that Ms. Masocco had similar background experiences and proved as willing as Helen.

Ed sent Helen a telegram, hoping his humor would help convince her to make their engagement official: "Congratulations on job. Now I won't have to work. Think it is swell. Am sending you car money and will write soon. Love, Ed" (punctuation added). The telegram is from Columbus, Georgia. A note in a small envelope is evidence of more attention and encouragement from Ed. Helen has written on the envelope "sent from Ft. Benning with beautiful compact, 1941." His note reads "My dearest, here's that belated birthday present . . . It should be usable on that new job. Lots of love, Ed." Her birthday was on July 6. Clearly, Ed wanted to remain on her mind.

Ed joined the U.S. Army upon graduation from Knox but stayed in close contact with Helen. He would not be rebuffed. After all, their eventual union had been foretold by all who knew them. I read a newspaper blurb, no doubt from the *Register-Mail* titled "R.O.T.C. Men Get Assignments For Reg Army Duty." It reads in part, "Those who will go to Fort Benning, Ga., are Dale H. Birdsall, Dean Lindstrom, Ed C. Roberts and Ted Szerlong, who will report June 30." A newly-printed name card taped beside the article reads "Edmund Condon Roberts, Jr." In the lower right-hand corner is inscribed on two lines "Second Lieutenant, United States Infantry." A few pages later I find a letter written from Columbus, Georgia that remains mysterious, as it is signed "Love, Cliff." When I review the names of the men in the article, I don't find any reference to a Cliff. However, the note may well represent the general impression of those freshly arrived to the deep South from Illinois: "Darling, arrived in Columbus about 8:00 Sat. night. We are amazed by 3 things. The red soil of Georgia, all the colored people & the southern drawls. Saw some of the Georgia peaches last night (not personally however). We'll take some pictures & send them to you. Will write long letter soon & send address." How the note ended up in my mother's scrapbook I can't know. It offers the first proof of horizons expanding beyond Galesburg and Chicago for Ed, Helen and their group.

Helen includes several articles about engagements and weddings of the young people I have watched mature through her scrapbooks and photo albums. Headlines read "Jeanne Garver is Honored at Event Monday;" "Jeanne Garver is Complimented at Shower Event": and "Jeanne Garver, H. Dean Koelling Wed in Kansas." Another with the headline "Florence Dexter is complimented at Event Monday" reads,

> Miss Helen Kost . . . entertained at a surprise shower on Monday in her home in honor of Miss Florence Dexter whose marriage to William Edwards of Pontiac will take place during this month. Fifteen guests were in attendance and bridge and other games were played. During the evening Miss Dexter received a series of notes and in this manner found three attractive electrical gifts. Refreshments were served.

An article about Flossie's wedding reads, in part, "The bride was attractively attired in a street-length dress of white crepe and wore a white glamelia shoulder bouquet. Mrs. Holstrom wore a light green silk dress and a peach glamelia shoulder bouquet." I'm reminded yet again of the sensibilities that have been lost in the 21st century, one obsessed with brief form and lack of formality. Such abbreviation permits—encourages—more volume and more inclusivity of voices. However, much of the craft of our life stories is sacrificed on brevity's altar.

Mother did accept Ed's engagement ring in August, and they planned a June wedding, which would allow her to teach for one full year. She was happy and satisfied with her teaching position, at last able to experience an adventure of her own. A newspaper article notes that she traveled with Miss Helen Fuhr "for a weekend visit at Ft. Benning, GA," and a telegram from Helen to her parents dated August 2, 1941 reads: "surprise of my life. Got diamond today. Awful happy. Love, Helen" (punctuation added). A note in her Bride's Book is more specific: "Got diamond ring August 2, '41 12:30 P.M. in Columbus, GA, Ralston Hotel." To write that Helen appreciated precise particulars would be to state the obvious. I admire the fact that she valued the detailed record not only for the present, but in consideration of a future when her memory might not be up to the task.

Photos depict her with the referenced Miss Fuhr, who Helen identifies with the nickname "Fury." An entire page of photos depicts scenes from the trip. The two women departed by train from an unidentified location to make the first change in Peoria and a second in Danville. Two snapshots depict "2nd Lt. Ed" in his swimsuit at the Ft. Benning officer's club, and a third completing a back dive and labeled "The Champ." Another depicts Helen sitting at the end of a diving board in suit and bathing cap, her left hand up to her face and labeled "showing my new ring—Aug 2, '41." I remember a story of her jumping off a diving board at one officer's club and suffering a wardrobe malfunction when she lost the top of her swimming suit. She told the story with drama, noting, "The top of my suit hit the water before I did." She commented with mock disgust that "Ed laughed harder than anyone else." In the final photo on that page, Ed is handsome in uniform, "Blondie" behind him, his arm around Helen who wears a dress and holds her purse and her ever-ready camera in front of her. It bears the jubilant label, "Just engaged!"

One of the most interesting and curious items that I find in response to the engagement is a letter written by John Kost, Sr. to Ed Roberts, dated August 13, 1941. The handwriting is on formal letter-head paper, the heading reading "John C. Kost, Lawyer." Its tone and formality so well represent the times that I include it in full:

> Mr. Edmund Roberts
> Fort Benning, Ga.
> Dear Sir:
> Your letter of recent date setting forth your drives and aspirations was received. Both I and Mrs. Kost were glad to hear from you, and we approve of the matter mentioned in your letter, and hope time may unfold as per your desire.
> You two have been closely associated since childhood, and I see no reason why you should be other than congenial and happy through-out life. Hope you may be forward with promotion, as that means much to your financial welfare.
> Will be glad to hear from you again, and your progress.
> Yours truly, John C. Kost

I recall again the photos of my grandfather looking solemn with his cane and white beard. A driver's license application reveals his height as only 5 foot 3. However, his formidable language would likely have brought any young soldier to attention under its scrutiny.

Helen includes additional mementos from her brief teaching career. She has written herself schedule notes in list form:

Meet – auditorium – 8:30
Assembly
Platform
Say hello
Pupils dismissed then
Have written on boards name of test, what supplies to have
  – notebook, pen, pencil, assignment
Be in my room. Pupils will come to see me

1:45
Don't hold them over in class
Dismiss when bell rings. (command discipline)
Don't let them go to locker during class
Be strict
Teacher's meetings on Tues morning – 8:00
Have on Board in English II
50¢ – workbook
90¢ – subscription to Current Events
90¢ collect Tues & Wed

Even across the decades, as an instructor, I can see similarities to my own time period. The reminders to her new teacher self to assert discipline and to be strict make me smile. She later found comfort in an authority role and would not need notes to remind her of this approach. A number of photos depict her with students and with other women labeled "teachers." Several are labeled "Roommates," in which she stands with a woman identified as Tressie. Photos of Ed labeled "Trip to Jacksonville, Fla, Labor

Day," are included, a reminder that they lived apart, but not alone. And their arrangements allowed for additional road trips and excitement. On the following page appears a group photo labeled "Jacksonville, 1941" that includes Helen, Ginny, Don, Helen's older brother Vic, his wife Mary, and daughter Mary Ann, and Ed, holding puppies, a mysterious prop. In another photo back in Illinois, Helen leans on a makeshift wall with a fellow volunteer, labeled "H.S. Concessions at Horse Show." Miss Kost obviously remains active and involved in her teaching appointment.

Helen continues to hear regularly from Ed, an established pattern that will not change later in their lives. He sends a note about his next assignment: "Got California. Wiring for seven days leave. Can leave here sometime Friday. Pick you up sometime Saturday. Will have at least 7 days at home." That note is not dated, but a telegram dated "Oct 9" reads "Trip uneventful. Weather good after middle of Iowa. Hope to get past Cheyenne tomorrow. Ed" (punctuation added). Helen has written in the corner, "on way to Camp Roberts." Ed lets her know in another note dated October 12 from Camp Roberts that he "Arrived in good shape. Signed to quarters. Letter will follow." I remember hearing about her stalling for a time when Ed wanted to advance the wedding date. Sometime in November 1941, she again refused Ed's plea that they marry immediately. She would not be denied her independent adventure, now curtailed to a nine-month season. Although Ed no doubt admired her *joie de vivre*, he must have felt more unsure as each day passed that the United States could avoid involvement in the war that at one time had seemed remote and unrelated. Now that he was officially a part of the military and learning more about the threat, his desire to marry the woman he had courted since their youth assumed a renewed sense of urgency.

My mother's hand-written note records the contents of a telegram that she sent to Ed on November 11, 1941, a testimony to his persistence. "Disregard letter. Will come. Don't change mind. It's too late now. OK with Smith and my folks. Inform yours immediately. Apartment idea fine. Lots of love, Helen" (punctuation added). The reference to the apartment and to her supervisor make clear they had engaged in some detailed alternative conversations. She later let him know that she would resign her job. She was convinced and happy to move into her new role sooner than planned. Ed's reaction had to confirm her decision. Taped beside her note is his response of November 13: "Happy beyond words. Feel we are doing rt thing. Hope you are happy too. Don't want you to come if not. Letter follows. Love." The lines provide more evidence of Ed's investment in a happy future not only for himself, but also for Helen. She has written in tiny script his name "Ed" below what I learned to call the "complimentary closing" in my own letter-writing instruction as a child.

Following their decision to advance the wedding date, Helen's days whirled in preparation. The newspaper noted her resignation from her teaching position. She shared with me later how much she enjoyed teaching, and she would return to teach French and Latin at the junior high level after her children were basically out of the house. In one doomed-to-fail effort, she tried to teach French to my high school boyfriend and me, but we all soon realized the error of that approach. It adhered to the common truth that children in many cases refuse to learn from a parent what they will accept as a lesson from another authority figure. Helen eventually chose again to resign from her formal teaching appointment. Her sense of hearing had diminished. Thus, she often had trouble understanding students when they spoke, which in turn caused them to become less respectful toward her. She likely would have enjoyed a long and fine teaching career with the proper resources.

Most of her friends and family members were thrilled over the impending wedding, although its timing, only a few weeks away and just before Christmas, meant that some would not be able to attend. Not everyone in her family, however, was quite as certain as she of the wisdom in pushing the wedding from June 1942 to December 1941. Her older brother John reacted to the news of her resignation with what he considers sage words from a brother who obviously cared a great deal about her:

> Well, I must say you surprised us by the news in your last letter. Personally, this took me aback more than if you'd written that you and Ed were married last summer. Of course we think we know what is best for you and offer you

> moral support in all you do, with our heartiest congratulations and best wishes for all sorts of happiness. I do wish you could have had a year or two of experience in teaching before you retired, and thus prepare for any eventuality, but everything you write is true. As the Ancients used to say, the garden of Aphrodite flourishes under the storms of Aries.

I enjoy his use of mythology to explain the conflict that we like to summarize as "Love conquers All." John, Jr.'s words were prescient, of course, but would not change her mind. Helen became just as determined to marry as she had been to not marry, her stubborn and decisive nature evident. John's reference to a possible marriage during the previous summer indicates that he well knew the habit of young couples to marry in secret when the woman's employment depended upon her single status, a strategy that my Aunt Ginny and Uncle Don had already used.

A newspaper blurb announced Helen and Ed's "Approaching Marriage Rites" to take place on December 18 in Grace Episcopal Church in Galesburg, after which they would live in Paso Robles, California, close to Camp Roberts. Almost immediately, however, it seemed Ed would not be granted leave to return home. A letter from the Office of the Chaplain, 90th Infantry Training Battalion, Camp Roberts, California dated November 13 to Helen's parents, John and Elsie Kost tried to mitigate against any feathers that news might ruffle. He explained that "it now appears that officers in our camp will be granted only Christmas and New Year's Day as holidays," necessitating that the December wedding would have to take place at Camp Roberts. Ed had enlisted the Chaplain, Paul M. Bourns, to help convince Helen's parents to make the trip to California, as he knew that she would be crushed if they couldn't be present. As I read his letter, I wonder whether such communications were routine for him. He executes what I would label in my classroom as "strong rhetorical strategy":

> Looking back to my own wedding and remembering the important part my parents played, I can understand some thing [*sic*] of the meaning of this particular ceremony to

> you as parents and to your daughter and her husband-to-be. Often unexpected adjustments have to be made in order to insure the happiness of those we love. I know that your presence at this ceremony will mean much to the young people, and hope that it can be arranged without too great inconvenience.

In one of the few hand-written letters from Ed, he states his case to Helen's mother. It is dated November 16. I have to admire his grit in making such an appeal to an adult he so obviously respected and likely feared, if only slightly. The fact that he writes directly to Elsie and does not include her father, John, is interesting. Perhaps he does so because they had already reached a gentleman's agreement regarding the fact of the marriage and wouldn't be as concerned with its date. I do not make any corrections to the original grammar or punctuation as I transcribe:

> My dear Mrs. Kost,
>
> I'm very sorry it has taken me so long to get this letter written but believe me I've never written so many letters in my life as I have since I got Helen's telegram with the good news in it.
>
> I hope that you have gotten over the suddenness of my proposal by this time. It did come more or less out of a clear sky but at the same time there was a lot of thought behind it. I tried to consider from all angles and used them all in arriving at my decision. I would like to have waited until June as we had originally planned but with the setup the way it is with the war and all if we did wait there's a chance we might never be married and after what we have meant to each other the years that we've spent together I feel that now is the time. Its not like we were hurrying to get married because of the war but we have been so close it seems only a more intimate continuation of our friendship and love. I feel that I can take care of Helen in a way so that

> we will both be happy. It won't be anything wonderful but then there are plenty of couples and families even living on less than $183 per mo. I don't owe anything but my car so that will help. If we live with this other couple as we have it planned now that will make it that much cheaper. We'll have each other which will be worth more than any material things we would otherwise have if we lived separately.
>
> I'm so glad that you and Mr. Kost approve. I knew that you would somehow because you have always been so nice to me. The old jokes about the mother-in-law will certainly never apply in your case as far as I'm concerned and never will. I think an awful lot of both you and Mr. Kost and always will. One hope I'm cherishing is that one or both of you can come to see the wedding. I have it pretty well planned now and I think it will be beautiful. The chapel here is small but very pretty inside; an ideal place for a wedding. A military wedding itself is very pretty and I'm sure you would be thrilled to see it.
>
> That's about all the news I have now. I would like to hear from you and any advice will be gratefully received.
>
> Your future son-in-law, Ed.

His letter offers much to admire, with its solid appeals and support for his argument. As he moves from logistical matters to the underlying fact, "we'll have each other" as worth more than any material considerations, he likely sealed the deal with a mother whose daughter's happiness remained crucial.

I find a letter that isn't signed, but I recognize my Aunt Ginny's handwriting. The letter provides a rare glimpse of her emotional side, one we children rarely witnessed among the adults in our lives. We were told that the tendency toward solemn practicality existed in our German genes. Ginny begins by joining others in expressing surprise at her younger sister's decision, especially her plan to relocate to California. However, she is supportive and writes, "I know I'd do the same thing if I were in your place." Already married to Don at that point and living in Arkansas where Don was likely stationed, Ginny adds, "you have no idea how supremely happy you'll be." She admits that she was so happy to learn Helen's news that she cried: "I know that when you get-together, you kids will wonder how and why you waited as long as you did."

While their own generation seemed elated for Helen and Ed, as evidenced in notes in Helen's scrapbook, the older did not. Based on Ginny's letter, Ed's parents, or at least his mother, seem to be causing the most conflict for the couple. Helen must have shared details about the gathering conflict with her older sister. Ginny offers the encouragement that perhaps Helen needs by writing that as Helen is doing what she believes to be right "in your heart . . . why worry what others think?" Ed's mother has apparently said or done something to cause Ginny to label Mrs. Roberts "selfish" and "jealous," but she believes that in the end, she will "come through," which will "be a feather in her cap." Helen's Aunt Jessie, a favorite relative, writes on the same subject and clarifies that the fact that the parents might miss the wedding would, indeed, be hard on all of them, but will be borne. About Ed's mother, she writes "Naturally it is a shock to her not to see her son married, and any mother hates to give up her son, but . . . she will have to make up her mind to it."

A letter from Ginny's husband, Don, followed, in which he emphasizes in typical big-brother fashion his support of her decision, writing, "if anyone has any objections you just tell them to see me and I'll put them straight." He adds, "I hated to see you waste many years of your life as a school teacher." I immediately notice the contrast between his attitude and that of her older brother and parents, perhaps emphasizing their different class values, or just Don's impetuous nature. Don notes that Ginny is feeling better and that "I hope your married life isn't as hard as hers. When you asked for advice, you sure came to the right person, after all she has been through." My siblings and I speculate that he might reference the multiple miscarriages Ginny suffered after their marriage in 1937 before they adopted our cousin Jim in 1954. Don includes in the letter that he hopes that Ed and Helen will visit them soon. However, by 1942 he will be back in the service, and he and Ginny will have joined

Helen and Ed at Camp Roberts. The two couples would become inseparable in the months before Ed departed, first for training in the Aleutians and then to Germany.

The details of Don's military involvement during the years following his graduation aren't completely clear. He taught physics during the Depression, the education that he earned proving a great benefit at a time when others could not find employment, although their income was slight. He and Ginny would settle in Pine Bluff, Arkansas later, a fact that had an enormous effect on the future of Helen's family. The reason for their original move to Arkansas we don't know. We do know that Don at some point drove a Swift Meat Packing truck for a time, as we have a photo of him sitting in the cab and looking out the window. He later purchased a feed and tack store with a partner, and eventually bought out his partner's share.

My sisters and I loved that feed store. It smelled of leather and grain and had an incubator room housing dozens of baby chickens. When we visited, Don let us sit in the saddles displayed on sawhorses and climb the hay bales stacked to a spine-tingling height in an enormous building behind the store. We also loved to hold the chicks, but my mother feared we would become attached and would want to take some home, so we weren't allowed to do so often. One of the most fascinating items in the store was the candy dispenser where Don would occasionally pop open the door to grab candy bars for us, a rare treat. I must have developed my taste for Pay Day candy bars there, as I don't recall Helen providing candy bars at home. We were strictly allowed a single eight-ounce bottle of soda per week, which was usually Coca Cola. We often attended the "Coke matinees" on Saturday, riding the bus downtown where admission to the Saenger Theater was two empty Coke bottles. But Don also gave us ice cold bottles of Dr. Pepper on the sly in the summer, cautioning us, "Don't tell your mother." He sometimes added a package of peanuts that we would share and drop into the dark brown liquid, burning with carbonation. (I was shocked during the summer following my 19th birthday when I worked in Connecticut in a branch of the Peace Corps to discover the locals were not familiar with Dr. Pepper, a mainstay in my Southern town). We all adored our Uncle Don.

As in many families, Helen's relationship with her brother-in-law would be a complicated one. He adds a P.S. to the letter that I hold: "Will you break down and write to me now?" I cannot know why she had refused to write to him previously. Helen would later feel immense gratitude for the part that he played in her children's lives during her widowhood and beyond. He enjoyed teasing her, as he did everyone, and she generally accepted it with grace. However, they argued, at times with passion, over different political and social views—she a liberal, he conservative. She also did not share my Uncle Don's negative attitude toward blacks in the South, nor his and Ginny's movement among the Southern upper social class in later years. But the fact is that Helen fiercely loved her older sister Ginny, and they remained extremely close throughout their long lives, sharing decades of one another's joys and pain. I would be with Helen in her last few hours of life in 1996, holding her as she struggled to stay. Minutes before succumbing to cancer and preceding her sister in death, she would whisper three times: "Ginny . . . Ginny . . . Ginny . . ."

Wedding plans had to be made within weeks. Several of those close to the couple sent their regrets. Ed's sister-in-law Polly writes from New Jersey that his half-brother Mike will be at a conference: "I so wanted Mike to be Bud's best man." Others send love, congratulations, words of wisdom, and encouragement, all of the traditional expressions. Aunt Jessie writes in late November of her sadness at not being able to attend the ceremony. However, she doesn't blame Helen for not wanting to wait until the summer, due to circumstances and uncertainty. She surely refers to conditions Ed confronted as part of the Armed Forces, particularly from the point of view of one who had lived through the First World War. By that time, everyone in Helen's circle knew that U.S. involvement in the world war was imminent.

Newspaper headlines and reporting content in November of 1941 could not be ignored by the public, nor could information from government resources. A timeline of reactions to an escalation in the war posted online includes the following published examples ("November 1941"):

> The United States pledged aid for reconstruction of devastated and occupied countries and for international economic rehabilitation (Relief of human needs offered little room for differences) (*Times*, November 2, 1941, p. 33).
>
> Czechoslovakia, Greece, Poland, and Yugoslavia concluded an agreement for a post-war bloc (To create a buffer against Germany and facilitate reconstruction as part of international economic rehabilitation) (*Times,* Nov. 4, 1941, p. 15).
>
> *The New York Times* Headline on November 4, 1941: **ARMY CONTRACTS IN DAY $270,717,040; Curtiss Wright Gets $107, 434, 037 Order for Airplanes and Plane Parts**
>
> *The New York Times* Headline on November 15, 1941: **103 REBELS KILLED IN SERBIAN BATTLE; Soviet Reports 15,000 Slain in Revolt by Bulgarians and Nazis**
>
> *The New York Times* Headline on November 20, 1941: **LONDON, Nov. 19 (U.P.) – German troops, in a new blaze of activity along the whole Russian front, have crashed through the northern flank of the Moscow defenses at Kalinin and are still advancing, Russian dispatches said today.**
>
> *The New York Times* Headline on November 24, 1941: **PRESIDENT AGREES; He Joins in 'Consensus' at Night Conference at White House** –WASHINGTON, Nov. 24 – Representative McCormack, Democratic floor leader

in the House, announced tonight after a bipartison [*sic*] conference with President Roosevelt that it was the "consensus" that anti-strike legislation providing for a "reasonable" waiting period in advance of walkouts in defense industries should be enacted by Congress.

From a Department of State Bulletin, November 8, 1941 – **(A PARAPHRASE OF THE REPLY OF PREMIER JOSEPH STALIN, DATED NOVEMBER 4, 1941, TO THE LETTER OF FRANKLIN D. ROOSEVELT OF OCTOBER 30, 1941)**:
Your decision, Mr. President, to grant to the Soviet Union a loan in the amount of one billion dollars subject to no interest charges and for the purpose of paying for armaments and raw materials for the Soviet Union is accepted with sincere gratitude by the Soviet Government as unusually substantial aid in its difficult and great struggle against our common enemy, bloodthirsty Hitlerism.

From Ambassador Grew:
"[U]nderestimating Japan's obvious preparations to implement a program in the event the alternative peace program fails, would be short-sighted. Similarly it would be short-sighted for American policy to be based upon the belief that Japanese preparations are no more than saber rattling, merely intended to give moral support to the high pressure diplomacy of Japan" (*Peace,* p. 775).

Secretary of State Hull warned the United States Cabinet that relations with Japan were extremely critical (Cf. Nov. 3, *supra* . *Peace,* p. 136).

London. Prime Minister Churchill again promised British declaration of war with Japan "within the hour" should

> America become so involved. (". . . every preparation to defend British interests in the Far East and to defend the common cause now at stake has been and is being made") (*Times,* Nov. 11, 1941, p. 4. Cf. Aug. 24, *supra.*).
>
> President Roosevelt and Secretary of State Hull urged repeal of sections 2, 3, and 6 of the Neutrality Act: (". . . the effect of failure [to repeal] . . . Our own position in the struggle against aggression would be definitely weakened, not only in Europe and in Asia, but also among our sister republics in the Americas") (*Bulletin,* Vol. V, No. 125, p. 379).
>
> "The proposals which were presented by the Japanese Ambassador on November 20 contain some features which, in the opinion of this Government, conflict with the fundamental principles which form a part of the general settlement under consideration and to which each Government has declared that it is committed. The Government of the United States believes that the adoption of such proposals would not be likely to contribute to the ultimate objectives of insuring peace under law, order, and justice in the Pacific area, and it suggests that further effort be made to resolve our divergences of views in regard to the practical application of the fundamental principles already mentioned" (*Bulletin,* Vol. V, No. 129, p. 462).

By November 29, about two weeks after Helen finally agreed to advance the wedding date, the United States warned Britain of an impending attack by the Japanese.

Simultaneously, though, a *Times* magazine cover featured a provocative Rita Hayworth, and articles focused on activities unrelated to war to keep readers grounded in the "normal." They included a national crocheting contest; the election of Frederica Fox of *Vogue* to head a fashion group; five women sweeping the field for the O. Henry short story award, unseating male winners for the first time in five years; and Congress legislating a permanent day for the Thanksgiving holiday. The public was entertained by fall movie releases including *The Maltese Falcon* and *How Green Was My Valley,* and by reads including *Curious George* by H. A. Rey (first in the series); *The Black Stallion* by Walter Farley (first in the series); *Nightfall* by Isaac Asimov (short story); *Mildred Pierce* by James M. Cain; *Between the Acts* (posthumous) by Virginia Woolf; *Black Lamb and Grey Falcon: A Journey Through Yugoslavia* by Rebecca West; *Reflections in a Golden Eye* by Carson McCullers; and *The Last Tycoon*, (posthumous) by F. Scott Fitzgerald. People still lived their lives, and, no doubt, thousands of weddings in addition to that of Helen and Ed were in the planning stage. But with the December 7 Japanese attack on Pearl Harbor only days away, theirs would be particularly vulnerable to war events.

- CHAPTER FOUR -

THAT TRUTH MAY EMERGE

The Greek recorder of myth, Hesiod, tells us that the nine muses inspired the production of art, history, science, mathematics, geography, drama and music. Of those muses, six proved necessary to the production of poetry in its many forms—epic, lyric, comedy and pastoral, tragedy, love, and sacred verse. History, based in the narrative story tradition, had as its muse Clio with her icon the scroll. The job of history is to record and relate, actions dependent upon facts and true events. History is generally read in dictated fashion; one must begin at the beginning and read directly until the end; the shortest distance between two points is a straight line—thanks, Mrs. Watson, my own high school geometry muse. Thus, the scroll, which provided the earliest means of recording on something other than caves and rocks, symbolizes well the pursuit of history.

Some claim that the product of history should be a better understanding of events, in order to avoid replicating mistakes in the future. Homer's bard did not bear the burden of that hope in the *Odyssey* or the *Iliad,* nor, I believe, did he offer history as a lesson. For the storyteller, history, in its broad brush strokes, may offer "the bigger picture." However, for humans to care about that general picture, they must be able to focus on individual detail, which art promotes. Select critics go so far as to believe that the goal of art is the fostering of civic awareness.

To adopt another artistic metaphor, history may offer a frame on which to weave plots, characters, and themes, but on its own cannot offer a personalized message for individuals. In contrast to history, a story should offer each member of the audience something with which to identify, an element to which each can point and think "that represents me" or simply intuit that truth. Homer's stories of war and combat, graphic depictions of the cleaving of limbs, beheadings, and debasement of corpses, rape, and pillage, offered entertainment and held audience attention, but who in an audience would confess to identifying or aspiring to be that father who betrayed his son, the brother who betrayed brother? Storytellers hope that their web ensnares the audience with its suggestion of personal truth, not of fact or reality, which are more the tools of history. Stories offer a truth that must be self-selected and applied through reader participation.

Thus, the beauty of the perfectly-balanced story lies not in its realism, but in its realistic delivery. An audience craves the truth of emotion, generally the motivation for characters' actions, because that truth is the one they may apply to themselves. They want to step inside the skin of the characters to stage their own re-enactment considering what they might have done if placed in the same situation. Shakespeare understood this aspect of his audience. In most instances in his tragedies, the main characters die, leaving those behind—indeed sometimes commanding them as they die—to relay details of the tragic story. An audience member might wonder, why did not Juliet simply run off with Romeo to Padua, rather than wait behind to trip the series of misunderstandings that led to their deaths? One of many theories is that in her innocent youth, Juliet still trusted the adults in her life to take actions that determined her best future. Unfortunately, they failed that trust and demonstrated the often-unanticipated effects of the inter-weaving with our lives of forces beyond our control. Stories demonstrate that as humans we lack control over our environment and its forces. Our true power is to choose how we react to those forces, and that truth may emerge as the only over-arching message of any story.

In November of 1941, Ed suddenly received leave from Camp Roberts to come to Galesburg for his wedding. Helen's joy is obvious.

She telegrammed Ginny with certainty, obviously wanting her older sister by her side: "Can't come to Arkansas. Want you both in wedding party. Date set eighteenth [of December]. Ginny come soon. Don by seventeenth. Not for Christmas. Send telegram collect. Send dress size" (punctuation added). She happily shared with Ed that Mike and Polly, her Aunt Jessie, and others could attend, and on December 6 sent a telegram that read, in part, "terribly happy . . . plans all made . . . showers galore. Awaiting your arrival impatiently" (punctuation added).

Then, abruptly, the terrifying events broadcast from Pearl Harbor, Hawaii on December 7 shocked the nation. Naturally, all leaves granted to military personnel were in jeopardy. The Japanese declaration of war would have weighed heavily on both Ed and Helen, as it did most Americans. They knew the world to which they awoke on December 7, in their youth always so accommodating, no longer existed. Still, he must have hated to send the dreaded wire to Helen: "Think leave cancelled. Will inform you as soon as certain. Love" (punctuation added). I can only imagine her reaction, as her recent elation turned to frustration in the aftermath of the Japanese declaration of war. A small disappointment to be sure when compared to the more serious events, but one that must have stung. Yet on December 8, good news would arrive: "Leave still granted. Home Thursday as planned" (punctuation added). In an oversized orientation book to Camp Roberts, Ed has marked the photo of the officer who issued his leave, immortalizing him as key to the completion of their plans.

Plans for events following the wedding remained understandably tenuous. Ed informed Helen that due to demands of the Christmas holiday, he could not book reservations on the Union Pacific Pullman or the Burlington Zephyr, as he had hoped. No doubt those choices would have best suited newlyweds. In 1941, the Zephyr had introduced an all-female service team called the Zephyrettes as part of their luxury approach (Hogan). Ed likely hoped to pamper Helen, knowing her expectations would be high, but those plans were stymied. He advises her to get tickets on the Santa Fe line, and to do so quickly. I find a postcard later with a photo of "One of the Beautiful New Club-Lounge Cars on the Santa Fe Scout." Helen's note reads: "left Galesburg Fri. Dec. 19th, 1941, 3:00 A.M. Arrived in Los Angeles Sun. Dec. 21st, at noon or after." On a train schedule, she has written, "Was 5 hours late to L.A. cause of troop trains (war)." Her passenger train would have had to yield to those utilized for military transport. Such consideration would soon become a crucial part of the public consciousness.

Despite the hectic schedule, Helen's mementos reflect the joy and excitement that buoyed even her hurried plan. Theirs would be a traditional church ceremony with all of the required attention to detail. In the scrapbook, I find a lengthy florist order. Her bouquet would contain lilies, white chrysanthemums, pink sweet peas, and she would wear red roses for her "going away corsage." In the many enlarged photos from my parents' wedding, the lilies that she carried in her bouquet are especially prominent. According to the order, additional flowers for the bridesmaids, junior bridesmaid, and the church decorations emphasized shades from pink to wine, complemented by white. These colors I must imagine, as I gaze at the black and white photos. Both mothers would wear orchids. Her students sent hankies and stationery, as she dutifully records, and one dinner party in her honor was termed a "hanky shower." I'm reminded this was in the pre-tissue days, making handkerchiefs a high priority. One of Helen's party gifts was a large silver bell given by the hostess: "Inside the bell was a red ribbon on which a poem instructed each guest to take a smaller silver bell from a decorated Christmas tree. In these bells the names of the betrothed couple and the date, January 18, were printed on red ribbons." (The January 18 date was in error, as the wedding would take place on December 18.)

At one in the "oodles" of showers to which Helen referred, a newspaper article makes clear how important her friends were to her with the headline "Wedding Date is Surprise News at Party Wednesday." Two of Ed and Helen's best friends announced their own engagement at Helen's party.

Finally, the article featuring the ceremony appears: "Miss Helen Kost, E.C. Roberts Wed At Grace Church." The description reflects the detail one might expect in an article of its day. Her dress is described as suiting her well with its "fitted princess body line, soft shirring at the front of the bodice, sweetheart neckline and long tight sleeves with points at the wrist." The article lists all of their Knox College clubs and activities and includes the fact that Ed is stationed in California. Two colored swatches, one blue and one green, are included with Mother's notes: "from the 'blue' I wore during the wedding." She references the old instructions to brides to wear "something old, something new, something borrowed, something blue." Her explanation continues, as she writes "Same as bridesmaids wore" and "from ribbon on going away corsage (roses)."

I still have my mother's wedding dress. I had hopes that I and/or one of my daughters might wear it. Unfortunately, our shoulders were too broad to fit into that "princess body line." When my younger daughter was in high school, we removed from the back of the bodice the long row of 20 satin-covered buttons, each of which fastened with a satin loop, so that she could wear the dress for a high school performance in which she portrayed Queen Elizabeth I. My mother greatly enjoyed that fact.

Helen and Ed settled into life at San Miguel near Camp Roberts military base. Mother would tell tales later about the close quarters they shared with another couple, laughing at the non-existence of privacy. Not only did circumstances prove challenging for newlyweds still becoming accustomed to one another, but also because they could hear every sound from their "roommates". Because the military had to establish bases so quickly in light of the war, most were not equipped for family living, and housing proved scarce. In one instance, Ed and Helen lived in a converted California chicken coup until adequate housing could be identified; she delighted in sharing that story. I later find photos of the Brazils, the couple with whom Ed and Helen shared the chicken coop housing. To add to the amusement, Mrs. Brazil was also named Helen. The fact that everyone faced the same challenges helped them to accept and even laugh about such circumstances. They had each other, and it all must have seemed like a grand adventure.

I find Helen's account of that period inscribed in her Bride's Book:

> I spent my first five or six nights alone from 11:30 on. Then the order was the officers could live off post if they had telephones. We had no telephone yet (new house), so Burt & Helen Brazil had us stay with them for 2 or 3 nights. Then we had our phone, and they had no place to live starting Jan 1st, so they lived a month with us—in a 2 room 18 x 20 foot house! Had a wonderful time and made 2 lifelong friends.

By spring 1942, Ed achieved a major personal goal when promoted to First Lieutenant effective February 1; Helen includes in her collection "A TRUE COPY," as noted at the bottom of the page of the official "Teletype," informing him of the promotion. A line in the Teletype directs the Camp Roberts commanding officer, "Do not radio or telegraph acceptance." It is signed as a certified copy by Dave W. Evans, 1st Lt., Infantry, Adjutant. In April, an article in the Galesburg paper shared the news: "Mr. and Mrs. E. C. Roberts . . . have received word that their son, Lt. Edmund C. Roberts Jr., has been notified of his promotion to a first lieutenancy, which occurred April 10. He is attached to the headquarters of the 90th battalion at Camp Roberts, Calif." Below the blurb in her scrapbook, Helen glued a first lieutenant's "bar" made of cloth, like that which would be sewn onto Ed's uniform. Below the bar is one of Ed's mother's formal cards. She has hand-written with underlining for emphasis above and below her printed name: "Congratulations & love to our new Lt and his nice wife. Mother & Dad." The Kosts' congratulatory telegram is also there, and Helen includes a photo in the other album labeled "1st Lt. Ed." Postcards from San Francisco on the next page show that Helen had taken the first of many treks into the surrounding area. Destinations about which she had read became real, and her ever-present curiosity about her surroundings was satisfied.

Helen includes clippings from the 1942 *Knox Alumnus* that list the many alums in service, along with addresses where they can receive mail. I see that "Lieut. Dean Lindstrom has been assigned to a new post" with an address at Morrison Field, West Palm Beach, Florida. The blurb about

Ed notes his promotion to First Lieutenant. Details about others include when one received his wings; that another is stationed on the U.S.S. *Wyoming*; that one "has arrived at his destination at an unnamed place (in some cases locations were secret); that one is "in the air corps at Sheppard field, Texas, the world's largest air corps technical training school"; that one "has accepted a government position as junior physicist in the signal corps" in New Jersey; that another "is receiving training as a weather observer in the aviation service with the Second Squadron"; that one, who while at Knox was among "the outstanding triple-threat backfield men in Siwash grid history, is in the army air school at Santa Ana, Calif." A separate column bears the headline "First Knox Women Join WAACS, WAVES." The daughter of the former head of the Knox ROTC is among the women identified, and a few pages later I discover a newspaper photo of her saluting her father with the headline "SIR DAD." On campus, on March 27 a "Victory Hop," or dance, is held in honor of "Knox Men in Service." Helen includes a program from the dance and writes on it, "sent Ed a present while he was at Camp Roberts." By that time in late March, they would know that Helen was pregnant. The Galesburg families were no doubt thrilled with the news.

His superiors recognized Ed's leadership qualities early on, and he was often assigned special duties. In the first days of my research, I received proof of that leadership quality that apparently grew even stronger over the years. After his WWII prisoner-of-war experience, an honorable discharge, and a brief stint in civilian life, Ed returned to the military, first as a Master Sergeant, but before long was re-commissioned to the rank of Captain that he held at the end of WWII. I received a touching e-mail from a private who had been trained by Captain Roberts following his re-enlistment. In the portion of the message that appears below, I have made no corrections or changes. He wrote, in part:

> When Korea broke out, the Captain received a letter from President Truman. He called a Company meeting. We all stood at attention and he told us that he just heard from

> the President and he asked the company first Sgt. Marvin Petersen to read it to us. I think Master/W.O. marvin Petersen alas Pete /alas Luke was his best friend. The letter asked for volunteers to go to Korea with the Captain (because he had already volunteered) to crush the North Koreans which were killing civilians After the leter was read, Captain Roberts said anyone who will volenteer to go to Korea with me, take three steps forward. Without any hesitation, everyone in perfect unison took three steps forward . . . That was the proudest moment of my life. There was no way that our Capt was going without us.

I'm touched by the sentiment of the message and marvel again at the strength of the ties among Ed's military group. I also pause for a moment to ponder the facts. I know now that Ed's best friend, Warrant Officer Junior Grade Marvin Petersen, will later die with him in North Korea.

A telegram dated May 16, 1942 from Ginny and Don informs Helen and Ed that they will be at Camp Roberts by June 1. They request assistance: "if you can locate nice place make deposit. Would like small furnished apartment. Fifty or more coming from here" (punctuation added). Considering the housing shortage that Mom described, I wonder whether they found that apartment, particularly in competition with 49 additional people needing a place to live. I find Don's name on a list of First Lieutenants in a booklet about Camp Roberts. On the final page, he is listed in the roster of "company "D" 90th Infantry Training Battalion."

Postcards depict the "World Famous Coconut Grove" in Los Angeles, and Helen notes that they all enjoyed "Freddy Martin's orchestra." Another card features "The Arcady: A Distinctive Apartment Hotel" on Wilshire Boulevard in Los Angeles and Helen identifies it as a place where the four stayed. Additional postcards are from the Redwoods of California in Yosemite National Park, depicting the enormous trees; one could drive a car through an arch-way cut into one. I flinch at the idea that a tree might have been sacrificed for the thrill of tourists, but then remind myself that in my parents' era they had scant if any awareness of the impending threat to such natural resources.

Helen glued that card onto the same page where a sheet of paper dated July 28, 1942, sent from the 19th Infantry Training Regiment shows that Ed would receive three days leave "on or about July 29." The photo album contains many pictures from the time spent in California, and in several, Helen is visibly pregnant. A number of the pictures depict Camp Roberts, with the 90th Battalion Officers' Quarters, the dispensary, a supply room, and Ed posing with fellow officers. Many show the couple at play—I find the photo of "Blondie" the car posed before the giant redwood through which they had driven. Additional photos from Yosemite National Park in July 1942, likely from the days of leave Helen had documented, depict scenes of a mountain stream and falls, and Ed sitting in a camp chair before a building with the label "our cottage." In separate photos, Helen and Ed feed deer, and I'm reminded that they both enjoyed taking pictures, recording their special events, as well as those occurring on a "normal" day. I think of the term "quotidian," a word I've always enjoyed, both for its sound and feel, its demand that the tongue, lips, teeth, palate all participate in its pronunciation—a word one can taste, a word that requires effort. What a spectacular term developed long ago to describe the not-so-spectacular, as in one's daily routine. Its application seems appropriate to what young military couples experienced in those days of pre-American involvement in WWII. I'm confident that it continues to apply to military families today, a quotidian that those of us outside of that life and its particular challenges cannot understand.

In September, Ed's mother, Muzz Roberts, visited San Miguel, where Ed and Helen lived. Photos show a blossoming Helen in maternity dresses, and one in a swimsuit walking away from the camera, ducking her head, beneath which she has written, "Ed & Helen have a water fight." A second photo shows her peering at her backside and calves, no doubt damp from the water skirmish. Ginny is in another photo, the first of many following the Roberts' move to California. The Sperrys will appear more often in Helen's records, both pictured and written, their three lives remaining intertwined for life.

Baby Boy Roberts arrived on November 22, 1942. A telegram to Mrs. Kost reads: "Bruce Ingram. Seven Three Quarter Pounds. Born Four Thirty PM November 22. Mother and Baby doing fine" (punctuation added). My brother Bruce Ingram Roberts was born in the Paso Robles Community Hospital, and I find a bill from the hospital for $55.50. Not surprisingly, multiple photos of baby Bruce now populate the scrapbook's pages. The label at the top of the first full page of such photos I find touching in its simplicity. Substituting for the dates Helen had regularly included at the top of other pages is the single word "Parents."

Ed and Helen continued to find a way to enjoy time away from the base, and I momentarily wonder whether Ginny, still childless, cared for Bruce in their absence. I can't imagine Helen and Ed taking him. I find a telegram from Ed dated January 17, 1943, reading, "Reserving room and table as requested for Saturday Night—Palace Hotel." As proof that they took advantage of the reservation, I find the hotel bill for one night–$5.00. Then I spot a label for a photo now missing from the album on a page dated 1943. The label reads "Ginny, Don, Rachel & Bill Sharp, San Miguel, triplex with us," supporting my theory that Ginny would be nearby to share in childcare. The fact that Ginny and Helen could live in the same building would have meant much to Mother.

I'm interested to find additional evidence of how Bruce's arrival altered my parents' lives, and how his care was affected by birth into a military family. A note dated January 28, 1943 from a physician indicates that "Baby Bruce Roberts under my care requires approximately 8 (eight) 13.5 ounce cans of irradiated evaporated milk per week." I assume that the note would allow Helen and Ed to make the necessary purchase at the base Commissary, an excellent military perquisite, due to lower pricing in comparison to goods in a regular retail store. More important, that physician would play a crucial role in my mother's future as a widow of war.

The ability to purchase at bargain prices at the commissary proved only one of the financial boons for active military and veterans and their families of WWI, WWII, and the Korean conflict. After Ed was killed in

Korea, my mother would continue to shop at the Pine Bluff, Arkansas Arsenal until she remarried. The military remained generous at that time to children of those killed in war. When mother remarried, our stepfather Bob did not adopt us, Ed's three kids. We retained the Roberts name and the right to continue to receive a small measure of financial assistance, all of which Mother would place in a savings account to help defray later college education costs.

Helen includes a bulletin and price list from the Camp Roberts Commissary in her scrapbook. The list "of subsistence stores for the month of January 1943" contains regulations, including the fact that only those with an account authorization card may purchase. Due to the needs of the military, the provision of certain supplies and articles could no longer be taken for granted. The bulletin notes that paper bags will no longer be supplied "for articles which are already protected against outside contamination, such as; canned goods, dry cereals, etc. . . . no more than three (3) cartons of cigarettes will be sold to anyone during a day's business . . ." Persons authorized to buy at the Sales Commissary read that "due to the current acute and nationwide shortage of butter, cheese, eggs, and meat (especially pork products) it has lately been impossible to fully stock these items for sale." Select listings perhaps interesting to today's readers include:

<u>CANDY</u>
Hershey's asst'd, bar .10
Kraft's Choc. Parade, Deluxe, box.67

<u>TOBACCOS</u>

<u>CIGARETTES</u>
Avalon, 200's, ctn.96
Camels, 200's, ctn1.20
(The 1.20 per carton price applied to all additional brands:
Kools, Lucky Strikes, Old Golds, Philip Morris, etc.)

<u>CIGARS</u>
Roi Tans, 50's box(no price supplied)
Santa Fe Fatties, box4.23
Van Dycks, 50's, box2.12

<u>CHEWING</u>, Star, 10 cent cut.07

<u>CIGARETTE PAPERS</u>, Book.04

<u>RAZOR BLADES</u>
Gillette, thin 8/s, pkg.12
Gillette, Blue 10's, pkg.32
Schick, Injector 20's, pkg.45

<u>TOOTHPASTE</u>
Colgate, giant size, can.26
Dr. Lyon's, 4.5 oz. can.26
Pepsodent, 25 oz. size, can.15

<u>PERISHABLES</u>
Butter, issue, 1# pkg..48
Eggs, 1 doz., ctn.53

<u>MEATS, FRESH</u>
Beef, Boneless, lb.32
Beef, Carcass, lb..23
Beef, liver, lb.36
Chicken, Roasters, lg..41
Pork, Butts, lb..28
Spareribs, lb..18

<u>MEATS, SMOKED, DRIED, CURED</u>
Bacon, issue, lb. .37
Beef, Dried, sliced, lb. .62

ONIONS, lb.04
POTATOES, U.S. #1, lb..03

<u>COFFEE</u>
Chase & Sanborn 1#, tin.27
Folger's 1# jar.29
Maxwell House, 1# tin.29
Monarch, 1# jar.29

<u>CEREALS</u>
All Bran, 10 oz. pkg.10
Barley, Pearl, bulk, lb.05
Bran Flakes, 40% Bran, 8 oz. pkg.08
Corn Flakes, 11 oz. pkg.08
Grapenuts, 12 oz. pkg.12
Oats, Rolled, 48 oz pkg.11

<u>FLOUR AND FLOUR PRODUCTS</u>
Aunt Jemima Pancake Mix, 40 oz .19
Flour, 5# sack, lb.03
Macaroni, 1# pkg.11
Noodles, Egg, bulk, lb..11
Spaghetti, 1# pkg.11

<u>FRUIT – CANNED</u>
Apples, #10 can.40
Applesauce, #2 can.07
Blackberries, #2 can.17
Cherries, Marachino, 5 oz. gls.12
Fruit Cocktail, #1 tall can.19
Peaches #2.5 can.16
Pineapple, Sliced, #10 can.51

FRUIT & VEGETABLE JUICES
Apple Juice, S&W, 12 oz. btl.14
Grape Juice, 16 oz. btl.19
Tomato Juice, #2 can.08

MEATS, CANNED
Beef, Corned, #1-12 oz. can.23
Chili C/C w/beans, 16 oz. can.19
Hash, Corned Beef, 24 oz. can.20
Mincemeat, 30 oz. jar.30

MILK
Evaporated, 14.5 oz can.07
Fresh, Qt..13
Powdered, Bkry. Only lb.14

NUTS
Asst'd, lb.28
Peanuts, 8 oz jar.19

PEANUT BUTTER
Peanut Butter, 28 oz. tin.50

SOAP & SOAP PRODUCTS
Borax, 20 Mule Team, 1# pkg.12
Lux Flakes, 12.5 oz. pkg.20
Poet's, Gran., large, pkg.23
Purex, Qt. Btl.11

CANNED FISH
Tuna fish, 7 oz can.14
Sardines, 15 oz. can.09

SOUP (Campbell's), per can.10

<u>VEGETABLES, CANNED</u>
Beans, Lima, #2 can.08
Bean Sprouts, #10 can.38
Beans, String #2 can.09
Beets, Sliced, #2 can.08
Carrots, #2 can.07
Corn, Sweet, #2 can.09
Peas, Sweet, #2 can.09

I am close to the final page of the scrapbook but make several additional discoveries. More evidence that the couples enjoyed some fun along with service exists in the postcards and notecards. One reads, "Sunday at Ciro's Gala Show: Special Entertainment." A telegram from Ed reads: "Reserving Table for Two Coconut Grove Evening February 21 Ambassador Hotel."

When I look online for photos from the Coconut Grove, I immediately find a historic shot from the 1940s. In the black-and-white photo, the room is enormous and packed with couples, both at tables and on a crowded dance floor. At another site, I learned that the 300,000 square foot Ambassador Hotel occupied 23 acres, and the Grove could seat 800. The roof appears to be of flexible material, resembling a tent. It had to be of some height to accommodate the numerous real coconut trees that stretch upward from the floor. I can see the art deco design in an enormous fireplace on one wall and arches and columns on another. Boxes lined the walls and a large staircase welcomes couples to the dance floor after they walk through a series of shops in the hotel. One entertainer commented in an online video that the Grove was normally so packed that couples could only sway, due to the crowded conditions. Opening in 1921, the hotel formed the lynch-pin of Wilshire Boulevard, which would grow up around it. The Grove attracted a long list of the most famous celebrities and talented musicians and many service-related couples following the war. Among the musicians was Harry Belafonte, as the hotel became one of the first to hire African-American entertainers.

In its early decades, multiple movies were filmed at the Ambassador Hotel, which also hosted the second and twelfth Academy Awards. I'm reminded that Robert Kennedy's assassination took place at that Hotel in 1968. Across from the Grove stood a modeling agency and the models sometimes paraded through the Grove. One photographer claimed to have taken the first professional photo there of sixteen-year-old Norma Jeane Mortenson, the future Marilyn Monroe.

Even after the Ambassador closed to the public in 1989, bowing to the evolving neighborhood, the Hotel continued to be used as a set in many movies, including *The Graduate, Pretty Woman, Apollo 13, Beaches, The Wedding Singer, Forrest Gump,* and *Fear and Loathing in Las Vegas.* The Emilio Estevez movie *Bobby* that recounted the Kennedy assassination used the Hotel, even as demolition had begun in 2005. After the discussion of various purposes and some litigation on the parts of the Los Angeles Conservancy and the Unified School District, the site was dedicated to a new school. Original plans included the use of Coconut Grove in the new design, but structural deterioration resulted in its destruction as well. The grand hotel entrance and one wall were incorporated into the school. As I view silent footage of the hotel prior to its demolition, it inspires awe, in the manner that luxurious, plush establishments can. I watch the camera scan across the massive lobby and linger on the hundreds of key boxes beyond the check-in counter. I think of my parents, excited and happy, admiring the enormous lobby fountain as they walked to the counter to be handed a key. I like to think of them at "the place to be" in Los Angeles in their era.

I return to the scrapbook and find a printed set of directions from the hotel, suggesting that visitors fill out a postcard and hand it to their waiter. The Ambassador Hotel will mail it, "and the recipient will treasure it as a token of your thoughtfulness . . . and a souvenir from the WORLD FAMOUS COCONUT GROVE." Of course, I find the referenced postcard, which Helen dutifully completed and mailed to her parents. In small, neat cursive script that fits the tiny space Helen writes:

> Dear folks –
> We are sure having a grand time acting silly, etc. Had dinner here tonight and were on the NBC coast to coast program at 10:30 (12:30 your time). Sure hope someone in G'burg heard us. If you buy some war stamps or bonds you can do anything you want in the orchestra. Ed sang & I played the drums & the rest of Freddy Martin's orchestra played with us. "This is the Army, Mr. Jones." Sure was fun. I've always wanted to play the drums. Some guy took a picture of me playing the drums & is gonna send me one. I'm dying to see it. He hands 'em in to the Blue Network. Ain't I the one? We sure have fun doing everything. We're gonna shop tomorrow and maybe go to a broadcast.
> Lots of love, Helen

I have treasured that photo of my mother, sitting so confidently behind drums, sticks raised. Becoming a mother had not changed her desire to make some noise whenever possible, and the Coconut Grove provided her an amazing venue. I also imagine my father singing and wonder which song he selected. I find the card they had to complete in order to participate. Ed signed on to purchase $18.75 worth of war bonds.

A baptismal certificate for Bruce dated March 21, 1943 bears signatures of Don and Ginny Sperry as his sponsors. In her Bride's Book, Helen includes a detailed account of what she describes as her "homes" between her wedding and September 20, 1944, when Ed would leave by ship for England to participate in what would become known as the Battle of the Bulge. Her first home she describes as "Tiny . . . all electric. Brand new. Bed in living room. Knotty pine walls . . . Bruce's first home." They remained there off and on while Ed was stationed at Camp Roberts.

Those first months together in California would end when Ed was assigned to the Aleutian Islands as part of the 138th Division. He would leave in August and wouldn't return until spring of 1944. Not only did

Helen and Bruce enjoy the support of the Sperrys, but Helen also had a cadre of friends, along with both extended families, waiting to see her. In April 1943, Helen returned with Bruce to Galesburg for a visit that lasted until June "while Ed was in the Calif. desert," she notes in her Bride's Book. Photos reveal her catching up with many friendships and using the opportunity to show off her new son. She also made the trek to Pontiac, Illinois to visit her friends Flossie and Bill Edwards. In the photos, doting grandparents and a great-grandfather obviously enjoy playing with Bruce, who at six months likely entertained them all. Helen's mother, Elsie, traveled with Helen for the return trip to California. Helen's Bride's Book notes that they first drove to Marchfield, California and lived at Elsinore for five days, then spent a month in Portland, followed by a month in Washington state. I'm impressed by such an ambitious undertaking. Photos along the way show their visits to John and Dorothy Kost in New Mexico, and Bruce in photos labeled "Portland, Oregon 7 mo" and "Everett, Wash. 8 mo." The next page of photos of Ed, Helen, and Bruce is labeled "Last week before Ed left for the Aleutian Islands, August 1943." From what I have learned about Ed, he must have been eager for the chance for his first test in an active military situation.

I find six pages of photos from Ed's time spent in the Aleutians where he gained that first experience. I closely study a small photo of him in uniform and high boots. He stands against a backdrop of snow in bleak terrain. It offers quite a contrast to the scenes from the spring of 1943 at the Coconut Grove. A much larger photo of a room depicts one wall covered in maps and lines of string stretching to documents on a table where additional maps of the islands lay. When I flip the photo over, I read "Umnak Is, Aleutians, Feb. 1944." I find a similar photo later that is labeled "Orientation Board," and I understand that the string-map contrivance guided the planning of military tactics. I decide to pause to read a history of the U.S. activities in the islands to supply context for the many photos and this chapter in my parents' story.

As I read at history.com about war activity on the Aleutian Islands from June 1942 through August 1943, I learn that the Japanese garrisons on the islands of Attu and Kiska represented the only U.S. soil claimed by the Japanese during the Second World War. Historians disagree over the ultimate reason that the Japanese wanted control of those islands, but all agree that their occupation challenged American morale. Between May and August 1943, both islands were reclaimed by U.S. forces, action in which Ed played a small part, arriving in time to participate in the invasion of Kiska. When I turn back to his photos, I immediately make connections to what I've read, as I see the names of those two islands in the descriptions.

Originally created through volcanic activity, both occupied islands were known for their challenging, frigid weather conditions. When troops were not suffering snowstorms, they encountered high winds, rain, and fog. Ed's photos emphasize the details I read in the description of the terrain. On the scrapbook pages labeled "ADAK Island," I find one photo labeled "Tanaga Mountain." Helen has added an arrow pointing to the sky and written the word "cloud" beside it, emphasizing the wonder of a cloud formation that fills the entire top of the photo. That Ed would take and preserve photos of Adak Harbor and a "Snow scene from Mt. Moffet toward Finger Bay" demonstrates his awareness of the unusual nature of their surroundings. It also emphasizes the fact that, like Helen, he believed in the importance of first-hand records of important and interesting events.

The photo of the "Officers' Quarters, Company D, 138th Infantry" shows what appears to be a small prefabricated one-level building surrounded on three sides by snow walls. A trench through the snow to its door allows for entry. I assume that the snow provided both insulation and camouflage for the dark building that contrasts starkly with the white setting. One photo shows two men sitting inside the Officer's Quarters in conversation, one holding a glass bottle. I'm curious about the head that I view from the back. The neck-length styled blond hair makes clear this is a woman, no doubt administrative personnel, but I'm still surprised to see her there. I'm reminded of the tradition of women in the U.S. military, although not in combat positions in that war. In another photo, a man stands outside a building with the name "CAPT.

CARRIER" in script lettering above the door; I see this man in other photos as well. An additional photo of Adak Harbor shows the "Truck co. mess Hall" in the foreground. The acute desolation of the surroundings helps me to understand how dependent upon the company of his fellow soldiers Ed could become.

When I return to my reading about the Aleutians, I see that the U.S. Command did not focus on the Japanese island garrisons on Attu and Kiska when first entering the war following the Pearl Harbor attack. However, troops eventually increased to 94,000 on the other Aleutian Islands. On January 11, 1943, several months before Ed would arrive, American forces moved onto Amchitka Island, which was about 50 miles from one of the Japanese garrisons. American blockades choked the flow of Japanese supplies, and on March 26th American patrols engaged Japanese ships in what would be labeled the Battle of the Komandorski Islands. Apparently unaware of the damage their fleet inflicted on that of the United States, the Japanese withdrew, losing a strong advantage. That is one of many examples of strategical mistakes that would not be made today, in light of technological advances, resulting in improved communications. On May 11, 1943, thousands of U.S. troops began a move to reclaim Attu and Kiska, their leaders assuming the mission could be accomplished in a few days. But due to harsh weather conditions and terrain too rugged for the ill-prepared troops, two difficult weeks passed before they accomplished their goal. The Japanese troops were outnumbered, and Americans suffered greater casualties from frostbite, in some cases resulting in gangrene and other physical challenges than from enemy fire. Although the Japanese eventually surprised American troops with a "bonsai" attack, moving straight through U.S. forces, they ultimately failed in their efforts to drive them from the islands.

When the sole land battle of World War II on American soil ended on May 30, 1,000 Americans had died in the taking of Attu. Having learned to better anticipate the grueling weather and terrain, U.S. forces prepared for a battle to regain Kiska in August. But upon arrival, American troops found a deserted island, the Japanese apparently having departed weeks earlier, their escape protected by heavy fog. The Battle of the Aleutian Islands formally concluded on August 24, 1943.

I peer at a photo of four men labeled "Jap Prisoners from Attu." The poor quality of the small old black-and-white photo does not allow me to see much expression, if any on the faces. Two are hidden by hats pulled low over their eyes. All of the men are dressed in jackets, gloves, and hats of various styles and no fences or compound are visible. They appear completely unremarkable. Another photo shows a group of ten "Jap prisoner guards," most of whom are armed, and I do see a wire fence in the background. Other photos of interest include Ed looking on during the "Award of Purple Heart aboard President Monroe," a ceremony that took place on one of the ships used to transport troops. In the officers' quarters in another photo, Ed sits reading in profile with a scraggly beard and unkempt hair, not a fashionable look in that era; the boredom during downtime must have been acute. I understand why he included a photo of "Cook's tent, Truck Co.," the smoke from a small vent pipe rising into the gray-white of its surroundings. He also includes a photo of a table, set with cups, saucers, and glasses, not an auspicious scene for a photo. The men obviously valued meal time and the relief it provided from their routine. I'm continuously thankful for the interest that both of my parents took in recording their activities; I feel confident that he took the photos in part to share with Helen during this, their first extended separation period. I can chalk my own love of photography into the column of parental gifts.

In a five-by-seven-inch photo with his ever-present reading material in hand (this appears to be a magazine) and smoking a pipe, I see 1st Lieutenant Ed Roberts more clearly. I again think how strongly my brother and two of his three sons particularly reflect Ed's features. I can now identify as the Officer's Quarters the building in the background of the original photo of him standing, armed in snow, that I had remembered before beginning this writing project. I'm sure the isolated quality of his stance made it linger in memory, after first seeing it as a child. In other photos, he stands before a different building; he walks in the front of a group of four men; he poses with two others; he stands without a weapon and has traded his helmet for a fabric hat—one hopes lined with warm material—with ear flaps. I find an intriguing formal photo of a Japanese woman, jarring in contrast to the additional photos. It is labeled "Sweetheart of Jap Commander—Attu," and I assume it was taken from that commander's personal items as a type of trophy. How odd that I gaze on her face, many decades and thousands of miles from where she, or at least her family, may still live. A more sobering thought occurs. What if Ed carried a photo of Mother and/or us when he was later taken prisoner, or when killed that may have taken its place in an album far from my existence?

A full page of photos is from the invasion of Kiska, several with landing craft visible; others depicting wreckage; all shots of the sea making me shiver, as I feel the cold of a wind that must have cut through even the warmest layers of clothing. The last of the picture groupings are labeled "February – May, 1944," and depict an air field; Ed dressed in various uniforms; Ed again reading in the middle of a group of five men in the Officers' Quarters; a photo of one man in a foxhole; other photos of Ed without a coat, reflecting the warmer temps; and spectacular mountainous landscapes. Although the photo is missing, I read the label, "Olivia De Haviland on visit." I recall having seen the photo of the movie star dressed in a fur coat and hat; it has likely been moved to another of our family collections. How glamorous and exotic she would have appeared in the stark landscape of winter war, a surrealistic sight. She later would make an indelible impression on me, as I watched the 1939 movie version of *Gone with the Wind*, already long in her past when she visited the troops. I'm reminded again of the fluid and contingent nature of time.

Telegrams in mother's scrapbook from Ed to his mother and one from Helen's older brother, John, to Ed indicate that Ed was in the contiguous states in the second week of April 1943, but the date confuses me. I know that he did not return from the Aleutians until almost a year later, and I find no other evidence that he was given leave to return to California for a visit, though apparently he did. Helen had been living in Galesburg in his absence, and the photos that follow his from the islands depict a happy Bruce in Galesburg in September and November 1943.

I observe photos new to me, once memories to others, as Helen moves on to live with Ginny and Don in St. Augustine, Florida from December 1943–March 1944. While there, she traveled a bit and enjoyed swimming in February, a novelty for a young woman raised in Illinois. I'm touched to read labels from two missing photos. The first reads "Bruce's 1st Christmas Tree (2nd Christmas) at Sperry's, Fla. Don got it from the woods." Don's habit of always cutting a live Christmas tree for the holidays apparently began long before I looked forward to those holiday white pines, cut for the Sperry living room. The second label helps me imagine the missing photo: "Dec 18, 1943, holding roses Ed had Ginny get me for our 2nd wedding anniversary. He was in Aleutian Is."

I picture Helen holding those roses with pride and satisfaction, a remembrance from her absent and still-attentive husband. As her scrapbook had revealed, Ed had quite the successful track record to maintain. He likely felt pressured to fulfill Helen's expectations, even while he was away. She lists on the "Anniversaries" page in her Bride's Book where the couple was and what she received for each of those celebrated dates. On their first anniversary, they were on the "Star Route out of Sanmiguel," and she was in bed with an infection, baby Bruce 26 days old. She received a red corduroy skirt, slacks, and a jacket. The second anniversary is the one on which she received the roses, as well as "Evening in Paris talc." On the third, she was in Galesburg, while Ed was "on the way to or had landed, from England." She received a "mink-dyed muskrat fur coat." She adds in parenthesis with an arrow pointing to the word "muskrat," the word "northern." I remember seeing the coat decades later hanging in our hall closet and wondering about the experience of wearing parts of a real animal on one's body.

In a letter to us thirty years later, Mom told us, among other unexpected information that "From early June 1943 till Sept. 1944 Bruce and I were in 10 different places counting twice at my parents'." Then she boomeranged back to the present and continued in her more recognizable vein, without skipping a beat, "Everyone should take more calcium according to the *Reader's Digest* (April)." Suddenly I recall as a child having to complete quizzes that she read aloud from the *Digest*. The quizzes were designed for children at certain ages in order to test intelligence that should fall in line with developmental expectations. She must have hoped to discover eventually that I had at last developed an I.Q.—the number that launched a million mid-20th-century American mothers into a frenzy of anxiety—to match that of my older music-prodigy sister, Kay. If so, she would be disappointed.

In the scrapbook, a telegram to Helen from Ed reads, in part, "Prepare to come to California within a month. Bring car. Get someone to drive with you. Will get gas coupons here if can. Details in letter" (punctuation added). She laughed telling us about that message and Ed's expectations that she could just jump in the car and "get someone" to drive halfway across the country with her, baby in tow. A photo, most likely from the Galesburg newspaper has a caption that reads, "Troops Back From The Aleutians." The blurb below the photo notes, in part, Lt. E. C. Roberts, jr. [*sic*], of Galesburg, Ill. (seated left) and other officers of the 138th Division are shown changing clothes after arriving at Camp Shelby, Miss. after nearly two and a half years in the Aleutians." The time period referred to the total years spent by American troops in the Aleutians.

The photo suggests yet additional missed opportunities in my learning more about Ed and his experiences. I see in the caption that one of the other soldiers was from "Cadde Gap" in Arkansas. I immediately recognize the misspelling of the name Caddo Gap, a community only about 30 miles from where my older sister Kay has lived for more than 30 years. When I contact her with the information, she tells me that the last name of the soldier may also be misspelled. A slightly different spelling would match that of a well-known family in her area, and she'll pursue that lead. Another of the servicemen, a captain at the time of the photo, is listed as from Marshall, Missouri, not too far away from my present home of Kansas City. With the aid of the Internet, I quickly locate his obituary. I had relocated to Kansas City a few years before he passed away and could have contacted him. I see from the funeral home website that he had been a career Army man, retiring as a colonel. Like my father, he had been called to military life. I leave a remembrance on the online memorial book. Whether the family is still reading postings at this point is doubtful, but I remain hopeful. Perhaps the men would have remembered returning from the Aleutians with Ed, perhaps not. At the least, I might have learned something about the shared experience I so want to better understand.

With a turn of a page, Ed has returned to Galesburg and is holding a skeptical-looking Bruce on a page labeled May–June, 1944. No doubt Bruce needed a little time to warm up once again to his father after the long absence. On the next page, however, Bruce is all smiles in his father's arms. Ed, dressed in a floppy hat, is standing knee-deep in water. I carefully remove the photo from the adhesive corners, traditional to scrapbooks of past eras that hold it onto the page so as to read the writing on the back: "at creek near Camp Shelby, Miss., July, 1944."

I reach the end of Helen's scrapbook. She so lovingly preserved it for our family, many of its treasures just now discovered, too late to inspire conversation with her. She has left me much, but I must turn elsewhere for additional information.

I gaze at three loose photo proofs of my father dressed in uniform. In two he wears the same V-shaped soft fitted traditional cap, the photos from different angles; in the other, he wears the traditional hard-billed hat with a leather strap and that supports the addition of a heavy metal eagle insignia pin. Our family has many of his various pins, patches, and insignia, most of which my husband can quickly identify, but which I have had to study in order to understand their meaning. I speak often in classes about the importance of iconography to the coalescence of any group, social, religious, or governmental. All militaries prove adept at developing such symbols that require interpretation by outsiders, forming a language specific and easily accessible only to the group. Such exclusivity promotes pride and a sense of reward for investment on the part of members. Only those formally initiated, via ritual and/or training, have access and permission to use those symbols as they are intended to be used. I have read recently of various groups who now call out military perpetrators, those who dress as military or speak of military service with no valid claim to do so. When I was young, boys dressed in military costumes, just as they dressed up like cowboys, their G.I. Joes close at hand. But in times of heightened military activity, we are reminded not to take the uniform lightly.

Ed Roberts took his membership seriously and with pride. Regardless of one's attitude toward combat, such devotion can be appreciated, if only on an intellectual level. As I study his photo, though, I look past the handsome uniform and the confident gaze and see the faces of my adult brother and his sons. Those faces of the next generations reflect an iconography of a family that Ed will never know. He did not experience our own family rituals, dress in our favorite team colors, appreciate our awards and honors, symbolized by pins worn on commencement robes, competition medals, and trophies, badges of various types, not only for my generation but for that of his grandchildren. But that possibility was likely not on his mind when these final scrapbook photos were taken. Buoyed and encouraged by the thousands of members of their military family, he and Helen prepared to face the unknown, optimistic about the future. Soon Ed would be in Germany as part of the 106th Division, captured in the Battle of the Bulge and sent to a prisoner of war camp, his brief previous respite standing in a stream with his son only a memory. He would begin service with the dear veterans who helped me sketch a memory I never shared, one they generously allowed me to adopt.

> November 6, 2006
> Dear Ms. Brackett,
> Please pardon the delay. I have been trying my best to remember any traits or habits of Lt. Roberts. but it has been too many years. Lt. Roberts was my platoon leader and even though I was a Sgt. orders came down the line and I had very little direct personal contact with the platoon leader. Lt. Roberts was not with us, as I remember, very long. Officers and non coms [non-commissioned men, like this message writer] were separated in the POW camps so we had no contact there.

I do remember his face well. He was a very nice looking man, soft spoken and kind to all of us. I was one of the original members of the 106th, shipped in among the first of the new members and we had, as I remember about 4 officers as platoon leaders come and go over the years. And I believe Lt. Roberts was the last.

- CHAPTER FIVE -

THEIR OWN STORIES

Arachne lost in a weaving competition to her teacher, the immortal Athena. The loss proved grave. Arachne had declared that were Athena to win, she would never again weave, the activity which brought her the greatest pleasure in life. Arachne so grieved the loss of her art that her teacher Athena took pity and transformed the mortal Arachne into a spider so that she might forever weave. The transformative tool was not the magic wand of the popular fairy, or the words of a magician's spell, but rather the tip of Athena's spear. Weapons of war have long been associated with the skilled telling of a story. The phrase "The pen is mightier than the sword" carries great cache, even though it flowed from a like instrument that wrote, "It was a dark and stormy night."

> Stalag XIIIC, Hammelburg, Germany – January–February 1945
> It was around this same time that forward artillery observer Sergeant Peter Gackis wife received the dreaded telegram. Gackis had also filled out a Red Cross postcard, but it took too long to arrive—the MIA telegram came first . . . A notice soon appeared in Gacki's local paper that he was missing in action.
> Alex Kershaw - *The Longest Winter* (183)

• • • • • •

Lt. E.C. ROBERTS IS MISSING IN EUROPEAN WAR: Galesburg Officer Gone Since Dec. 16; Other Casualty News Reported
First Lt. E.C. Roberts, Jr., 25, Galesburg soldier who has been in the army since he was graduated from Knox college in 1941 and received his commission, has been missing in action in Germany since December 16, the war department last night notified his wife, Helen . . . The young man is the son of Mr. and Mrs. E.C. Roberts . . . He and his wife, the former Helen Kost, have a two-year-old son, Bruce.
The Register-Mail, Galesburg, IL newspaper clipping – undated

• • • • • •

Wednesday, October 25, 2006 9:00 PM
Mr. Kline,
Thanks to your help, I have heard from several members of your group, two of whom remembered something of my father, and almost all have sent me their own stories, which I highly value. I anticipate meeting you, so that I might thank you in person.
Personal Correspondence – Virginia Brackett

• • • • • •

I have the roster that Gen. Goode published on March 25, 1945 at Lager-Hammelburg of the officers at Hammelburg Oflag XIII-B.
"1st. Lt. Edmund C. Roberts, 0-405053, POW # 25476."
I'll send a copy of page 18 which has his name.
Personal Correspondence – Virginia Brackett

• • • • • •

According to the website of the WWII Museum in New Orleans, the United States suffered 418,500 military and civilian deaths in WWII.

During the first years of my research, I received information about the war experience from many who did not know my father, but who wanted to share their own war memories. One objective of this book is to share those stories, both brief and lengthy, with readers and to celebrate their generosity. Although each may focus on a similar experience, each account varies to include its own details in distinctive delivery. In some of the messages presented throughout, I have made a few grammatical changes for the sake of clarity, but no changes to content.

Oct 12, 06
Dear Virginia,
In response re: your father-

I was deployed to Europe early March 1945, in the infantry. Was issued weapon M-1 below Paris & sent to the front lines. Spent 7 days, six nights in a 4048 box car—not knowing where we were—and ended up near Adahen Ger, in Black Forest, assigned first to Co K 3rd Inf. Regt which was attached to 106 Div. The 3rd are (is) the oldest Regt in our history, they guard the tomb of the unknown soldier in D.C. Then was transferred to 106th 422d Regt Co D. We guarded German prisoners. Another soldier & I were assigned to a Pup tent in the woods. I . . . can't remember anyone now-except two Sgt's. I'm sorry I can't relate any other data than that. Our outfit later was [transported by] trucks some place in . . . of Germany. After that I ended up with 89th Inf. Div. at Rouen, France was then deployed to South Pacific via USA. Records were changed . . . in USA and I ended up in V CORP Headquarters at Ft. Jackson, S.C.

I did remain in the reserves for a total of 21½ years service. I'm sorry I can't help you re: your father.

• • • • • •

Robert L. Blackwell
October 6, 2006
Dear Mrs. Brackett

As per our telephone conversation, I am enclosing a copy of my history in the service, which included time in Company D. I remembered your father Lt Roberts, when he interviewed me when I was assigned from Ft. Benning Ga to Co. D 422nd 106 Div . . . He was a well liked officer and got along with the men very well. We were not together at any time when we were in Germany.

The person I remember the most was Charles Smith, who is deceased. He was the head chef for Co. D, and I wrote some about him in my story. I hope you enjoy my story even though it does not mention you father. If I can be of any further help with your endeavor, let me know.

Yours very truly,
Bob Blackwell

One thing in my story is not correct. I wrote that the bombing when we're in the railroad track in Cologne Germany actually took place in another area.

I decided to enclose a few pictures.

1. Map of Europe with a line drawn the route that was taken after we were captured.
2. This is a picture of the area where out train was sitting when we were bombed.
3. Picture of me which was taken right after I got out of the service.
4. Picture of my wife and me taken recently. In May of this year we celebrated our 59th wedding anniversary.

Following WWII, a letter from the Army Ground Forces Headquarters, Office of the Commanding General dated 6 November 1945 to Ed expresses "my very real appreciation for the important part" that he played in the war. "Without you, and others who like you unselfishly gave up civil pursuits to defend the civilization we cherish, our brilliant and complete victory could never have been achieved." It is addressed to "Captain Edmund C. Roberts, Junior," reflecting his promotion from lieutenant to captain following imprisonment. The letter concludes "I am sure you will resume your duties as a citizen with the same loyalty, leadership and devotion that have marked your service as an officer. You go to your home with my wishes for your good fortune in the future." It is signed by Jacob L. Devers, General, USA, Commanding.

As I consider the importance of service during WWII to those to whom I've spoken, I find special meaning in a one-sentence paragraph in the Devers letter: "Your military organization and the friendships you have formed therein will be a source of great satisfaction to you for many years to come." The crucial role that the VFW (Veterans of Foreign Wars) organization played in veterans' lives for decades following the world wars proves the sentiment in that sentence. In addition to such community organizations that helped preserve relationships, individual battalions, regiments and companies found ways to extend opportunities for continued contact over many decades. I became familiar with a few such groups as I participated in several reunions of Ed's 422nd battalion of the 106th Division from WWII and, on one occasion, with a meeting that included anyone from the 106th Division. In the spring edition of *The Cub of the Golden Lion*, the publication of the 106th Battalion, one mini-reunion was highlighted with the following introduction:

> They are older now, much older than they ever thought they would become.
>
> Each year for the past fifty-eight years, the surviving members of the 106th Infantry Division's "Golden Lions" hold a mini-reunion with their brothers in arms. Every year, their ranks become smaller. This year, only fifteen of the more than fifty members in Michigan were able to attend. But like they have every year, they made it.

I read that the group's speaker for the occasion concluded his presentation by projecting on the wall a paraphrased excerpt from The Saint Crispin Day's Speech from Shakespeare's *Henry V* Act 4, Scene 3 (1599):

> This story shall the good man tell his son;
> And this day shall ne'er go by,
> From now to the ending of the age,
> But we in it shall be remembered-
> We few, we happy few, we band of brothers;
> For he who shed his blood with me today
> Shall be my brother

The article continues, describing the emotional reaction of the group as they remembered "buddies killed." "Tears filled their eyes . . . for loved ones and comrades that have lost their own personal battles through the years; for the memory of pain, wounds, captivity, escape, cold, hunger and rescue that each . . . struggled with over the years." The account includes specific experiences of two of three former POWs present at the reunion. The details of one follow:

> Jack Gillespie was captured on December 16th. He was marched to a rail station, brought to Berlin and interrogated. He later was sent to Bavaria and marched to Czechoslovakia. He was imprisoned there until the Russian guns could be heard moving west. He then was rescued by the British under Gen. Bernard Law Montgomery, and flown to northern Germany on "Monty's" private plane. He weighed less than 90 pounds when he was released. He still suffers from his captivity.

The article notes that one widow continues to attend the reunions twenty years after her husband's death. Children of veterans, like me, attend and identify themselves, hoping to discover information about their fathers from those with whom they served. The group continued to gather for large and small reunions until only a handful of men remain to make the trek. During the ten years or so that I dedicated to the process of producing this book, all but one or two of those who assisted me to better understand the events of 1941–1945 involving my father passed on.

When my husband and I moved from Chicago to Kansas City, we again packed our hundreds of books for transport. I decided to do a better job of arranging them in our new home than we had in the past, so that we might more easily locate specific books in what became a large library composed of both of our collections. I returned to one of several sets of shelves where we had placed books in loose categories upon unpacking. I read the title on one spine—*Dark December*—and didn't recognize the book at first. The title suggested a mystery, of which my husband is a great fan, and I wondered whether it might be one that he brought to the marriage. I pulled the obviously old book down from the shelf and opened it. Then began what I like to describe as events that would be at home in the plot of a B grade movie. A letter that I had never seen fell from the book, so startling me that I momentarily froze, staring at it where it rested on the floor. It would prove pivotal to my investigation. It read:

ROBERT E. MERRIAM
Office: 1463 EAST 55th STREET
Telephones: BUTTERFIELD 7411-7412
CHICAGO 15, ILLINOIS
Residence: 1321 EAST 56th STREET
Telephone: HYDE PARK 5267
CHICAGO 37, ILLINOIS

December 1, 1947
Mr. E. C. Roberts, Jr.
1447 North Broad Street
Galesburg, Illinois

Dear Mr. Roberts:

I was very happy to have your recent letter concerning my book "Dark December," and I was very much interested in your story about the two regiments in the 106th Division. As a matter of fact, I was aware that a large number of these people put up a very gallant fight, but the leaders appeared to have lacked this individual drive. This is not my own opinion, but that given to me by almost every Allied commander with whom I spoke, and by the Germans who captured your Division.

I am sure you understand the difficulty in a short book of this type of completely satisfying all of the units who were in the battle. If I didn't mention the units of the 106th Division which fought on after the first few days, it was an oversight, (although my memory tells me that I did go into this subject.) You can rest assured that I have read all of your Division history and most of the messages and other information, including reports of officers who were freed after the war was over.

I would be very happy to talk with you sometime if you are in Chicago. Don't hesitate to give me a ring.

Sincerely yours, ROBERT E. MERRIAM

I had indeed stumbled upon a mystery, although not of the fictional type that I anticipated. This mystery centered on two individuals, the author/storyteller, Mr. Merriam, and an original actor in the story he told, Captain Ed Roberts (retired at the time). As for the strategy of the leaders of the Allied Forces that embroiled the newly-constituted, untried and under-trained members of the 106th Battalion in the Battle of the Bulge, little mystery exists. Historians and theoreticians agree that the decision to assign that Battalion to a location open to German attack proved not only foolish, but deadly to many. Generals wrongly believed that the Germans would not push through that specific area, and they gambled heavily on that belief. A summary of the details involving the

106th in *The Cub*'s spring, 2003 publication suffice for the needs of this narrative:

> TYPE OF DIVISION: Army of the United States
>
> NICKNAME: Golden Lion Division
>
> SONG: "Onward Lions of 106 to Victory," words and music by Frank Power
>
> ACTIVATION DATE: 15 March 1943. INACTIVATION DATE: 2 October 1945, Camp Shanks, NY
>
> COMPONENT UNITS: 422, 423 and 424 Inf Regts.; 81 Engr Combat Bn; 106 Cav Rcn Tp (Mecz); 331 Med Bn. Div Art: 589, 590, 591st FA Bns (105 how) and 592 FA BN (155 how). Sp Tps: 106 QM Co, 106 Sig Co, 806 Ord Co (LM), Hq Co, MP Plat and Band. TRAINING UNDER ARMY GROUND FORCES. The division was activated at Fort Jackson SC, and was assigned to the III Corps of the Second Army.
>
> DEPARTED U.S. FOR FOREIGN DUTY: 10 November 1944
>
> DATE ENTERED COMBAT: (Division) 10 December 1944
>
> COMBAT DAYS (DIV): 63 RETURNED TO U.S.: 1 October 1945
>
> BATTLE CREDITS: (Division) Northern France, Ardennes; and Rhineland.
>
> SUCCESSIVE COMMANDING GENRALS: MG Alan W Jones from 15 Mar 1943 through Nov 1944; MG Donald A Stroh from Feb 1945 to inactivation
>
> DISTINGUISHED UNIT CITATION: 81st Engr Cmbt Bn for 16–23 Dec 1944 action in Germany.

> COMBAT HIGHLIGHTS: On 11 Dec 1944, the 106th Infantry Division went into the line in Belgium. It was a quiet sector. Five days later all the hell of modern war broke loose in that sector. The full force of Von Rundstadt's breakthrough spearhead came up against the 106th. The regiments of the division absorbed all the power which the Germans could deliver at that point. Only a handful of men from the regiments came back, but it could be said of the division as a whole that it went down fighting. The German attack started 16 Dec 1944. The enemy turned its guns on the 422nd and 423rd Inf Regts and followed up with infantry and tank assaults.

I find in Helen's collection an account in a curiously small booklet, about half the size of a graphic novel, on which the one from *The Cub* might be based. The cover of the booklet is missing, and the first remaining page is numbered "3" and titled "Index of Division Histories." While I find an Acknowledgement page, I find no credit to an author or to any particular organization. I assume it is military produced. It contains condensed historical accounts for all 106th Infantry Divisions, as well as those titled "Americal" [I look up this term and discover that it refers to what was later known as the 23rd Infantry Division. The group activated on the island, New Caldonia in 1942 following the attack on Pearl Harbor as the only division formed off U.S. territory in WWII] and "Philippines"; for twenty Armored Divisions; for the Airborne Divisions 11th, 13th, 17th, 82nd, and 101; and for the First Cavalry Division. Pages following the account of the 82nd Airborne are missing from the worn booklet. The wording of the account of the 106th is quite similar to what I have read thus far in *The Cub* but contains more descriptive rhetoric than I would expect to find in an official publication. For instance, in describing the Nazi attack, it reads, "von Rundstedt was on the loose with his and the Nazi's last desperate bid for victory. His main spearhead struck the 106th with pulverizing force." I return to *The Cub* account but keep this booklet close at hand.

> On 23 Dec the division pulled back to reorganize, but was thrown into the line once again the next day. It finally helped to halt the Germans on the north side of the salient between Stavelot and Manhay. During the gigantic German offensive the 106th suffered 8603 casualties, which included more than 7000 men missing. Before the last big drive into the Reich could gain momentum, the division was pulled back to Rennes France for rehabilitation. While there it also constituted the reserve for American troops investing the St Nazaire and Lorient pockets. When the Germans began to surrender by the thousands in April and early May 1945, the 106th was rushed east to take over the partly-built prisoner of war cages and to handle the masses of humanity who were milling about in American held territory. The division in June 1945, had a strength of 40,000 men, three times the size of an ordinary Infantry Division, because of the gigantic task it had to undertake on caring for prisoners and displaced persons. Late in June the division had headquarters at Bad Ems, and was disposed along a 340 mile front. The division sailed for the US in late Sep 1945 and was inactivated upon arrival in this country.

I return to the booklet and read another highly descriptive passage that follows the notation of the 8663 casualties suffered in the Battle of the Bulge. It applies the 106th moniker of "The Golden Lions" to the division and describes it as "now tempered in the hottest crucible of the western front." When I carefully turn back to the Acknowledgement page, I read the reason for the publication:

> In due time, historians will weigh data, not now available, to write the authentic histories. In the meantime soldiers who served with them are impatient to read what their outfits did, to remember the names of their commanding officers, the stations where they trained, when they went

> overseas, what were the component units, what were the principal actions and what awards were made to minor units or to the divisions themselves.

The final paragraph on that page reads: "As the years pile up, the hardships, the suffering and even the differences of opinion will mercifully fade. The luster of the glory will grow brighter. No divisions in our military history have added more glory to its pages."

A still smaller publication about the actions of the 106th, little larger than my palm, its full-color cover still intact, contains a statement on the first page that by now rings familiar. Written by Donald Stroh, Major General, Commandin [*sic*], it states,

> When the history of the Ardennes fighting has been written, it will be recorded as one of the great strategic allied successes of the war in Europe. Tactically, for the 106th and the other American divisions involved, it was a bitter and costly fight. But it becomes increasingly clear that the Germans expended in that last futile effort those last reserves of men and material which they needed so badly a few months later. The losses and sacrifices of the 106th Infantry Division paid great dividends in eventual victory.

I glance down at the opening paragraph, which begins "Dec. 16, 1944: Springing from the bleak vastness of Schnee Eifel with the speed of a coiled snake, Field Marshal von Rundstedt's desperate but mighty counter-offensive struck toward Belgium and the Ardennes."

As the coverless booklet predicted, details of the battle and subsequent capture of most surviving members of the Battalion have been rehashed, revisited, and reshaped through the lens of history. In general, it is believed to represent one of the great failures on part of those in command of American forces. That revisionist telling is not the focus of this book, which instead seeks to present the story of the Battle of the Bulge through the words of those individual men actually on its lines.

Some details regarding the military point of view, as reviewed above, at the time may prove important to those stories. Helen saved various newspaper articles and communications sent from the military to Ed that help supply context for his contemporary reaction to the various accounts of the battle.

Ed's indignation at one man's report of the battle and what he perceived as the short shrift that his battalion and his regiment, the 422nd—as well as that of the 423rd—specifically received is understandable. He was there and witnessed the individual sacrifices that a broad analysis of military strategy generalizes through numerical figures. The tiny history booklet that opened with the statement by Major General Stroh comments:

> Surrounded, the 422nd and 423rd fought on, Ammunition and food ran low. Appeals were radioed to HQ to have supplies flown in, but the soupy fog which covered the frozen countryside made air transport impossible. The two encircled regiments regrouped early Dec, 18 for a counterattack aimed at breaking out of the steel trap. This bold thrust was blocked by sheer weight of German numbers.
>
> The valiant stand of the two fighting regiments inside the German lines was proving to be a serious obstacle to Nazi plans. It forced von Rundstedt to throw additional reserves into the drive to eliminate the surrounded Americans, enabled the remaining units and their reinforcements to prepare the heroic defense of St. Vith, delayed the attack schedule and prevented the early stages of the Battle of the Bulge from exploding into a complete German victory.

Helen includes one summary article titled "Battle of the Bulge" from an unidentified newspaper in her scrapbook, along with one titled "U.S. Casualties in German Drive Listed at 40,000." These are in addition to articles from the Galesburg paper featuring Ed and one other local man taken prisoner. The headline: "Lt. E.C. Roberts is missing in European

War: Galesburg Officer gone since Dec. 16; Other Casualty News Reported" ("Lt. E.C. Roberts"). In addition to contemporary articles, she also includes articles printed during the few years following Ed's return. One by William Strand is titled "Bulge Battle—Proud Chapter in U.S. History; GI Courage Routs Hitler Bid for Victory." The article is described as the third of five by Strand, "who was at the Ardennes front" and uses the term "epic" in describing the battle (Strand).

Later articles look back to certain aspects of the war, and Helen has naturally saved those that relate to Ed's experience. An article by Kenneth Koyen titled "General Patton's Mistake" chronicles Patton's error in the use of "a task force," rather than the strength of a "combat command" to free Hammelburg, where Ed and other officers were kept as POWs. Koyen later explains that "'a combat command'" is a measure of military strength as specific as the word 'brigade.' . . . usually half the flexible fighting force of an armored division." It would likely include "a medium tank battalion, an armored infantry battalion, an armored field artillery battalion" and support such as "mechanized cavalry, tank destroyers, engineers, heavy artillery and sometimes air support . . . a powerful force." A task force "could mean anything from a couple of beat-up cavalrymen in a peep—the tankers seldom called it a jeep—to a couple of companies or a major offshoot of a combat command." Koyen sums up his point by writing, "Patton sent a boy on a man's job."

Ed had been interred in the Hammelburg prison camp, along with Patton's son-in-law Lieutenant Colonel John K. Waters, who had been a prisoner for three years. While the damage done to the prisoner of war camp by the attack led by Captain Abraham Baum helped liberate many prisoners, it did not rescue many who were sick or injured. I know from family stories that Ed and two or three others escaped the camp, one of the three dying in the attempt to reach American forces. I will learn later in an article written by my father that he escaped with three other officers, and I'm unsure whether anyone died during the attempt, as I find nothing to confirm that fact. That escape may have taken place before or after Baum's drive, which would have weakened the compound, making escape easier, but, as evidenced by the possible death of one of

Ed's group, not assured. But Ed did enjoy an audience with General Patton, which I'd been led to believe was, in part, for the General to collect intelligence regarding the prison camp, ostensibly due to Waters' presence there. Some theorized that Patton ordered the task force due to the Waters imprisonment in that particular camp, although Patton later stated that he only knew with confidence that Waters was at the camp nine days following the attack.

I track down information on Mr. Koyen online and discover he was a longtime freelance journalist. More importantly, according to his obituary, he:

> was on the staff of the 'Paris Herald' in that city when World War II began in 1939. He served as an officer in the Armored Force of the Army of the United States in Europe in five campaigns and was awarded two Bronze Stars. During the war, he was on his division's G-2 (Intelligence) staff and wrote the combat history of his unit, 'The Fourth Armored Division, From the Beach to Bavaria'" ("Kenneth Albert Koyen").

One can see in the article that Mr. Koyen's concern partly focused on the attitudes of the men in combat at the time that he wrote his story, which was after Patton's death (Koyen).

Koyen notes that Patton had made the statement in "a personal journal published in The Saturday Evening Post." Patton wrote, "'I can say this—that throughout the campaign in Europe I know of no error I made except that of failing to send a combat command to take Hammelburg." Interesting in light of my reading about the various events of the war decades later, Koyen adds that Patton wrote, "with a self-confidence that history may not seriously question." However, those soldiers who served in Patton's 3rd Army "may not be prepared to say that their commander made only one error."

Individuals in every area of the Armed Forces have continued telling stories many years beyond their experience. *The Cub* has served as an excellent source of such stories for me. Quotations from those stories, welcomed by its editor in every edition, invite readers into the personal experience that history with its more general goal may overlook. The publication also contains a "Historian's Message . . ." column. It signals an awareness of history's varied versions of events and emphasizes the importance of learning history other than the battalion's own, such as that of the locations where combat occurred and of the geographic locations where they hold reunions. In one column, the Historian's remarks prefacing the collection of WWII photos that follow make clear that some important stories would never be shared: "I fully realize that many of you don't want to re-live your experience. I understand. If you care about your buddies and their experiences, I recommend that you read their stories. You will learn a lot about them that you never suspected" (Schaffner). An additional benefit to the relation of stories is that one, perhaps, learns something about one's self in the re-telling of personal experience. A poem from the fall, 2002 issue captures the survivors' sentiment:

> My First Reunion
> We were there, that winter long ago
> We survived: many of our comrades fell.
> Twin enemies were the weather and the foe—
> The never-ending cold and the bursting shell.
> Conceived of this ordeal of fire and icy earth
> this brotherhood of old men came to be;
> a kinship stronger far than that by birth
> was born when we were young, across the sea.
> Of the ties that bind, others cannot know,
> but we were there, that winter long ago. (Carver)

The poet is identified as Dale Carver, Poet Laureate of the 106th Infantry Division Association, and the poem appeared as a tribute to his memory. As I continue to ask the question, why did my father return to the military with so much at home at stake, the identification with his comrades expressed by Mr. Carver could provide at least a partial answer. The dedication to Ed Roberts' memory and helping that memory remain a living entity on the part of two individuals that I eventually identified via my correspondence—John Carrig and Frank Trautman—support that possibility.

Memory, and the crucial nature of the act of remembering, remain the foremost theme of many military publications. One featured activity of the 106th Infantry Division Association was a collection of funds that supported the purchase of a memorial to be placed at the Andersonville (Georgia) Museum and Memorial to all of the U.S. Prisoners of War. Dedicated on May 25, 2003, it ensures, according to the Association President, "that the men of the 106th Infantry Division who suffered the indignities of being a prisoner of war, and sometimes death, under horrific circumstances, will long be remembered." The program from the Andersonville Memorial Dedication contained the following statement: "TO ALL AMERICAN SERVICEMEN AND WOMEN WHO HAVE NOT RETURNED FROM THEIR LAST ENGAGEMENT." Accounts of additional, sometimes more personal, memorials followed in later editions, such as one erected to "The Last Five Hundred Men of the 106th" in Belgium. The spring 2012 edition of *The Cub* included a feature that focused on the memorial. One 106th member, Herb Sheaner, and his family traveled to Belgium for a tour of the area that served as battlefields during the Ardennes Offensive. They were met by a young man named Carl, a local who had "adopted" the 106th Infantry Division as a child, his class visiting the site on a school field trip. According to Sheaner, Carl "fell in love with the Division and learned of its difficulties and hardships. Today he is our Belgium 106th Division Liaison and local Historian."

Sheaner recalls his military activity as the group drives along the road that played a crucial part in the fate of the 422nd Regiment. They eventually arrive at the area where the last men from both the 422nd and the 423rd "were surrendered" after a decision by their officers on December 21, 1944. Sheaner writes, "I was there. We were hungry, without sleep, cold, numb, without food, with little or no ammunition, no fire support, no medical help for the wounded and facing the promised deadly fire of concentrated German artillery that evening of December 20th." At that spot, Carl "nailed a memorial on a tree," and Sheaner signed it "as a member of that surrendered group." As of the time of the writing of the article, the memorial remained, awaiting "the arrival of any survivor to sign his name to the new 106th Infantry Division Memorial." Carl later established a website, a tribute to the division from a member of a grateful younger generation at www.106thinfantry.webs.com.

One veteran's story extended far beyond the Bulge. He spent decades searching for answers about his brother's death following imprisonment as a POW. The two Vogel boys did everything together growing up, separated in age by only about 18 months. The only children in their Jewish family, the older brother Bernard was called "Jack" by his adoring younger brother Martin. Both took draft deferments in 1942 in order to attend Brooklyn College, but as U. S involvement in the world war intensified, deferments were canceled. After Jack's drafting into the 106th Battalion and deployment to Europe in the fall of 1944, Martin was acutely affected by his absence. The appeal of higher education without his brother diminished, and he signed up for duty the following year. Martin became part of the 372nd Engineers and served as a guard at the end of the war in Germany's Bad Kreuznach. Martin came home, but Jack died in a prison camp, and the family later buried him. They had been notified by the war department that he had been taken as a POW but received no additional details, other than that his body was found with those of a number of American POWs in a cemetery near Berga, a small town in eastern Germany.

Martin began to wonder what had happened to Jack, as did many family members of the soldiers removed from the cemetery and returned home. Although Martin did not know it at the time, one of his uncles began to make inquiries. The uncle located and contacted several POWs from Berga who had returned to the U.S. Their responses contained few specific details, as the men didn't want to write about what had happened to them. However, their correspondence made clear the despicable conditions of their imprisonment. One man who witnessed Jack's death wrote that he "was made to work in the mines" and that he, like all of the POWs "suffered from malnutrition," which "made him easy prey to pneumonia, he didn't have the strength or will to fight the disease . . ."

Jack's family soon understood that conditions at the Berga POW camp proved far worse than at most other camps. According to Martin's account, on September 3, 1946, before a military tribunal at the Dachau concentration camp, Berga's commanders were charged with "assaulting and killing POWs . . . and deliberate mistreatment of prisoners." This information became available in the book *Soldiers and Slaves: American POWs Trapped by the Nazis' Final Gamble* (2005), written by *The New York Times* journalist Roger Cohen. Although American POWs volunteered to testify at the tribunal, none were called. The tribunal did see written testimonies from a dozen POWs. Both former commanders, Sgt. Erwin Metz and Capt. Ludwig Merz received severe sentences, but both sentences were later reduced. By 1955, both men were released from prison.

Many years later in the early 1960s, Martin received his uncle's correspondence from a cousin. While traveling in Italy, he discussed his brother's experience with Mitchell G. Bard who was in the process of researching for his book, *Forgotten Victims: The Abandonment of Americans in Hitler's Camps* (1994). Although he learned a few details through the years about the POW camp, Martin remained frustrated over the lack of a full explanation for his brother's death. In the 1990s at his wife's class reunion, Martin met Dan Steckler, a Berga survivor, but like the man who wrote the letter to Martin's uncle decades earlier, Steckler provided little of value. Adding another piece to the puzzle, in 2003, PBS aired a Charles Guggenheim documentary titled *Berga: Soldiers of Another War*. Martin found it informative, but it offered no new information specific to his brother.

At last in 2008, a friend told Martin to check a CNN website for an article published on Veterans Day titled "WWII vet held in Nazi slave camps breaks silence: 'Let it be known.'" Martin was amazed to discover that the veteran finally sharing details was the same man, Anthony Acevedo, who had responded so vaguely to his uncle's inquiry in the 1940s. Acevedo had broken his silence to express "anger that the government had never recognized what he and his fellow soldiers had endured at

Berga, and it [the article] quoted from his diary. Among his recollections were the last words of a young soldier named Bernard Vogel." His details about early imprisonment at Bad Orb matched those of other veterans. Almost 5,000 men were crowded into barracks— "sewage flowed into trenches . . . the prisoners grew so hungry that one of them attacked the camp's cook with a cleaver in an effort to steal food from the kitchen. Until the Nazi guards could find the culprit, they made everyone stand outside for 12 hours in the snow."

I paused in my reading of the article to think about my father, awarded a purple heart due to frostbite sustained while forced to stand barefoot in the snow, just as Acevedo described. I did not know until reading the article whether that practice was generally punitive or in retribution for an unacceptable act on the part of the other soldiers. It could have been for either reason in Ed's case.

The guards at the first prison camp where the POWs were retained demanded details about the prisoners, particularly information regarding "their pasts, their families and their ethnicities . . . a clear violation of the 1929 Geneva Convention, which states that POWs must not be coerced into disclosing anything more than their names and ranks." Acevedo was tortured as part of his interrogation, the Germans inserting "needles in my fingernails." Dog tags revealed the religion of the American soldiers through an initial: "*C* for Catholic, *P* for Protestant, *H* for Hebrew." In January 1945, the guards gathered all the troops, including "Cpl. Anthony Acevedo of the 7th Infantry Division and Pfc. Bernard 'Jack' Vogel of the 106th," and demanded that Jews step forward. When few obeyed the command, the guards arbitrarily grabbed others "who supposedly looked Jewish, including Vogel, as well as troublemakers and other 'undesirables,' including Acevedo," and a group of 350 men was loaded onto a train and sent to what Acevedo described as "a slave camp."

Cohen and Guggenheim included in their accounts that many Eastern Europeans, including children, already at the camp wore the Star of David on "striped uniforms." When Americans arrived to free the camp, they at first, according to Acevedo, "thought we were Germans, camouflaged, when they saw us in the shreds of clothes." Acevedo weighed 149 pounds at the beginning of the war and weighed 87 pounds when liberated. The most inflammatory detail of his account was his statement that following their delousing and feeding, "each soldier had to sign a 'Security Certificate for Ex-Prisoners of War,'" that held them to secrecy regarding conditions of their imprisonment. The reason given was "in order to protect 'the interests of American prisoners of war in Japanese camps' and future wars." Many would not have discussed the experience anyway, due to shame about their own actions under the horrific circumstances or for other reasons. Those who later chose to break silence found they often were not believed.

The enormous public reaction to the CNN story prompted Drash to continue his investigation and publication of additional articles. Readers lobbied "for a response from the Secretary of the Army, who . . . ordered the Pentagon to investigate." Members of Congress joined the fight for "long overdue recognition of the 'service and sacrifice'" of the 350 soldiers. According to U.S. Army Maj. Gen. Vincent Boles, "the Army's intent in having the prisoners sign the 'Security Certificate' was solely to prevent them from talking about escapes and those who had tried to help them escape. 'We didn't explain it correctly, and it was construed as a secrecy document.'" His representative shared this information at a long overdue recognition ceremony in Orlando, Florida on June 6, 2009. Drash subsequently visited the Vogel household on multiple occasions, and Martin shared later government documents that he received with Drash as well. The article containing that information was sent to me by the veteran I came to know as a good friend throughout my research, Frank S. Trautman. Written by Katherine Duke, it appeared as the cover story in the fall 2009 edition of *Amherst* magazine (14-21).

I recall reading in Alex Kershaw's *The Longest Winter: The Battle of the Bulge and the Epic Story of World War II's Most Decorated Platoon* that while in Hammelburg, the POW camp in which Ed was held, some men did experience "the closest bonds of their lives" with their fellow captives. However, that was not true in every barrack; in some, "dissent and discord were the norm." Hammelburg housed officers, who were separated from enlisted men. They stole or bribed guards for food and spent sleepless nights fearful others would take it. Some officers "refused to salute senior officers—they had failed so badly during combat, they no longer deserved respect." But the detail that stuck in my mind was that much anger focused on one "106th Division senior officer, Colonel Charles C. Cavendar." He was placed "in official command" of the officer POWs. A few weeks after the division was captured, in early January, he complied with "a German order to provide a list of Jewish POWs from the 106th Division, only to have his own officers refuse to cooperate" (184-85). I wondered whether Ed might have been among them.

As I continue to leaf through the many editions of *The Cub* that Frank shared with me from his own collection, I find the following remembrance in the "In Memoriam . . ." section of the fall 2002 copy:

> Guggenheim, Charles E. 424/E
> Date of death: October 9, 2002. Charles Guggenheim, 78, winner of 4 Academy Awards and 12 nominations—an achievement equaled only by Walt Disney—for his documentary films. One of the most memorable was a biography of Robert F. Kennedy made shortly after the presidential candidates [*sic*] assassination in 1968. In 1969, "RFK Remembered" won an Academy Award for the best live-action short subject. He was a veteran of the 106th Infantry Division and member of our Association . . . A few weeks before his death he completed his final film, the story of 350 American POWs—many of them from the 106th—who were removed from Stalag 9-B to the slave labor camp at Berga, a branch of the infamous Buchenwald concentration camp. The film is scheduled for release next April. Most of us remember him for his graphic award-winning documentary "D-Day" which was viewed during the 50th anniversary of World War II. As befits a local residents [*sic*] of such prominence the Washington Post carried

> a very large obituary in the Metro section as well as a 2 page "appreciation" in the Style section.

I think of Guggenheim at work selecting and arranging details about an event in which he had been so intimately involved decades after its occurrence. I think of him at work adding his own to the many judgments of the men who served and those who led them. I think of him at work re-shaping the events that brought those men together through sometimes perverse serendipity to produce a multitude of combinations and possibilities, in a mathematical sense. I assume that theories of coincidence exist that could be applied to those various combinations and possibilities. When I first learned as a young person of the concept of the revision of history, I did not understand. How could facts be revised? With maturity I came to understand, as do we all, that facts are simply facts—they do not equate to history. The perspective of time serves as a catalyst to its shape and appearance, as do personal perspectives. And there exists a myriad of such perspectives, a myriad of planes through which information may be refracted.

I notice a story in the September–December 2012 *The Cub* edition because its author, Murray Stein, is among the veterans who I met and conversed with during what became much more than mere research about my father and his fellow soldiers. It focuses on Harold (Sparky) Songer, Murray's comrade who was a "lifer," serving in WWII, Korea, and Vietnam and in the Air Force as well as the Army. Murray shares his recollections of their military service as part of the 106th, beginning with their training at Camp Atterbury. As related by Stein, "someone forgot to throw a rail track switch and the troop train collided with a freight train," incinerating all duffel bags and clothing. He could find no official information regarding the number of men killed and injured in the collision. Upon reaching the Belgian front, Songer remembers being assigned with Stein to guard duty: "The Germans were in pillboxes all along the front. [We] could see each other, and everyone thought the war was almost over and we would be home for Christmas." He quotes from a broadcast by reporter Cedric Foster titled "The Story of America's

106th Infantry Division," of which I have a copy, and then adds that by December 15, the German movement with "vehicles and big guns" was obvious. The American troops were told, "not to fire and give away our positions." Songer found that amusing, as the Germans obviously knew the position of the troops. As of 6:00 A.M. on December 15:

> The Germans stormed the 50 mile Belgian front with 88s mounted on tanks, artillery, buzz bombs and rockets. The earth shook and we were being hit by shell fragments raining down from the trees. "Was I scared? Hell, yes," Songer said. On that first day, a German sniper shot several men in Songer's company. Sgt. Sammy Pate was setting up our 60mm mortar with Stein, when he was shot and killed by that sniper. Sparky was shot in the chest and flipped over yelling I'm hit, I'm hit. Songer was saved by a large spoon in his breast pocket that enclosed the bullet in the spoon . . . The bullet bent the spoon and fell in his pocket.
>
> Murray Stein, Songer's bunkmate in the horse stalls in England, shares identical recollections of the battle. "Sammy Pate and I were setting up our 60mm Mortar," Stein said. "Sparky was with us. The Germans were shooting from their tanks. Shrapnel was falling all around us, Sammy and I stuck our heads up to make sure we had clearance for our gun to get that sniper. Sammy was hit and killed, he never knew what hit him. Sparky was hit and yelling that he was shot. That spoon story really happened. I was there."
>
> One of our Squads was pinned down, out in the open Stein said, and we knew we had to get that sniper. Sparky and I sent up some shells and we got him. On the fourth day, Sparky said "we had used up all our ammo, no food and water, and the weather didn't allow for our Air Force to assist us. The situation was desperate, many of our young soldiers were wounded and killed. We were ordered

> to destroy our equipment and our Regiment commander decided to surrender . . . the German SS troops lined us up and marched us in that freezing cold to a barn lot for the night. We were frozen and hungry and frightened . . . We were packed into Box Cars and after six or seven days, we arrived in Stalag 4B. Murray and I were then split up. I was sent to Stalag 4A near Dresden . . . we worked on the railroads in that freezing cold, and our food ration was a ladle of 'soup' and a slice of bread for the day . . . I endured continuous pain from a blow I had taken on my back. That injury plagues me today. I had spinal fusions in 1958 and 1970, followed by back operations in 1984 and 1985 . . . I went to the second 106th Infantry Division Association meeting, I believe in 1948, and found no one there from my Co. I/423. I was afraid that many of them might have perished in prison camps. Many years later, by chance, the brother of our Sgt. Sammy Pate . . . met Murray Stein at a convention in Amarillo, Texas and called me . . . I called Murray after finding out that he had retired as the Postmaster in Brooklyn, N.Y. We decided to meet at an upcoming 106th Association Reunion, and talked and talked and cried . . . (17-20).

Some stories of the Battle of the Bulge wander from the ending brought by death and suffering to tell instead of joyful beginnings, offering the paradox common to the human condition. One *Cub* story titled "How My Marriage Came About Because of the Battle of the Bulge" depicts the bittersweet element to many tragedies. Its author, Hampton J. Dailey, had been separated due to illness requiring hospitalization from his friend Kenneth Peterson following their internment at Stalag XII A and later Stalag IV B from December 19, 1944, to mid-March 1945. Two weeks before liberation on April 19, 1945, Hampton saw Ken again on the floor of a different hospital. His friend suffered from malnutrition and jaundice as a result of a brutal work detail. He told Hampton that he feared he wouldn't make it out of the hospital and asked his friend to be sure that his watch went to his parents.

Kenneth died on April 11 during an R.A.F. air raid on a nearby railroad. Following 30 days of convalescence in England, Hampton spent ten days on a hospital ship before arriving at Staten Island in New York and made it home to nearby New Jersey on the same day. He wrote to Kenneth's parents and returned the watch, and they then invited him to visit the family in Minneapolis, Minnesota. Kenneth's cousin Shirley Mae Femling met Hampton at the bus depot, and he subsequently spent two weeks in Minnesota where he met various family members. After rejoining the military following about three months of furlough, he contracted pulmonary tuberculosis and spent nine months in a sanitarium before release. During those many months, he continued to correspond with Shirley and eventually asked her on Valentine's Day, 1946 to marry him. At the time of his writing his story, they had been married for 43 years. He closed by telling about their children and writing, "It took the irony and the tragedy of the Battle of the Bulge to give me a dear wife . . . We praise God He was able to take a situation of utter sorrow to bring about a joyous union" (Dailey).

A *Cub* article in the May–August 2012 edition summarizes the experience of the 106th Division in the factual detail used by historians, but with the tone of a writer possessing first-hand experience. It begins:

> Bleialf is a German town just over the Belgian frontier. The Germans call the area northeast of Bleialf the Schneed Eifel: the Snow Mountains. The forested heights seem to be a continuation of the area west of Bleialf that the Belgians call the Ardennes. In mid-December, 1944, the men of the US 106th Infantry Division called the area the front line.

The article explains that the 106th Infantry Division was considered "green," benefitting from only seven weeks of training in England prior to placement at the front. During the summer prior to their placement near Bleialf, the battalion had lost trained personnel, "raided" to replace casualties in France. Those gaps were filled by replacements "from the defunct Army Specialized Training Program, which had given qualified men the option of attending college after training. When that program was abruptly canceled, the men went from carrying books to carrying rifles."

Shipped out of England on December 6th, members of the 106th moved into the line to replace veteran troops of the Second Infantry December 11-12. Some of the original troops expressed surprise upon seeing their replacements arrive wearing neckties. The "hand-off" was brief, a risky operation that demanded all remain as quiet as possible. The "rookies" took over the Second Division's "dispositions and defensive plans," to the dismay of Commander Major General Allan W. Jones. The newest group to "the entire theatre had to cover a sector better than three times as long as the book said they should . . . spread along a 22-mile sector." The risky placement was based on "a calculated gamble on the part of Supreme Headquarters Allied Forces Europe (SHAFE), which believed the area of the Ardennes to be "a comparatively safe part of the front." The area marked by "rugged hills and few east-west roads" made it seem "an unlikely area for large-scale movements by either side. It seemed a good spot for a rookie outfit to cut their teeth with some combat patrolling before taking part in the conquest of Germany."

The detailed account of the results of such a disastrous placement includes that the Germans expected to gain control of Bleialf in a half-day of fighting. Dressed in white for camouflage against the snow, ground troops appeared "ghostly," emerging in the early-morning hours from the woods to engage the 106th. Under-armed and under-manned, the entire battalion was overcome by enemy troops, but they held the Germans back for four days. The detailed account of their strategic use of arms and maneuvers provides evidence of a failed operation, but not for lack of spirit and determination on the part of members of the doomed battalion.

My mother saved accounts of the action later sent to my father from various sources. One that doesn't indicate a source is titled "Operations Against the Enemy of the 106th Division 7 Dec to 31 Dec." Beneath printed dates, the information moves chronologically through time and informs as to what each group experienced and how they participated on each day. I scan through, looking for references to my father's 422nd infantry regiment, Company D; the 422nd is almost always referenced along with the 423rd. On December 19, "422nd and 423rd Inf Regts were out of contact with Div." and yet "maintained and improved defensive positions west of OUR RIVER." The account concludes with a description on December 25th, 1944 of the attempt on the part of the division "to reorganize and supply." By that time, Ed's group was captured. The account is type-written, and at the bottom of the final page appears the name, "Charles A. Brock, Lt. Col. G.S.C. AC of S, G-3."

My mother was reading accounts in the newspaper, including one dated December 28 from London that contained the sentence that one account "asserted that the United States 9th armored division, and the 4th, 28th and 106th infantry divisions" either were "wiped out or reduced to minimum strength." A bulletin from the German High Command bragged that "Yesterday [Wednesday] 21 enemy tanks were shot up. The booty in guns and anti-tank guns has increased to more than 300 since Dec. 16." On the flip side of the scrapbook page, she has glued an article titled "Why Nazis Caught Allies Off Base: Not One but Many Serious Errors." A small article announces, "U.S. Officers' Prison Camp on Soviet Route," detailing that the camp "lay in the pathway of the Russian drive through northwestern Poland," but it would turn out not to be the camp to which Ed was eventually taken. Other articles list the enormous losses along the Western front during December that pushed the total American losses since D-Day to 33,912.

Finally, on January 11, 1945, Helen received a telegram. She must have opened it with great trepidation; I feel confident that her family was around her, as it was delivered to her childhood home address in Galesburg. She may have read the following aloud:

> The Secretary of War desires me to express his deep regret that your husband First Lieutenant Edmund C. Roberts Jr has been reported missing in action since sixteen December

> in Germany. If further details or other information are received you will be promptly notified.

My father was now officially MIA. A headline from a January 15 clipping from the Galesburg newspaper reads, "One Knox county Soldier Killed, 3 Hurt, 1 Missing," and it references the news received by "Relatives of First Lt. E.C. Roberts, Jr., 25." Another headline reads "Roy Sharp and Keith Holloway are Safe Now." A January 21 article begins, "It was a 'quiet sector' they handed the 106th Infantry division, fresh to the front and rarin' to go, on Dec. 11. The quiet ended in a shattering eruption of fire and steel five days later; in another two days two regiments and supporting artillery and armor of the Golden Lion division were wiped out."

Helen continued to chronicle events and information. One article contains the news that Major William Beaty, leading a task force named for him, regained the embattled city of Vith and "lost only a few men . . . where lst December American youths of the 7th armored and 106th division fought on for three days beyond the time they were supposed to. Hundreds of them fell on the shell and bomb-pocked ground." She has underlined that the attack against the 106th started at 5:50 A.M. on the 16th. She glued in a transcript of the Foster broadcast "The Story of American's 106th Infantry Division," dated January 21 with the remark at the bottom of the cover, "Reprinted in response to many requests."

My eye goes to a plain type-written document that has the heading "C-O-N-F-I-D-E-N-T-I-A-L." It is from the headquarters of the 106th Infantry Division and is also dated 21 January 1945. Its subject: "Recognition of Accomplishment," and it is addressed to "The Officers of the 106th Division." The document generously praises the accomplishments of the Division throughout "a period of thirty-four days of practically continuous close combat with the enemy . . . the physical hardships endured, the constant exposure to rain, sleet, and snow in freezing temperatures, and on terrain over which it was once considered impossible to wage effective warfare." It lauds the men's "stubbornness of will . . . fixed tenacity of purpose, and grim and determined aggressiveness of body and spirit." The document quotes a statement by the

Secretary of War: "although partly overrun, our 106th Division made a gallant stand in Ardennes." According to the First Army Commander, Lieutenant General Hodges, the men did "a grand job," and "By the delay they effected, they definitely upset von Rundstedt's time table." The document closes with a personal statement by its author, Herbert T. Perrin, Brigadier General, U.S. Army, Commanding:

> It is a gratifying thing to any man to know that the organization to which he belongs is highly regarded . . . In my service I have belonged to many organizations in which I have been proud to claim membership because of their prior deeds of valor and success. My greatest pride is that I can wear the Lion on my shoulder, for all the world to know that I am a brother in arms of the men of the 106th Division. I know you share that pride with me, as well as the calm confidence that we will always accomplish whatever we are asked to do.

While Ed Roberts would not view that communication while imprisoned, a line at the bottom of the second page states that it was reprinted on May 22, 1945.

Captain Edmund C. Roberts, Jr., undated.

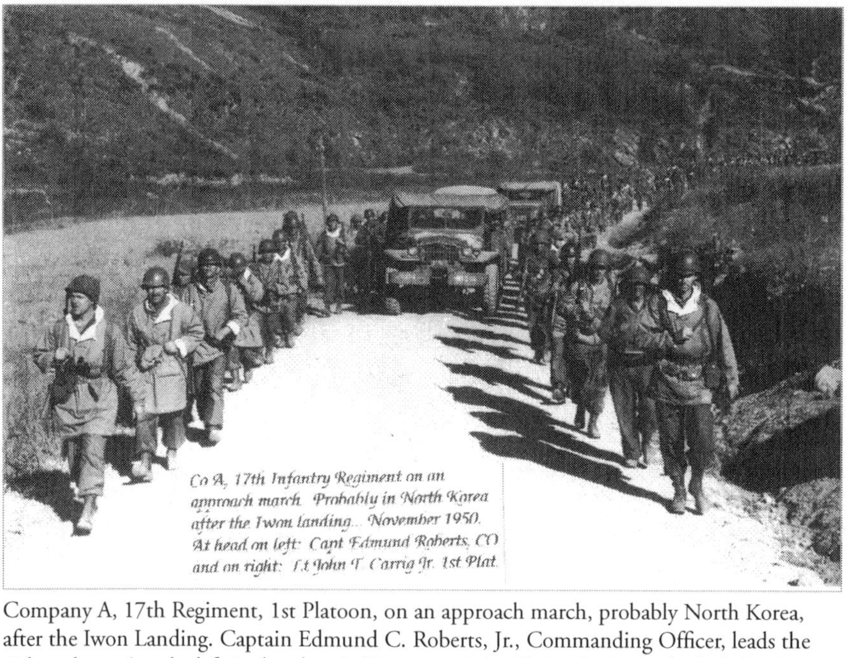

Co A, 17th Infantry Regiment on an
approach march. Probably in North Korea
after the Iwon landing... November 1950.
At head on left: Capt Edmund Roberts, CO
and on right: Lt John T. Carrig Jr. 1st Plat.

Company A, 17th Regiment, 1st Platoon, on an approach march, probably North Korea, after the Iwon Landing. Captain Edmund C. Roberts, Jr., Commanding Officer, leads the right column (on the left in the photo). Lieutenant John T. Carrig, Jr., leads the left column (on the right in the photo). Circa November 1950. Sent to Virginia Brackett by John T. Carrig, Jr.

Captain Edmund C. Roberts, Jr. in the Aleutian Islands, 1944.

Mary Virginia (Ginny) Kost Sperry and Don Sperry, circa 1937.

Helen Kost in performance. Left to right: Betty Miller, Helen Sugart, Helen Kost, Jeanne Garver, circa 1932.

Helen Kost Roberts holding a hat with her sister Ginny Kost Sperry in Los Angeles, 1943. Ed Roberts and Don Sperry were stationed at Camp Roberts.

Helen Kost Roberts performing with Freddy Martin's orchestra in exchange for a war bond purchase at the Cocoanut Grove, Hollywood, CA. The performance was broadcast on the radio. Ed Roberts, not pictured, chose to sing. January, 1943.

The World Famous Cocoanut Grove...Los Angeles Ambassador

Postcard Helen Kost Roberts sent to her parents from the Cocoanut Grove, Hollywood, CA, given to patrons to post during their visit, January, 1943. She wrote "Ain't I the one," referencing playing drums with Freddy Martin's orchestra, hoping the family had heard the performance on radio.

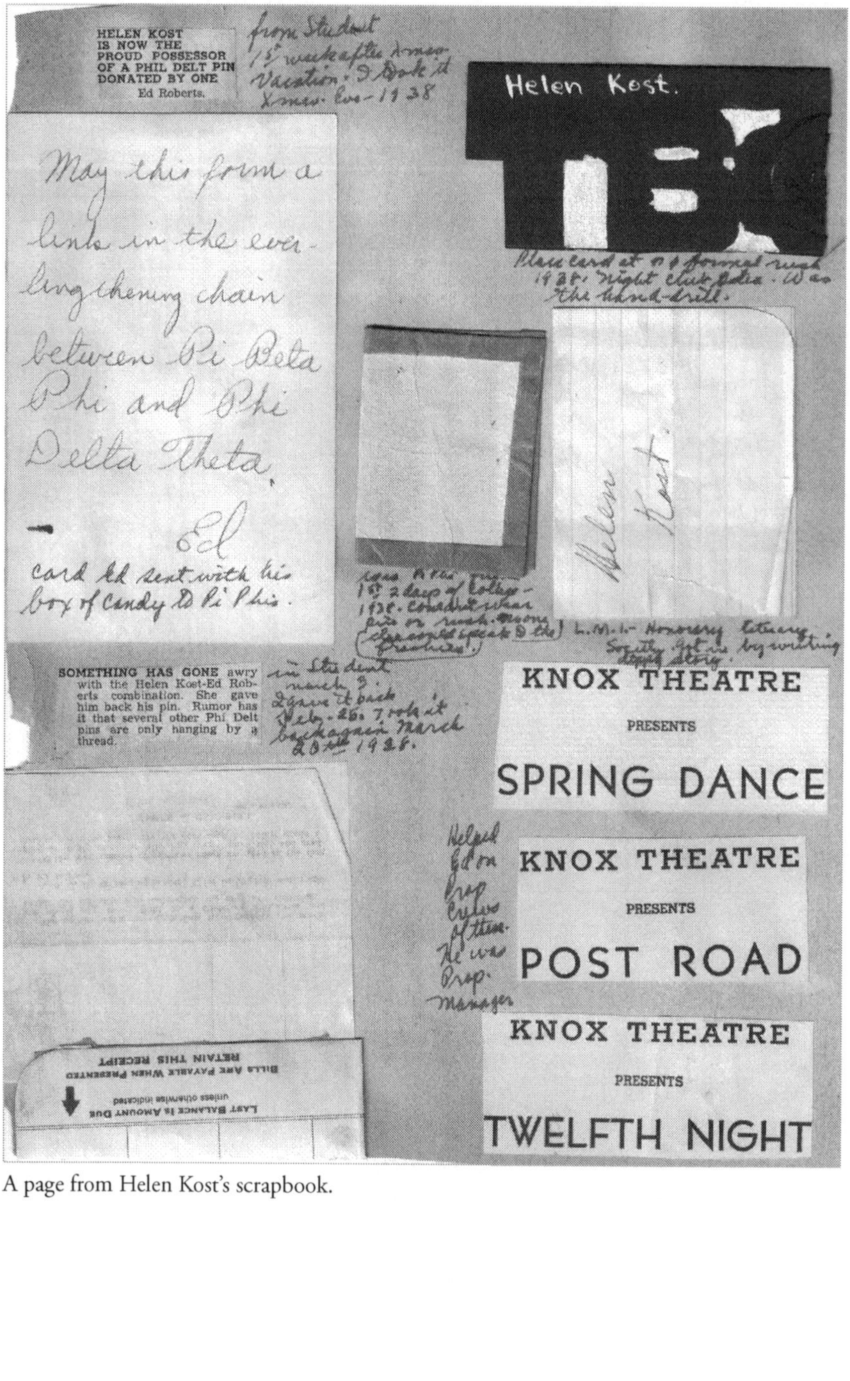

A page from Helen Kost's scrapbook.

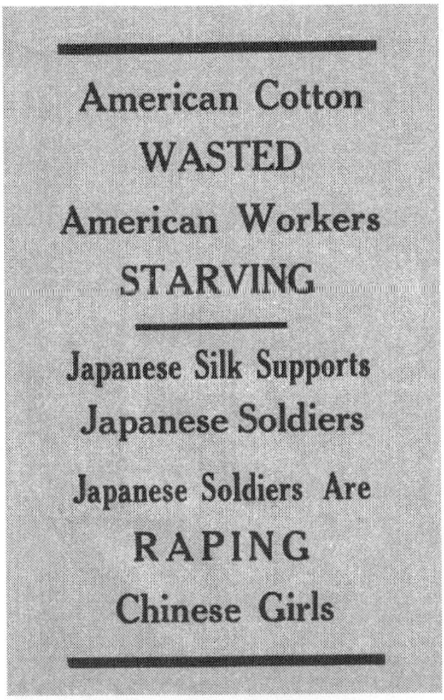
American Cotton
WASTED
American Workers
STARVING

Japanese Silk Supports
Japanese Soldiers
Japanese Soldiers Are
RAPING
Chinese Girls

Anti-Japanese propaganda handbill, probably from WWII.

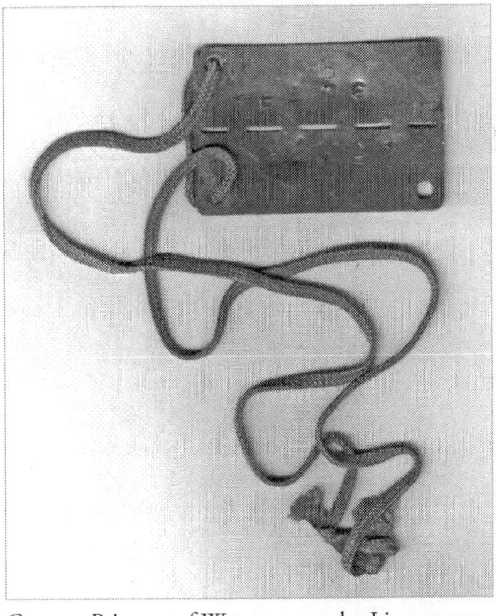

German Prisoner of War tag worn by Lieutenant Edmund C. Roberts, Jr., while imprisoned in Hammelburg, Germany, 1945.

The Bronze Star awarded to Lieutenant Edmund C. Roberts, Jr., by General Patton for actions during WWII.

Tank goggles and U.S. Army 7th Division sleeve insignia worn by Captain Edmund C. Roberts, Jr. in Korea, 1950.

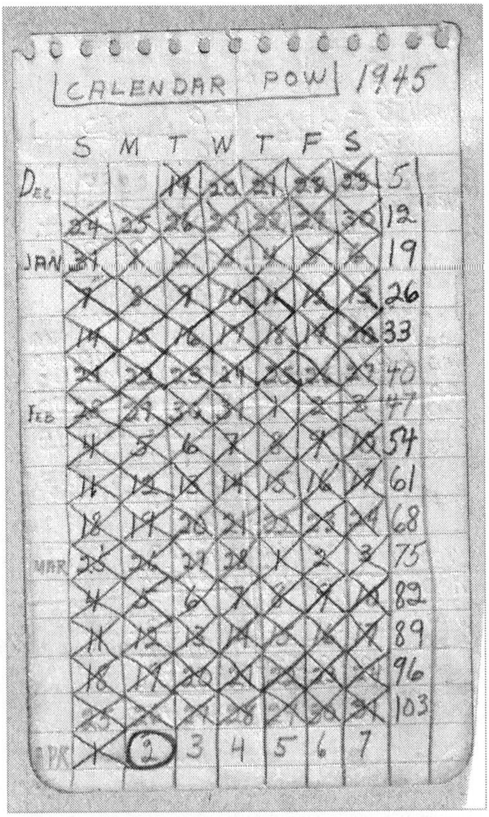

A calendar of days kept by Lieutenant Edmund C. Roberts, Jr., until escape from German Prison Camp at Hammelberg, 1945.

Helen Kost Roberts' military spouse ID pin from Ft. Benning, GA, 1945.

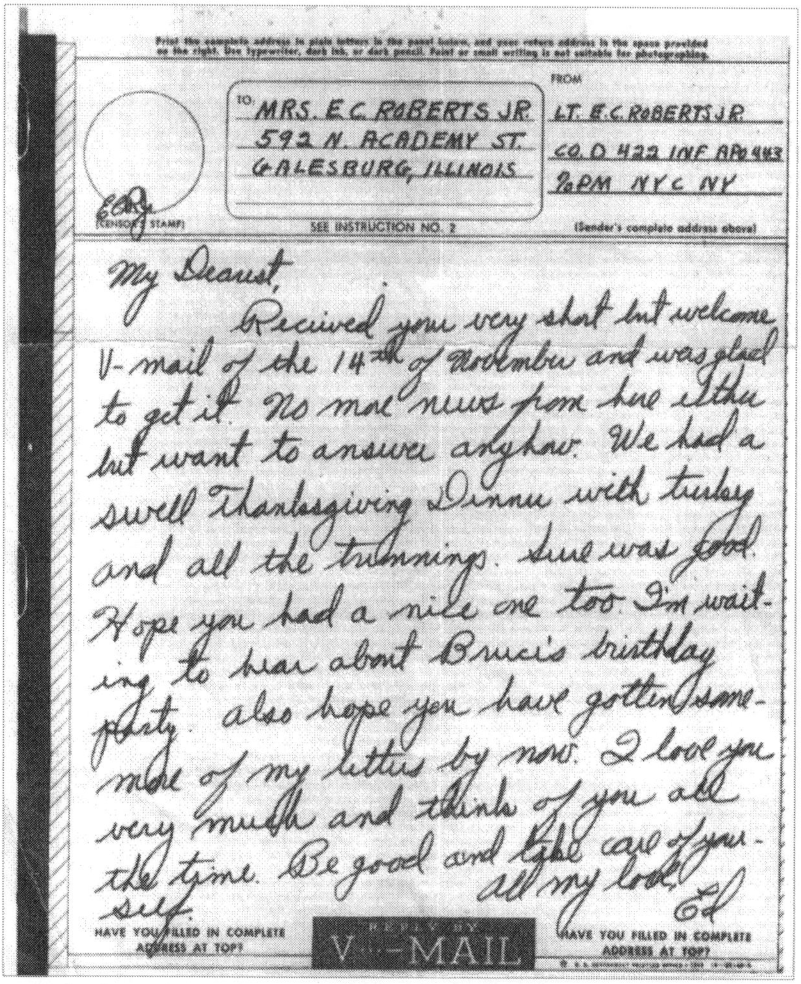

Print the complete address in plain letters in the panel below, and your return address in the space provided on the right. Use typewriter, dark ink, or dark pencil. Faint or small writing is not suitable for photographing.

TO: MRS. E.C. ROBERTS JR.
592 N. ACADEMY ST.
GALESBURG, ILLINOIS

FROM
LT. E.C. ROBERTS JR.
CO. D 422 INF APO 443
% PM NYC NY

(CENSOR'S STAMP) SEE INSTRUCTION NO. 2 (Sender's complete address above)

My Dearest,

Recived your very short but welcome V-mail of the 14th of November and was glad to get it. No more news from here either but want to answer anyhow. We had a swell Thanksgiving Dinner with turkey and all the trimmings. Sure was good. Hope you had a nice one too. I'm waiting to hear about Bruce's birthday party. Also hope you have gotten some more of my letters by now. I love you very much and think of you all the time. Be good and take care of yourself.

All my love,
Ed

HAVE YOU FILLED IN COMPLETE ADDRESS AT TOP? REPLY BY V-MAIL HAVE YOU FILLED IN COMPLETE ADDRESS AT TOP?

Example of V-mail.

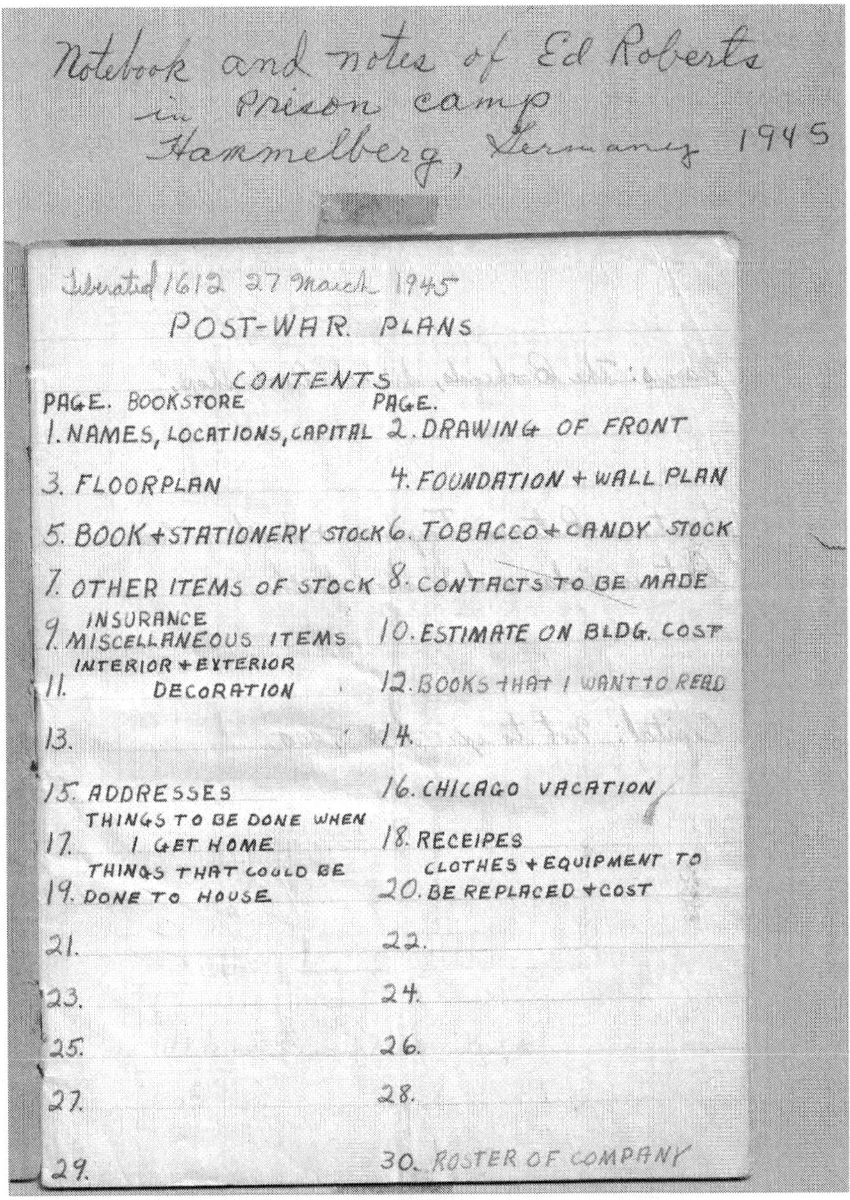
Notebook and notes of Ed Roberts
in Prison camp
Hammelberg, Germany 1945
liberated 1612 27 March 1945
POST-WAR PLANS
CONTENTS
PAGE. BOOKSTORE
PAGE.
1. NAMES, LOCATIONS, CAPITAL
2. DRAWING OF FRONT
3. FLOORPLAN
4. FOUNDATION + WALL PLAN
5. BOOK + STATIONERY STOCK
6. TOBACCO + CANDY STOCK
7. OTHER ITEMS OF STOCK
8. CONTACTS TO BE MADE
9. INSURANCE
7. MISCELLANEOUS ITEMS
10. ESTIMATE ON BLDG. COST
11. INTERIOR + EXTERIOR DECORATION
12. BOOKS THAT I WANT TO READ
13.
14.
15. ADDRESSES
16. CHICAGO VACATION
17. THINGS TO BE DONE WHEN I GET HOME
18. RECEIPES
19. THINGS THAT COULD BE DONE TO HOUSE
20. CLOTHES + EQUIPMENT TO BE REPLACED + COST
21.
22.
23.
24.
25.
26.
27.
28.
29.
30. ROSTER OF COMPANY
Table of Contents for notebook written by Lieutenant Edmund C. Roberts, Jr., while prisoner of war in Hammelburg, Germany, 1945.

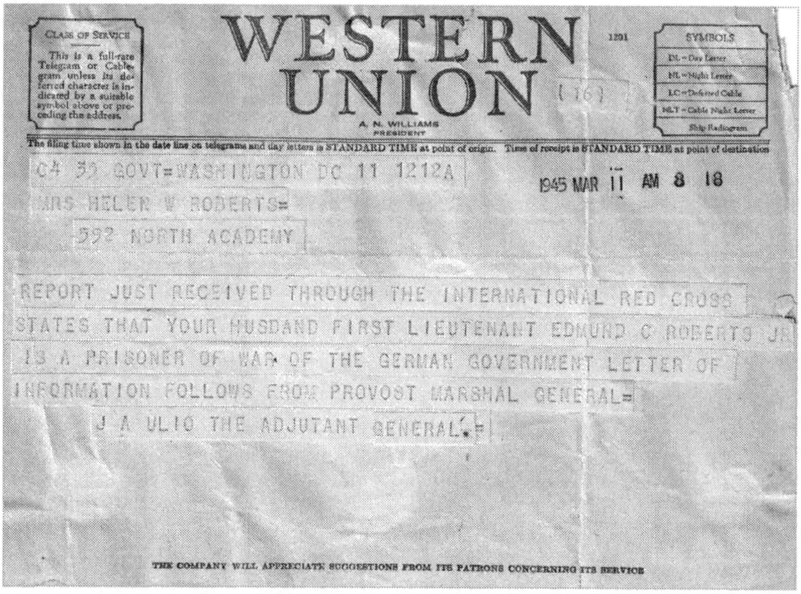

WESTERN UNION

A. N. WILLIAMS
PRESIDENT

CLASS OF SERVICE
This is a full-rate Telegram or Cablegram unless its deferred character is indicated by a suitable symbol above or preceding the address.

SYMBOLS
DL = Day Letter
NL = Night Letter
LC = Deferred Cable
NLT = Cable Night Letter
Ship Radiogram

The filing time shown in the date line on telegrams and day letters is STANDARD TIME at point of origin. Time of receipt is STANDARD TIME at point of destination

C4 35 GOVT=WASHINGTON DC 11 1212A   1945 MAR 11 AM 8 18

MRS HELEN W ROBERTS=
592 NORTH ACADEMY

REPORT JUST RECEIVED THROUGH THE INTERNATIONAL RED CROSS STATES THAT YOUR HUSBAND FIRST LIEUTENANT EDMUND C ROBERTS JR IS A PRISONER OF WAR OF THE GERMAN GOVERNMENT LETTER OF INFORMATION FOLLOWS FROM PROVOST MARSHAL GENERAL=
J A ULIO THE ADJUTANT GENERAL.=

THE COMPANY WILL APPRECIATE SUGGESTIONS FROM ITS PATRONS CONCERNING ITS SERVICE

Telegram from U.S. Government to Helen Kost Roberts informing her that Lieutenant Edmund C. Roberts, Jr. was being held as a prisoner of war in Germany.

Edmund C. Roberts, Jr., circa 1929.

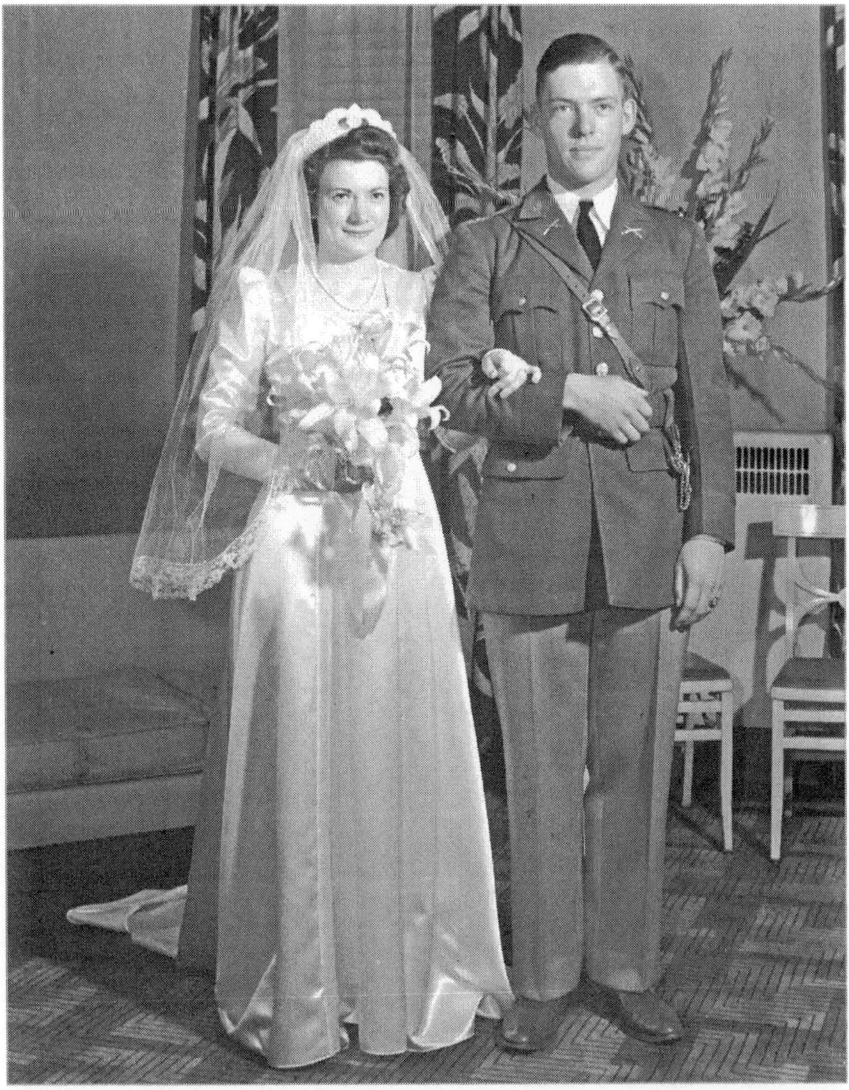

Lieutenant Edmund C. Roberts, Jr. and Helen Kost Roberts, Galesburg, IL, December 1941.

Lieutenant Don Sperry and Lieutenant Edmund C. Roberts, Jr., December 1942.

- CHAPTER SIX -

"THE REAL DIRTY BUSINESS"

Helen Kost Roberts Ferranti wrote often to us, her children, from the time that we attended summer camps, through all the small journeys of our childhoods, and regularly after we left home for college. I did not select a university close to home, and I did not understand my classmates who did. Among their top criteria for a university was that its location allowed them to drive home every weekend if they wanted to, and they were sure they would. I did not share their desire, and the university from which I earned my first degree was at that time a six to seven-hour drive from my parents' house, the last two hours on mountain roads. I was just far enough away to not allow for a comfortable weekend visit. With cell phones not yet in existence and no phone in my dorm room, I called only when necessary, using the main dorm phone, and later that in the sorority house. The calls went through "Ma Bell," and were classified as long distance on my phone bill, costing money. My family exchanged letters, preferring not only the stamps that cost pennies but the intimacy letter writing encouraged. In my case, the letters perhaps provided the opportunity to my budding writerly instincts to be more eloquent than I would be in speech. Letters also proved more surreptitious than a phone call with background noises that suggested guilty pleasures would allow. The "round robin" letter eventually suggested by my mother became a mainstay of our family even after her death, until the arrival of the Internet.

The round robin envelope arrived thick with promise, containing a healthy serving of news from each member of our family. Each of us would remove our old letter, which had made the rounds to all in the family circle, including Ginny and Don, replacing it with new news and responding to all questions and discussion points in the other letters. The opportunity to read our previous letter at a month's distance provided some curious perspective on our own lives. We then dutifully addressed a bulging envelope that often required tape to secure its flap, applied the appropriate amount of postage, and dropped it into the mailbox closest at hand, addressed to the designated next recipient. An enthusiastic letter writer, Helen bequeathed the desire to write long messages to others to me, although my grasp on that singular talent loosened with the arrival of instant messaging. I still prefer e-mails to texts, a nod at least to my letter-writing history in an electronic age. My sister Kay enjoys posting well-crafted messages to Facebook, the effort they take to compose obvious. We seldom skip articles of speech or conjunctions, or any of the additional fussy grammatical organs of communication. When my mother died, I composed a final hand-written letter to be buried with her, she with her love of first-class mail.

Before I begin to review Ed Roberts' letters, I pause to think of the facts about his WWII service that I held true as I matured. He joined the military right after graduation from Knox; he and mom married; Bruce was born; he spent a lot of time in the snow in far-away military destinations; he entered the actual fray at the end of WWII; he was captured but escaped from a German prison camp; his feet were frozen while in the POW camp, for which he received a purple heart; he came home and Kay and I were born; he re-entered the military; he was killed in Korea when I was eight months old.

Of course, while I was young, I had heard many accompanying stories with details I did not worry about investigating to prove their veracity. For instance, when Ed was elsewhere, and my mother went into labor with Bruce, Don had to drive her to the hospital. He became so flustered that he couldn't remember Helen's name when asked to identify her and to explain the situation. Those kinds of stories. Part of the family mythology included my father holding an audience with General Patton, and one of Patton's aides delivering military decorations to him on the tarmac as he boarded the plane home. I suspect this tale to have perhaps been mistakenly construed over the years, or it could have sprung fully grown from my own imagination in earlier years. I settle in to hopefully find facts that support my favorites among those stories.

Following preparation at Camp Atterbury, Ed shipped overseas to England for a brief, eight-week training period in preparation to be stationed on the European continent. The only record of that period that I find among all the boxes and folders of artifacts is one letter via V[ictory]-mail and a tiny photograph. In the photo, Ed stands still, posed, his hands at his sides. He is photographed from the side, a large bandage wrapped around his head. My mother wrote on the back of the photo, "Ed Roberts, Jr. place unknown probably England Nov 1944." Below her notation is a round stamp that reads "Passed by U.S. Army Examiner Base 1717." V-Mail messages remained brief, the result of a successful U.S. attempt to save money and time in delivery of communications during the war by photocopying the original letter and shrinking it to a sheet approximately five-by-five inches. This message is not dated. However, in it, Ed refers to "a swell Thanksgiving Dinner with turkey and all the trimmings." He has no particular news to share and hopes Helen had a nice holiday. He waits "to hear about Bruce's birthday party" and hopes she has received his letters. He closes, as he will all of his letters with minor variation: "I love you very much and think of you all the time. Be good and take care of yourself."

Shortly after beginning my search online for Ed's fellow servicemen from WWII, I received an e-mail claiming that Ed had placed money in an English bank, its balance now blossomed to millions of dollars. If I would just send money . . . While I had received similar messages from that would-be member of Nigerian royalty, as have we all, this effort to scam money, transparent in its intent, I find more personal and troubling. The sender obviously found my request for more information about my father on the Web, one of thousands, enough to contribute to a scam industry. I know that I should not waste more than a moment of my energy meditating on the ethical boundaries others feel free to challenge with the application of wit and imagination that could be so much better invested. I thank my parents again for instilling in me a sense of ethics based on the Golden Rule, a simple statement that we can recall and apply even in our most stressful moments. The list of intellectual and spiritual gifts from my parents continues to grow.

I did learn from Mr. Jack Dixon Walker a few details of the time between the battalion's preparation at Camp Atterbury and its arrival in France. He explained in a letter, from which I include un-edited excerpts below, that he and Ed were assigned to DO Company 422 Regiment at about the same time. He had trained for the infantry at Camp Benning, Georgia and was sent to Atterbury "to help fill out the 422nd regiment requirements to have so many officers and men to fill out various jobs for overseas shipment" as a Division. He explained that he and Ed knew of one another, but not in a personal manner, adding, "I found him to be an effective leader." The group first arrived at the Firth of Clyde, Scotland and then boarded a train to a "small Quonset village in England." Less than a month later they were "sent to the English Channel for transport of France." In what he labels a "snafu," the ship that preceded theirs:

> struck a floating 'mine' and sunk. Their ships finally rushed at the beach in a landing craft 'Tank' the front of the LCT lowered and each soldier with his pack on his back, rifle (M1). The pack was loaded with clips of 7 rounds of ammo and I guess 6 or more clips in pockets of the pack.

He tells of stepping into a "hole" where a chain fastened to the door caused the butt of his rifle to strike his First Sergeant's foot. The Sergeant was not pleased. Once on land, the men "paired up and made a 2 man tent." A few days later "we were aboard 6 x 6's they were called Red Ball Express." He described their quick replacement of the "82n airborn" division as follows: they picked up their machine guns, and the 422nd set their weapons in the vacated spots (Walker).

Ed typed a fairly lengthy letter to Helen on December 5, 1944, which must have been gratefully received. While each of them might write regularly, circumstances in the military did not guarantee receipt of mail and packages. His letter confirms details of the various accounts of the group's activities that I've read during research.

> Well I haven't had a chance to write to you for several days but there were definite reasons for it. I'm now somewhere in France amid mud, rain, and sleet. The weather right now isn't a whole lot different from the Aleutians and the worst part about it is we are in pup tents whereas up there we at least had nice warm huts. I guess the fun is over and we will soon be getting down to the real dirty business of which this is the first. Things are wet all the time, but thanks to some of the things which I had up there and the stuff which I brought along I'm doing pretty well. Nearly everybody has wet feet most of the time but thanks to the overshoes which I brought along mine have done alright so far.

I recall the frigid terrain from the many photos from the Aleutians, as well as almost every account from the Battle of the Bulge referencing the terribly cold conditions. I knew the military issued certain garments, and I hadn't thought about men being able to supplement with their own supplies. I learn later this is still a regular practice. Unknown to Ed as he wrote this letter, he would soon stand as a prisoner for hours in the snow without shoes.

> I haven't had a bath for several days and don't expect to for some to come. Yes, we are really the old dirty rough infantry but everybody seems to be in pretty good spirits in spite of everything. I wish I could tell you about some of the things I have seen, but that is out I guess for a while. I am so thankful that all of you are home safe where no bombs can get close to you because if you could see what concentrated bombing can do you wouldn't believe it. It is just like the pictures of it that you have seen of it but a lot more appalling. The war isn't over yet by a long shot and I sure wish the

> people there could see some of the things that I have seen and they wouldn't be so sure it was all gone and done. The French countryside is not an awful lot different from the English except it isn't old and decrepit like the English. The destruction shows in only a few places and the rest of the countryside is very pleasant and peaceful. You would hardly know the war passed here only a few weeks ago.

I wonder whether Ed in his phrase "all gone and done" refers to predictions about the end of the war; those voices had grown stronger in the early 1940s. That false sense of comfort likely contributed to the Division later being stationed in what should have been a safe location, but all would discover within days the error of that assumption. He had arrived late to combat and was reporting observations as a newcomer. As he relates, what he had seen in England had shocked him and offered a contrast to the quiet—for the moment—French fields and cities. The lack of destruction in France had a simple reason—the country surrendered to German forces. England had sworn never to surrender and bore the brunt of German attacks.

I recall reading in modernist writer Virginia Woolf's diary entries about the destruction of London and the effect on her, an individual who also lived through World War I, as a thoroughly English woman who had emphasized the importance of connections to various geographic locations throughout her several diaries. The sensory imagery of the screaming sirens especially lingers. Two Woolf family homes in London were damaged and then destroyed in the fall of 1940. The half-ton of bombs dropped by the Germans destroyed the location of their famous printing concern, the Bloomberg Press while she and her husband Leonard were in the country nearby.

Woolf's September 18, 1940 diary entry begins "We all need all of our courage" as she wrote of the bombing of Mecklenburg Square, describing her reaction to learning "that all our windows are broken, ceilings down, & most of our china smashed at Meck. Sq. the bomb exploded." She later reemphasizes her thoughts, writing, "As I say, we have need of courage." In October, the bombs fell again, this time on Tavistock Square, part of the destruction that occurred as the bombers intended to obliterate railways and air force bases. The Woolfs were scheduled to travel to London on October 18. On October 17, she wrote ". . . the Siren, just as I had drawn the curtains. Now the unpleasant part begins. Who'll be killed tonight? Not us, I suppose. One doesn't think of that—save as a quickener . . . Every day seen against a very faint shade of bodily risk."

Shortly after arriving in London and visiting their residences to discover what might be salvaged, Woolf recorded not only her reactions to personal losses but also her acute observations. In the October 20 excerpt below, the "tube" refers to the underground public transportation system, which provided an enormous, city-wide bomb shelter. Her abbreviations of common terms are not difficult to understand. More difficult to comprehend may be her attitude toward loss. Her reactions run the gamut from regret to ambivalence to grief, suggesting the complicated nature of war and its losses to both those directly engaged, and those who suffer collateral damage.

> The most—what? —impressive, no, that's not it—sight in London, on Friday was the queue, mostly children with suitcases, outside Warren st. tube. This was about 11.30. We thought they were evacuees, waiting for a bus. But there they were, in a much longer line, with women, men, more bags & blankets, sitting still at 3. Lining up for the shelter in the night raids—which came of course. Thus if they left the tube at 6 (a bad raid on Thursday) they were back again at 11. So to Tavistock sq. With a sigh of relief saw a heap of ruins. Three houses, I shd. say gone. Basement all rubble. Only relics an old basket chair (bought in Fitzroy sqre days) & Penmans board To Let. Otherwise bricks & wood splinters. One glass door in the next house hanging. I cd see a piece of my studio wall standing: otherwise rubble where I wrote so many books. Open air where we sat so

> many nights, gave so many parties. The hotel not touched. So to Meck. All again litter, glass, black soft dust, plaster powder . . . Books all over dining room floor. In my sitting room glass all over Mrs. Hunter's cabinet—& so on. Only the drawing room with windows almost whole. A wind blowing through. I began to hunt out diaries. What cd we salvage in this littler car? . . . No raid the whole day. So about 2.30 drove home. L. says 10 [pounds currency] wd cover our damage. Cheered on the whole by London. Damage in Bloomsbury considerable. 3 houses out in Caroline place: but miles & miles of Hyde Park, Oxford & Cambridge Terrace, & Queens Gate untouched. Now we seem quit of London . . . Exhilaration at losing possessions—save at times I want my books & chairs & carpets & beds—How I worked to buy them—One by one. And the pictures. But to be free of Meck. Wd now be a relief. Almost certainly it will be destroyed—& our queer tenancy of the sunny flat over . . . But its odd—the relief at losing possessions. I shd like to start life, in peace, almost bare—free to go anywhere. (Woolf 330-31)

The Woolfs would never again live in the city, taking residence in the country where Virginia committed suicide on March 28, 1941. Ed's letter continues:

> It is fun to read the French signs and try to recall some of the things I slept through with Mrs. Arnold, and I think if we are here long enough I will parlez vous pretty well. We all have a French book with a lot of phrases in it so it isn't hard to talk to some of the people.

I recall the card that Ed gave to Mom with an untranslatable—or, rather, a nonsensical when translated—message on it written in French. I'm familiar with the sleeping-in-class syndrome, having looked out over my own students to see eyelids drooping. And now that I think about it, almost always young men succumb, rather than young women. All of these thoughts make me smile.

> The old typewriter is going fine but the outside of the case is rather muddy right now. However I will take the best care of it possible because I know you want it back some day. It works swell right now. Got a new ribbon for it just recently.

I typed my first stories and even an early-effort novel in high school on an old typewriter of my mother's. I can't believe that it might be the one to which my father refers, although I like that thought. I have a letter from the military to my mother that apparently was enclosed with Ed's belongings, sent home during December 1945, a full year following the Battle of the Bulge. The second lieutenant who signs the letter reminds Helen, "My action in transmitting the property does not vest title in you. The items are forwarded only in order that you may act as gratuitous bailee in caring for them, pending the return of the owner." I still shake my head at the delays experienced during wartime, to be expected with so many, many men involved. Two ten franc notes are clipped to the letter, money that must have been in the "envelope and contents" mailed to her. Perhaps there was a chance that the typewriter was a world traveler, delivered home at a different time. Ed continues,

> Got a letter from you just before we left England and you hadn't heard from me. I sure hope you have by now and I hope you got the second cable. The reason I sent the anniversary greetings is because I knew I wouldn't get a chance to send those later. My thoughts will be with you on that day and be very good and take care of our little boy.

I think of Helen's careful notations in her Bride's Book of three anniversaries and what she received from Ed. I'm reminded that the missing photo in her album was of red roses, the anniversary gift the Sperrys had helped deliver to her while Ed served in the Aleutians. This anniversary greeting would have been the fourth in the group of nine that she would eventually receive. Traditionally, the tenth anniversary is marked by a gift of tin, having been preceded by gifts of paper, cotton, leather, fruit/flowers, wood, candy, wool, pottery, and willow. Clearly, my mother preferred the gift appointed for the fourth anniversary—red roses played an important part in all of their celebrations, including their wedding.

"Whatever happens to me will be for the best I feel sure and keep your old chin up." This line rings as the most important to me in my search to know Ed Roberts, in my wondering what precisely motivated his return to the military following this obviously harrowing experience. I'm struck again that he could consider himself as an entity apart from his family. Apparently, faith, whether in religion or in simple destiny, played a strong part, at least in his early motivations. My eldest suggested to me as I worked on this book that another type of faith may have supported his military career—his faith in my mother's inherent strength and ability, as well as the support system of family, all of which she would require to care for their little family on her own.

Ed next writes of their hometown friends and companions:

> Haven't seen either Roy Sharp or Weatherbee for some time but they are here all right, I know. Ran into a fellow on the boat coming over who used to live in Galesburg and we talked over several people that we know. He went to high school about the same time John did I think.

The John Ed refers to is likely Helen's oldest brother, John Kost, Jr., the one who had taught at the same school where she taught for a brief time following her college graduation. I recall having seen Roy Sharp's name in a headline from the Galesburg paper reading, "Roy Sharp and Keith Holloway are Safe Now." It reported the Sharp family had received letters from Roy dated December 26 and January 1 that noted how busy he had been, but with few details regarding the German advance. In at least one, "He mentioned having seen Keith Holloway and that he was all right. This was the first news his parents . . . had received since before the German advance December 16. This morning the Holloways received a letter from their son but it had been written December 16." While the article isn't dated, it obviously appeared sometime after the first week of January. It reinforces the crucial nature of letters received in many communities like that of my parents in 1943, 1944, and 1945. They were important to families of those who wrote them but could also be substantially valuable to other families whose sons and husbands a friend might mention. Ed's letter concludes:

> I'm typing this sitting on an ammunition box in our supply tent with the rain pouring outside. It rains everyday here and that is no lie. The rain is ankle deep right now but so long as I can keep all my stuff with me I'm fine. It is beginning to hail outside right now. Write soon and I will try to do the same although don't count on it. I'm thinking of you all the time.
> All My Love, Ed

I must assume that some of this "stuff" would have been included in what was shipped home to Helen later, following Ed's capture. I'm again reminded of O'Brien's short story, Ed's experiences personalizing the importance of the items that the soldiers selected to carry with them.

I consult the rendition of activities of the 106th Division written by Lt. Col. Charlie Brock to learn of Ed's activities between December 7th and 10th, 1944. The men relocated from the vicinity of Limesby, France to that of St. Vith in Belgium, the town that would figure so prominently in the tug-of-war between Allied and Axis forces during the next few months. The Division relieved the Second Infantry Division on about December 11th, according to the account. On December 12th, the 106th Recon Troops joined the 424th Infantry and other groups and maintained and improved defensive positions. On December 15th, "enemy activity consisted of sporadic arty [artillery] fire and minor patrol activity." The 106th didn't engage the enemy until the chaos that erupted in the early morning of December 16, detailed by the various personal accounts of the veterans that I had received.

The report notes that the "Infantry and the town of BLEIALF were subjected to heavy arty fire and at daybreak the enemy had succedded [*sic*] in some infantry." In the hours that followed, orders were changed a number of times, as planned reinforcements and supplies did not arrive. By December 17th, orders were as follows: "Troops will be withdrawn from present position only if position becomes untenable." Enemy troops forced that untenable situation as they surrounded the 423rd Infantry and other groups in the 106th. The 422nd, 423rd "and units with them" lost contact with the 424th. Ed's company—the 422nd —is one that was captured prior to December 21, when the report notes that "Fighting within the ST VITH sector and the steength [*sic*] of enemy armor and inf made the holding of the ST VITH area questionable," although some groups "continued to repulse enemy attacks" along certain fronts. By the following day, the "fall of ST VITH became eminent. All units were pulled back to form a perimeter defense." On December 23, the division "made successful withdrawal," and the few groups remaining underwent reorganization and attachment to new divisions on Christmas Day. According to an article headline dated January 25, one month later, "Ruined St. Vith regained at low cost to Yanks" ("Ruined"). Such a timeline, now so clear to us at our perspective, would have remained invisible to those involved in the actions that created it.

I return to Mr. Walker's letter. He described the action from one participant's point of view:

> The Germans hit our forces and broke out of their holding positions and forced us to move out of their way. They had anti aircraft [*sic*] arterial weapons and we basically had only some light machine gun and mortar tubes. Lt. Edmund C. Roberts and our other Lt. were leading separate but jointly focused "recon." They were far enough over toward the

> crest of the hill to see that the Read beyond the crest of the hill was jam packed with horse drawn artillery, tanks, men ready to fight their way to the Netherlands to divide the English troops and generally disrupt the line that became the Bulge in the manner we have all become to understand as the bulge in the line of the battle of the bulge. Even then Lt. Edmund C. Roberts was using his skill and savvy to save our lives by surrendering all of us and telling us to destroy our weapons and to come toward the crest of the hill where the German soldiers lined us up in a column of two's and march [*sic*] toward the rear of their column. If memory serves me, I gave Lt. Edmund C. Roberts the inside of my compass as they separated the officers from the enlisted soldiers. I reasoned that the Germans would not search the officers as thoroughly as they would us. After the war was almost over, I remember speaking to Lt. Roberts and asking him whether the compass helped. He indicated that it had as they were almost free lancing wanting to resurrender to our forces.

I'm unsure of the meaning of his final statement. I wonder whether my father might have utilized that compass in his escape from the POW camp. Although Mr. Walker would not see Ed again, I find Walker's name on a list in a booklet completed by Ed Roberts during his imprisonment, discussed below.

On January 11, 1945, Helen received a telegram: "The Secretary of War desires me to express his deep regret that your husband First Lieutenant Edmund C. Roberts Jr has been reported missing in action since sixteen December in Germany. If further details or other information are received you will be promptly notified. Dunlop Acting the Adjutant General" (punctuation added).

Cedric Foster's broadcasts about the war had become a touchstone for many. The Kost and Roberts families were among thousands who tuned in to learn war news that listeners often could not find until later in the slower-to-arrive newspaper reports. Foster continued to report on the war after it concluded, and the nation continued to learn facts just then surfacing. His "The Story of America's 106th Infantry Division" was broadcast on January 21, 1945, and I find a script copy glued to a loose scrapbook page in Helen's possessions. It begins, "Tonight for the first time, there may be told the story which, in its dual aspects, is one of the most tragic and yet one of the most glorious episodes in the history of American arms . . . the story of America's 106th Infantry Division." His phrase, "tragic and yet . . . glorious" would continue to loom large in the varied descriptions of the Battle of the Bulge, and particularly that of the 106th that would unfold in various re-tellings and revisions over the next many years. At some point during Ed's service, Helen had begun a correspondence with Foster and developed a strong relationship with the broadcaster. That relationship would become a vehicle by which Ed's, and later Helen's experiences would be shared with an enormous listening audience. When Foster visited Pine Bluff in 1954, Helen would meet him and preserve the moment in a large black and white photo.

Helen would not receive the telegram from J. A. Ulio, The Adjutant General, informing her that Ed had been captured until March 11, 1945, two and a half months following the Battle of the Bulge. It read "Report just received through the International Red Cross. States that your husband, First Lieutenant Edmund C. Roberts, Jr. is a prisoner of war of the German Government. Letter of information follows from Provost Marshal General" (punctuation added). In Helen's photo album, I see three small black and white photos of her, two inches by three inches that Ed must have had with him in battle. One shows her standing before a porch in a bathing suit top with shorts, and the writing in blue ink on the back of the photo notes, "yellow bathing suit," with a black ink additional notation reading, "Helen Kost Roberts in FL Dec. 1943." A second photo of Helen dressed in a skirt, blouse, and dress jacket, hands in pockets standing in front of a sign reading "Oldest House: Open to Visitors," also bears a blue ink notation on the back: "In St. Augustine, Fla., Jan. 1944. Blouse for Xmas from Sharps," in likely reference to their childhood friend, Roy Sharp, and his wife. Helen's name again follows in black ink. In the final photo, she steadies a tow-haired, shirtless toddler who is standing on a porch railing. The blue ink explanation reads, "Bruce—15 months," and below it appears their full names added later in black ink. Each one bears a lavender-colored oval stamp. Within each oval appear the curious notations, "69 Gepuft D4." Mother's note beside each offers an explanation: "stamped at the German Prison Camp where Ed Roberts was," one with the addition, "end of Dec '44 – April '45."

I well recall my mother talking about the relief the family felt when they received word about Ed's capture and imprisonment. She also told us with her usual theatrical flare, hands on hips, how annoyed she was that Muzz Roberts, Ed's mother, received a letter from Ed before she did. The tease in her voice didn't betray any real anger but knowing now after my review of so many of her artifacts the possessiveness that Muzz felt toward her son, I understand that at the time my mother probably was irritated. It would not have hurt her feelings, as she wasn't prone to such injury, but more her sense of equity and decorum. She held unrealistic expectations, of course, but all of her children matured having been trained to consider the effect of their actions on others, preferably *before* acting. I add my learning the value of that approach to the list of "pros" of having been born to Ed and Helen Roberts.

Our family has copies of four letters that Ed wrote to Helen while imprisoned. While the letters are dated, we don't know exactly when my mother received them. I assume that, as was not uncommon during the war, the family may have received the letters and known that Ed was imprisoned before Helen received the official telegram that informed them of his capture. Three of the letters are written on postcard-sized paper, and Ed repeats some lines word-for-word in two letters. Strict restrictions were placed on content that the prisoners could share. As Mr. Walker explained, the enlisted men were separated from the officers early on, with the officers sent to Hammelburg (also spelled Hammelberg in various accounts) where they received better treatment than did the enlisted men.

On January 23rd Ed wrote: "My Dearest, I'm still in good health and in good shape. Food is OK and we have been issued more clothes so are nice and warm. Winter is cold here. Don't worry. Lets hope we spend birthdays together. Keep smiling and praying as I think of you all the time. All my love, Ed." The next letter, dated February 2 is the most lengthy, but contains little detail. Still, it must have been a treasure to my mother and to their families.

> My Dearest,
> My monthly letter to let you know that I'm still well and getting along fine. The weather has turned warmer and that helps a lot. Got my Esquire subscription changed to your address. I also have a book coming from the Infantry Journal which you might write about. It is a picture book on World War II. I hope you and Bruce are fine and also the rest of your family. Tell everyone hello for me. Of the officers that you know the following are here with me: Kirl, Hewitt, Weigel, Turner, Fisher, Mason, Hereth. Captain Porter and Houghton are all right but they are not with us. We don't know what happened to Hotaling. I hope you didn't send many Xmas packages because I didn't get any of them. I lost all my clothes and everything so now I'm open to any presents which you can buy and put away. We'll have a shopping spree and don't forget the Xmas dinner I missed. I love you very much and think of you all the time.
> All my love, Ed.

The third letter, dated February 9, reflects the plans Ed made while a POW. They include a return to their beloved Chicago.

> My Dearest,
> Well, there isn't much that I can say. I'm still getting along all right but life is very monotonous. But then so long as I can be alive and come back to you soon that is all that matters. We found out that Capt. Porter and Houghton are all right but we still don't know about Hotaling. I'm looking

> forward to that 30 day leave and lets hope I get rehabilitated at Mayo General or Atterbury. We will go to Chicago again and to Fisher's wedding. I love you very much. Take care of yourself and Bruce.
> Love, Ed.

The name "Hotaling" stirs a memory, and I search through the many responses that I received to my queries to those who might have known my father. I find one to William Hotaling, a possible source sent to me by another correspondent. I never received a reply, but I'm thrilled to think that this man that my father cared about while imprisoned survived to live a long life. In another letter from a William P. Dohoney, DDS, Major, USAF Retired, he writes that he recalls Ed joining D Co. 422nd in the summer of 1944, assuming the position of Executive Officer to Capt. C.R. Porter, D Co. commander. However, he did not remain long in the company and has no information to share about Ed. He mentions that "at that time I had three second lieutenants answering to me, and John Robb," who I would meet later at the veterans meetings I attended, "would have been under the command of one of them." One of the three that he identifies is William E. Hotaling. The intricacies of the puzzle I continue to assemble serve as both a challenge and a motivation for me to continue. Dr. Dohoney does yield some interesting additional detail, as he describes events. I do not edit the excerpt below:

> Once again, the old Army separation of officers from the men, even into different POW camps, resulted in a situation where the only ones who would have been around your dad would be other officers . . . the people (enlisted men) who are most apt to remember him (the men of Co D), were disbursed into different camps. Originally, . . . ALL of us were in Bad Orb, known as Stalag IX-B, but the Germans quickly sent most of us to Hammelburg . . . The rest of the POW's at Bad Orb then either remained there or were sent off to various work camps, other POW camps,

> or to the infamous Berga am Elster (Stalag IX-A?), if the Germans thought a prisoner was a Jew . . . and worked down to skin and bones . . . or death, in many cases . . . I never remember seeing your dad at either Bad Orb or Hammelburg. If he was at Hamm, then he probably was also on the long march from Hammelburg to Moosburg POW Camp, were most of us were liberated and saw General Paton 'in the flesh.' I assume you are familiar with the story of the famous Abe Baum 'Raid on Hammelburg' when patton forces liberated us from the camp for a few hours and then we were all recaptured and march the whole way into Bavaria and into Moosburg POW camp (located east of Munich).

Of course, I learned as a child that my father was not among those recaptured, but those that made a successful escape, meeting with Patton on his own as an escapee.

My father's briefest letter, dated February 23, would have been written about a month before he escaped: "My Darling, I am still in good health and everything is fine. The weather is warmer and we have received Red Cross food packages. I think of you all the time and live for the day when we can be together again. Take care of Bruce. All my love, Ed."

I find among the many papers "Parcel Mailing Instructions" issued by the Headquarters Army Service Forces in Washington D.C. They list the size and weight requirements for parcels, as well as "permissible items which may be included" for POWs. One heading that catches my eye reads "Items for Children," and I shudder. Helen has pasted onto the page four pre-printed labels furnished to her. Two are orders addressed directly to a (the individual adds the specific name of the company) Tobacco Co. that can substitute as a money order. The other two labels distinguish the package as "Prisoner of War 'Personal' Parcel," and will be sent via New York City.

A letter from the same source dated March 1945 is addressed "To the Next of Kin of American Prisoners of War in the Hands of the Enemy." It begins with a reference to "the recent glorious successes of Allied Armies which resulted in the release of thousands of Americans interned in the Philippines and a lesser though equally important number in Europe" and explains that the office has been "swamped" with inquiries. While the task of "informing next of kin" that loved ones have returned is "pleasurable," it also brings challenges. One statement that focuses on those still imprisoned makes clear that the source wants to ensure "that our own people in the hands of the enemy have all of the benefits of the Geneva Convention" and to be sure all POWs return in "the best possible condition." Surprising to me is the inclusion of the fact that some sources have made comments "to the effect that American treatment of German prisoners of war has been 'soft.' That is untrue. American treatment has been firm and fair." The claim is that the U.S. has followed the Geneva Convention, but has not gone beyond in application to its prisoners.

I find only one letter written by Helen to Ed, dated April 1, 1945. She expresses delight with the mail exchange, letting him know that she had received his letters, as had his parents. She employs the same phrase that he had to her, writing "Keep your chin up, Honey. I know you will," adding "I love you so very much and think of you all the time." She describes the beautiful Easter she and Bruce enjoyed and their activities, promising to develop the photo film that captured the day, ostensibly to send him photos. She asks whether he has access to a chaplain, and then returns to describing the promised photos, some of which captured Bruce's "swell" birthday party from the previous fall and his "grand" presents. She writes, "he sure is a good little boy and you are sure going to love him when you see him." She includes details about people he knows, and I see a dark black mark blocking one word that concludes the sentence "Harold is in . . ." I imagine she must have been referring to the location of a friend in the military, blacked out by a censor. She concludes, "I only live for the day when we can be together again, and continue our happy life. Your statement that you have decided to stay in Galesburg, instead of the Army makes me extremely curious as to what you plan to do here. I love you, Honey, with all my heart." Helen seems surprised that Ed would consider leaving the service, so they must have discussed the possibility of his becoming a career officer. The reason she has the letter becomes clear when I look at the address section. It is stamped "Returned to sender . . . undeliverable as addressed." Of course, Ed was no longer in Hammelburg by the time the letter would have arrived in New York and/or Germany.

In addition to the letters written by Ed, Helen includes artifacts from the prison camp. I find a piece of lined paper from a small pocket-sized notebook that Ed fashioned into a calendar. He drew squares to represent days and has written the day number within each square. It begins with Tuesday, December 19, and concludes with April 7. All of the numbers are crossed through until April 2, which is circled, with the next five days left untouched. At the end of each row, he totals the days. The final tabulation is 104 days spent imprisoned; he escaped the camp on March 27. He stopped counting on the calendar at 103 days with March 31, but April 1 is also "X'd" out. I assume that April 2 must have been the day that he arrived at his Ally-controlled destination. Beside the calendar, Helen pasted a newspaper article titled "Lt. Ed Roberts to Come Back: Prisoner of Germans Writes Wife of Return; No Other Details." It reads:

> Until 1st Lt. Edmund C. Roberts returns to the states, his wife and parents here probably will be without information how he gained his freedom from a German prison camp for officers at Hammelburg, Germany, following his capture December 16, during the last major German offensive in Europe.
>
> There is a lot of reason for speculation regarding the officer's release from the prison camp. After it was first learned weeks ago that he was a prisoner, relatives here learned that another prisoner with him was a Cincinnati, Ohio, young man. Contact between families of both was immediately established and continued by letter and telephone communication.
>
> It became known that the Cincinnati officer had escaped from the German prison and because in Lt. Roberts' letter

> he mentioned that he was returning with the Ohio man, the question as to the possibility of the lieutenant having also escaped resulted.
>
> Having closely followed war news, relatives of Lt. Roberts had read that American prisoners at Hammelburg had been liberated and when they failed to hear from him after that occurrence, they naturally were concerned. Now because of the lapse of time, it seems possible that he too might have fled the camp before its liberation.
>
> In his letter which was written April 2, Lt. Roberts stated that although he had lost a lot of weight, he was feeling fine and was safe. At the time he wrote he was with an American cavalry unit.

My mother received two telegrams, one dated April 24 and one dated April 25. The first informed her that her husband "returned to military control" and was "hospitalized" due to "battle causes" on April 5. The telegram that arrived the next day noted that he will be "returned to the United States within the near future and will be given an opportunity to communicate with you upon arrival."

While I find the letters and calendar intriguing, particularly as they are written by his hand, another artifact that Helen saved is my favorite. It is glued to a scrapbook page, above which Helen wrote, "Notebook and notes of Ed Roberts in Prison camp, Hammelberg, Germany 1945." I have poured over every page of the small booklet many times. At the top of the first page is a note added after its contents had been recorded: "Liberated 1612 27 March 1945." The title of the first page reads "POST-WAR PLANS." It is a Table of Contents (TOC) of the lists that follow, for pages 1-30. The first time my younger daughter saw the book, she clapped her hands and said, "Now I know why I love to make lists! Look—he even made a list of his lists!" I add this item to my own mental list of the gifts bequeathed by my parents to their offspring.

I read a note in my mother's handwriting: "The heads of Knox College, Galesburg, Ill, had promised Ed the job of supervising the building of, and being the manager of, a college book store, if and when he retired from the army after WWII. It didn't work out, though we did go back to Galesburg Aug. 1945 – Oct. 1948." Many of the Items from the TOC constituted plans Ed made for the future book store. They included:

1. Bookstore Names, Locations, Capital
2. Drawing of Front
3. Floor Plan
4. Foundation & Wall Plan
5. Book and Stationery Stock
6. Tobacco & Candy Stock
7. Other Items of Stock
8. Contacts to be Made
9. Insurance Miscellaneous items
10. Estimate on Bldg. Cost
11. Interior & Exterior Decoration

Each of these pages contains extreme detail, and I'm impressed by the illustrations and the building plans. On the Floor Plan he includes a tobacco counter, jewelry counter, stationer and Book Counters, Public Pay Phone, Storeroom, Rest Room, Magazine Counter, two windows, Book Shelves, Coke Machine, two display tables, candy counter, cash register, heating, plant, filing cabinets, office, wrapping counter, small white border fence, and clothes rack. He adds color details: "Exterior paint battleship grey with black roof."

On another page, he includes his tobacco and candy stock lists. For some reason, he has numbers up to 46 on the tobacco list, and has filled in product names for lines 1-11 (Camels, Luckies, Chesterfields, etc—these are cigarettes), then skips to 15 – 30 (Prince Albert, Raleigh, Briggs, etc.—I recognize some names as pipe tobacco, which my stepfather used), and concludes with 40-46 (White Owl, Harvester, La Polina, etc.—I follow a hunch and discover these are brands of cigars). The candy and gum list is long and includes many brands not only familiar but among my own favorites: Hersheys, Milky Way, Mounds, Nestles, Clark, Butterfinger, O'Henry, as well as some I don't recognize—Walnettos and Dr. IQ. I locate illustrations of early Dr. IQ candy wrappers on the Internet. His final entry, number 31: "Either Fannie Mae, or Martha Washington box candy, Whitman's."

I walk over to my dresser where I locate the old Fannie Mae candy box that had been among my mother's possessions; the company originated in Chicago in 1920. It holds some of Helen's costume jewelry. On another page, on the list titled "Contacts to be Made," I find the name Hallmark Greeting Cards. The Hall family members are great philanthropists in Kansas City, home of Hallmark, its offices a few miles from where I now live.

On another page with the heading "Addresses," he lists 29 names, many with specific addresses, including street numbers. I'd have greatly benefitted had I read this list when I began my search for men who knew him—on the bottom of the list is the name "hotaling," with a New York address. I experience again a moment of sadness that I could never locate Mr. Hotaling. My favorite page is titled "Chicago Vacation," on which he plans activities in a three-day itinerary. I have visited most of the locations he has included—the Palmer House, still one of the grandest hotels in the city and Berghoffs on the Loop—we ate there just before it closed in 2005. Plans for one morning include "shopping, fool around," and in the afternoon, "show, fool around, catch train." The list also notes that he will "Go to 6th Service Command about commission and active duty order."

On his list of "Things To Do When I Get Home," he includes "Go on picnic with both families" and "Get [a] malted [milk] at Hawthorns." I read among the list of "Recipes I Want to Remember," "Coney Island Sauce; Waffle Sandwich, Candy Pie, King Edward Toast, Fruit Pancakes, Baked Alaska," and names of various drinks. My favorite item on this list is "Candy Tart; wrap candy bar in dough, bake, serve with ice cream." Simple, and certainly sweet. I find a note stuck between the scrapbook pages in my mother's handwriting. She wrote, "Ed said the most talked-about subject by the POWs was food. They would describe lavish dishes they planned to concoct when back home. They were mainly desserts.

They'd talk about food by the hour. They received about 1300 calories a day. Ed lost 35 pounds in three months." Ed concludes the list with "items of food to keep at home all times: jelly beans, gum drops, ice cream, marshmallow sauce, Nestle milk choc. bars, honey." I think of my pantry, well stocked with some of those very items, and add another item to my inheritance—my unrelenting sweet tooth.

The final two notebook pages contain lists with the headings, "1st Plat," "2nd Plat," and "3rd Plat" with a total of 162 names. As will happen for me multiple times as I work on this project, I feel a stab of regret as I recognize now the names of men I found through my investigation and have spoken with. Why did I not study this list earlier? What a thrill to have told them about the booklet and that their names appeared on a list that helped occupy my father's thoughts while in prison camp.

I scan through the smeared pencil cursive writing and pick out names of several men I now know, Wesley Eckblad among them, the Wesley who died soon after I made contact with him. I find the notes I took during our first phone conversation. He recalled having sent something to my mother upon learning of Ed's death, but he didn't know what. He told me of his work supporting "men who had not been treated well" after the war, and of "20 boxes of personal letters and articles" that chronicled his efforts. He told me he would look through that collection in an attempt to find a copy of the letter he wrote to my mother. It will be "easy to pick this out—it's a person, not a document." He paused and then asked of my father, "Did he go to West Point?" When I replied that he did not, Mr. Eckblad said, "He had all that West Point graduates should have." He wrote to me on October 5, 2006. Ill for several years, he had continued to work for the benefit of veterans, serving as commander of a Long Island, NY POW chapter. As for his own experience, he wrote that in WWII he was:

> one of about 110 American POW soldiers who were put in a group under control of the Germans. We were isolated and treated as slave laborers in the last three months. Ten died. It was truly cruel conditions. When we were liberated

> the government really couldn't care for us properly. All effort was focused on ending the war in the Pacific. I was fortunate—I was so weak I needed hospital care.
>
> There were . . . 90,000 POWs in German hands. Not until 1980 did Congress begin to try to "catch up." But by this time my friends would have nothing to do with the Veterans Administration.

I saved his voice mail on my answering machine for more than a year.

The familiar names continue; Black, Padgett, Robb—then I stop. I see the name "Trautman." Frank Trautman quickly became a good friend, from my initial contact forward. In his September 23, 2006 email reply to me following my query sent to him, along with others on a list of members of the 106th Association, he wrote,

> Tis a bit of serendipity . . . About three weeks ago Lt. Roberts was a part of a discussion on former members of DO Company 422nd. The 106th Division Association was enjoying their 61st reunion in Newark, New Jersey. Time has taken its toll on former members of DO Company all over 80 years in age. Of course memories have waned accordingly. First your father, then 1st Lt. Roberts was one of two officers I admired out of our officer staff. Mind you I was only an enlisted man but I was able to talk with him and be of ease. In fact it was our opinion that he ran the company. I will not discuss the Captain as that would not be polite. He took his duties of command as a professional member of the military. I do not know his background but . . . I believe he was from Galesburg, Ill. At the time we were captured, not time or space to relate, many of his fellow officers appeared to be in a quandary. May I note 80% of the DO Company members were qualified for OCS [Officer Candidate School] but declined for many basic reasons. The IQ on average was above 130—not a typical

> infantry company. [Frank later earned an engineering degree]. I recall your father to be a nice looking man who dressed well as an officer.

He added that another member of the group, now a retired pharmacist, had recalled seeing Ed in 1948 at the second reunion in Indianapolis, and he knew that Ed later reenlisted and worked in some aspect of recruiting.

Thanks to Frank, I attended a September 8, 2007 meeting of the 106th in Kansas City that took place within weeks of our contact. The gathering fell firmly under Frank's descriptor of "serendipity." The timing proved amazing. When I met Frank in the lobby of the appointed hotel, his warmth and enthusiasm overwhelmed my husband Edmund and me. I recorded our conversation in a noisy hotel lobby.

We began by exchanging again our basic information. I was Ed Roberts' daughter, in search of information about him. My husband Edmund had served as a medic in Vietnam. Frank had been an enlisted man in the 106th and was captured at the Battle of the Bulge. He explained that he began his military experience as part of ROTC in college, which helped pay the tuition and bills that he could not have otherwise afforded. He joked that his membership reduced his costs at Ohio University from $300 to $90. He left college for a time, joined the Reserves and returned to finish his degree, then was called to active duty. After capture at the Bulge, he was a POW in Stalag IX B Bad Orb until the camp was liberated in spring, 1945. As I listen to the tape, I hear that we are interrupted by a woman selling drinks. Frank declines, sharing that he already had two drinks during earlier celebrations. He continues, saying that he met Ed Roberts at Camp Atterbury. He adds that he has served as the Camp Atterbury representative for years. "Your father was very athletic, a real military man," he remarks. He tells me of another member, Dr. Doxie, who might remember my father. "He was a prisoner of war with Kurt Vonnegut." I'm stunned by this information. As an English professor, I must know more about that experience, and I ask Frank to send me Dr. Doxie's contact information later. The call to dinner is issued, and we move into the dining room. Frank guides us toward a table where he has reserved two seats for us.

I can't recall ever having felt so immediately at ease in a new group as I did with those wonderfully accommodating veterans. They treated me as if I were a celebrity. I experienced in a minute fashion the camaraderie that must have served as a buffer against the severity of events that my father and his fellow servicemen endured, conditions beyond imagination for those of us not present. The regret over missed opportunities that immediately strikes me upon reading Frank's name has by now grown familiar during my research process. However, it intensifies in this instance. Frank greatly admired my father and would have so loved seeing his name on that list.

The program following dinner began with two awards, both for service to the 106th Association. The citation issued by the Board to one of the veterans is the Order of the Golden Lion, Commander Class. A second citation—Companion Class, Order of the Golden Lion—is issued to the wife of the long-time editor of *The Cub*, due to her devotion to the Association. I later learn that Frank received the Order of the Golden Lion the previous year.

Ed Roberts returned home on the S.S. *John Ericsson*, and I find various artifacts from the ship, including the list of duties that a group of Officers will undertake. There I read of Ed's assignment as Troop Adjutant. A menu dated Thursday, April 26, 1945 from the farewell dinner is formally printed with a brown and white drawing of a many-sailed ship in mid-voyage, with the line at the bottom, "United States Lines." A humorous newsletter with the title "Seaweed Gazette" printed during the trip makes clear the high spirits of the group with its silly comments and observations. One column is titled "Deck Poop" with the blurb that a "red-head from Brooklyn who dances with a USO troupe aboard the ship has been elected 'Miss Penicillin of 1945' by patients in the hospital." I find a photo of Major General Manton S. Eddy of Chicago receiving a kiss on each cheek from his wife and daughter clipped from a newspaper.

The line beneath the photo notes that he returned from Europe with 7,000 other men. The hand-written explanation in blue ink beneath it is Ed's, not Helen's, an unusual addition to the scrapbook. He wrote, "Had interview with General Eddy at Tauterbach, Germany on 3 April 1945."

Helen includes an article with the headline "List Yanks Released from Nazis," on which Ed's name appears under the "Downstate" list ("List"). Another undated article headlined "Escape Took Four Days," at last allows me to read detail about his escape. It begins by noting that Ed, Helen, and two-year-old Bruce are visiting Ed's aunt, Miss Jessie Roberts, along with his mother, "the former Miss Winifred Aylesbury" (Muzz Roberts), while on a 60-day leave from the military:

> He was decorated with the Bronze Star after a personal interview with General Patton along with 12 others who were the only ones to report at that time, from 1,000 prisoners liberated by a spearhead of our troops. Fighting with the 422nd infantry of the 106th Division at St Vith, a division that is said to have been practically cut to pieces, Lieutenant Roberts was taken prisoner there after his group had been cut off from supplies. During the imprisonment he lost 30 pounds and both hands and both feet were frozen. In this country he was reported as missing.

The article explains that the spearhead could not accommodate so many prisoners and that 200 were selected. The remaining group of 800 were instructed to "make their own way or to continue to submit to German imprisonment." About 100 chose to escape. The group hid by day and moved by night, encountering "many perils," breaking into smaller groups and losing track of one another. Ed's group of thirteen "made contact with an American cavalry unit after four days." When they later met with General Patton, "they learned that neither the spearhead of rescuing troops, the chosen 200 rescued, or any of the others that started with him had been heard from." Ed didn't know their fates at that time, though many later surfaced.

A much lengthier undated article from the Galesburg newspaper carries the headline "Lt. Ed Roberts has Interview With General: Patton Entertains Local Officer for Half an Hour After He Escapes German Prison." In the article, the Cincinnati serviceman previously referenced is identified as Lt. Fisher. It begins with humor, recounting how my brother Bruce was far more impressed with the locomotive that brought his father home than with the strange man he had now come to know as his father. The entrapment of Ed's company and lack of supplies and ammunition was again described. Details about the prisoners' march to their first POW camp included that they did not eat for two and one-half days and then were herded into small boxcars, in each of which 50 men crowded. The group had to lie down in shifts, so tight was the enclosure. While traveling, they each received a quarter loaf of bread and some sorghum-like liquid. The article describes as "Quaintly" the action of the Germans who feigned generosity at Christmas. They handed out packages, one per five prisoners: "It was irony as the packages only contained uncooked foods," which the men lacked means to prepare.

They arrived at the railroad yards at Limburg during an American bombing raid that missed the cars, but "bursted doors of the cars." One group ran to a nearby "small earthen depression," which immediately received a direct bomb hit, killing ten and wounding 40 soldiers. Eight days later, the prisoners reached Bad Orb, previously a Bavarian Alps resort, where they received weak tea and greens in which wood and worms were discovered. The nighttime meal consisted of a small amount of bread. They had little protection from the bitter cold. Eleven days later the officers moved to Hammelberg, located 60 miles east of Mainz on the Rhine. The food did not improve with weak coffee, watery soup and dinner bread as their fare. I well know the horse tooth that came from a bowl of POW camp soup, still in the box where my mother kept it, sitting now in the same dresser drawer in my own room.

The article recounts the arrival of the spearhead and Ed and Fisher's choice to escape. They ate raw turnips and were able once to trade soap to a German family for "bread and bacon." On Easter Sunday the two men became separated from two other friends and watched as they were re-captured by German soldiers "retreating from the front lines." They hid in the forest, and at one time the enemy came "within a few yards of them." When they could no longer hear the enemy, they moved quickly toward the sound of "small arms fire a few miles away," hailing a tank force "by waving a white towel." After convincing the drivers they were escaped prisoners, they enjoyed K rations, a meal they said they would remember forever as a "highlight in their eating history."

The next details validated one of the most exciting of the stories I heard when young. The men met with Patton: "possibly a tough hombre in battle, the general was a brilliant and generous host. What was discussed in that conference cannot now be told, but it was a thrill for a couple of young officers who thought they had experienced every emotion before this interview." After viewing the movie *Patton* starring George C. Scott, I inevitably conjured Scott's face and demeanor—even the rough sounding voice he adopted for the part—from his stirring portrayal of the iconic general when I imagined their meeting.

The article continues by confirming the tale that I had been most unsure about: "The next day the two were waiting at an airfield for a plane to fly them back to France when an aide of General Patton dashed up to the men. Representing the general he decorated them with the Bronze Star for their heroic flight behind enemy lines." I had imagined this scene as a child, eventually conflating the fog, mystery, and drama from the final scene ("Here's looking at you, kid") in the Humphrey Bogart movie, *Casablanca*, which I viewed at some point. My ability to mix and stir various details into one delicious fantasy that I would visit again and again marked my youth and carried over into my adult life. The true details of this scene and this particular story, however, will now remain clear.

Naturally, with the alacrity of a child, I easily fantasized about new scenes, original to my overactive mind and often unshared with others. I recall during several of my walks home from grade school imagining that Ed Roberts had re-appeared after years in a Korean prison camp, the remains sent home to my mother all a mistake, those of a different sad victim. He would open the door when I arrived, dressed in uniform, and say hello. After all, he had been captured before and declared MIA and no one knew where he was for some time, so this story did not seem that far-fetched. He had also escaped once before—why could he not do it again? I worked out in minute detail how we could all live together, my step-father and half-sister included, a brave new version of a blended family. I did worry briefly about Helen having two husbands and the resulting conflicts that could cause, but lacking detail about the nature of such conflicts, I dismissed them to the realm of adult problem-solving. I focused more firmly on my having two fathers, a situation filled with promise.

In the final pages of the last photo album I've consulted for my project, there appear various pictures and artifacts that feature my father's life following his return from WWII. Many show various groupings of family members, he almost always wearing his uniform. I find a surprising label beneath a photo now missing, the white ink a stark contrast to the black page: "4 escapees from German prison camp, Ed, Bruce Fisher, John Mason, Joe Herth, Cincinnati, June, 1945." I recalled the article referencing the fact that Ed and Fisher were separated on Easter Sunday from two others, whose re-capture they witnessed. I learn from the later article written by Ed that Mason and Hoerth (Ed's spelling) did escape with Fisher and him. Was this gathering part of a specific military reunion? Again, some facts I can't know. I later locate the missing photo along with an eight by ten featuring the four men and see Bruce Fisher's face for the first time. I will learn soon that he continued to play a part in my parents' lives.

A return home meant a return to the activities most loved by Ed and Helen. I find a souvenir photo from "The Latin Club" in New York City of Ed, Helen, Mike Thompson (Ed's half-brother) and Mike's wife Polly. The inscription with the names also reads, "21 June 1945 26th birthday of Lt. Ed C. Roberts, Jr." The room behind them is packed with celebrants. I find a postcard dated July 10 written to Helen's parents that begins "Dear Folks" and tells them what a wonderful time she and Ed are enjoying at the Shelborne Hotel at Miami Beach, Florida. I assume they are there for a vacation. However, a second postcard notes, "Here's the gorgeous hotel we live in." I'm unsure why they would be living in a hotel, and I don't remember hearing about that stage of their life. Then it becomes clear they are there awaiting another assignment for Ed who is participating in an interview, selecting his camp as she writes the card. She includes details about their activities, beginning, "We are with Fisher most of the time," and I can safely assume that "Fisher" is the same Bruce Fisher included in the previous list of prison camp escapees. I recall having seen a list of assignments for Ed and others "for the duration of the voyage" ordered by a Transport Commander, which would have applied during the trip home from Europe. I revisit the list and see the assignment, "1st Lt. Edmund C. Roberts, Jr. . . . Troop Adjutant." Below that assignment, I read "2d Lt. Bruce Fisher . . . Blackout Officer." The two had obviously shared much, and any such military friendships begun by Ed would be immediately accepted by Helen.

I find a booklet among Helen's possessions in another box titled "Welcome to the AG&SF Redistribution Station Miami Beach, Florida." As I carefully turn the pages of the aged publication, I understand my parents' stay in the hotel. The booklet details the process of redistribution that soldiers returned from Europe and Asia will undergo. The inside cover depicts a young military couple, he holding a suitcase, both looking hopeful, with the comment, "You will be met at the railroad or bus station in Miami, and conducted to the Redistribution Station in Miami Beach, across Biscayne Bay. Every married returnee is urged to bring his wife with him." The "Message of Greeting" on the first page is offered by F.E. Uhl, Major General, U.S. Army Commanding. It reads, in part:

> The Redistribution Station has been established so that your experience and your records may be carefully studied to the end that your next assignment will be most useful to the Army. This study will, of course, involve a certain amount of routine and processing. However, these will be simplified in every way in order that you may have a maximum amount of free time for rest and relaxation. Except from the

> schedule in connection with your processing, your time in Miami Beach will be completely free.

Now I understand how Helen could write with such enthusiasm about their experience in Miami Beach. However, the first page of the booklet also carries a reminder: "As an overseas veteran, you will be looked up to. The impression you create will serve as a standard for others. In accepting this responsibility, you will be expected to exercise at all times the greatest care in maintaining the courtesy and military bearing of a soldier." Still, many of the photos in the booklet stress the R & R that this time should represent. A photo taken from the air of the Miami Beach shoreline has superimposed labels that identify by name each of 18 different hotels to which couples might be assigned, every one of them steps from an inviting beach. The caption beneath one photo of a "beautiful sanitary swimming pool" offers an alternative for those who may not prefer the "saltwater surf." Sketch classes in a well-supplied art studio are available, as was miniature golf, real golf, volleyball, deep-sea fishing, a chapel for every faith, and archery, along with the fun in the water represented by photos of couples in swimming suits, arms linked, running in the surf.

Helen writes that they will know in a week where Ed will finish his military service. I also find photos of Bruce with Ginny and Don, Don still in uniform. Many of the photos make me smile. In one, Bruce Fisher jumps from a swimming pool diving board, Ed on his back. In another, Ed and Helen are deep sea fishing with Fisher. They are assigned to Ft. Benning, and I find a group picture from September 1945 with each man's name dutifully listed on the back. Lieutenant Fisher is there, and the knowledge that the two friends remained together for a time brings to me a moment of perhaps irrational happiness to realize that they reaped together the rewards due to their war efforts. Beside Ed's name appears the word "Captain," and Fisher has moved from second to first lieutenant, indicating they received the promised promotion for those who were Prisoners of War. Among mother's possessions, I find a round silver metal badge she had to wear at Ft. Benning, her photo in the middle, and the number "39546" beneath her youthful face. She wears a serious, but not gloomy expression, that of an adult, matured by experience since her college days at Galesburg. I learn the names of another couple that became close friends, the Coopers; their son Bill appears in many photos. Ed and Helen appear in two photos with a group enjoying what may be an officer's club, clipped from some type of a magazine, probably featuring Ft. Benning. My brother Bruce now wears his trademark goofy boy grin in photos, as I watch him changing rapidly, the way of toddlers who too suddenly seem to depart babyhood. The final photo in the scrapbook is loose, stuck against the spine to prevent it slipping from the pages. It is out of order, dated on the back November 1944. I know now, as my mother could not know then, the symbolic value of the photo. In the picture, our Uncle Don holds Bruce on his shoulder, just as he would support us all in the years to come.

- CHAPTER SEVEN -

"ALL THE ADVANTAGE AFFORDED BY HINDSIGHT"

• • • • • •

I noticed your father was held at Stalag 9B.
Do you happen to know if your father was wounded during captivity or contacted frostbite? Was he awarded the Purple Heart for such wounds?
Personal Correspondence – Virginia Brackett

• • • • • •

11/23/06
Virginia Brackett,
Thank you for the kind words, and your father for his sacrifice. I was surprised he has received his Purple Heart. Since the initial authorization during 1996, many former POWs are not aware of the entitlement.
Regards,
Robert E. Johnson
Personal Correspondence – Virginia Brackett

I find a certificate in another group of artifacts, which I will soon investigate closely, certifying that Ed was awarded a Purple Heart posthumously for his mortal wounds in Korea. I'm uncertain for which sacrifice the

Purple Heart medal that I have was awarded. Certainly, he would have been eligible to receive one for having been killed in Korea by a sniper, but he should also have received a purple heart for the life-long suffering he would have sustained as a result of standing barefoot in the German prison camp snow and sustaining frostbite. The fact that a serviceman *deserved* a decoration did not equate to the *receipt* of one. A typed page dated June 14, 1945 to "Former Members of the 422nd Infantry" informs those members of a formal request "for award of Combat Infantryman Badges and Medical Badges to all qualified personnel (including those killed) retroactive to 16 December 1944." Although "no unit awards or citations have been made" former members of the 422nd "are entitled to wear 2 battle stars (Germany and Ardennes) on the ETO ribbon, and 2 overseas service stripes." A list of "officers known dead or still missing" is included, and all officers are urged to "take action NOW to submit recommendations for any awards they feel their men should have."

Elsewhere among my mother's artifacts, I find a strip of paper bearing the following undated typed message: "The Purple Heart decoration is being sent under separate cover from the Philadelphia Quartermaster Depot and a delay of approximately forty-five days may be expected for engraving and shipping." I read more about the 1996 legislation that allowed former POWs to apply for the Purple Heart medal, a decoration initiated by President Washington to reward those injured or dead during combat, whose profile it bears:

> No former prisoners of war of any service, living and dead, who were wounded or injured during captivity before April 25, 1962, were eligible until Congress passed legislation as part of the 1996 National Defense Authorization Act.
>
> Prior to the 1996 legislation, for instance, none of the 140,000 U.S. service members who surrendered to the Japanese in the Philippines in May 1942 could qualify for a Purple Heart. Also ineligible were the thousands of former POWs who came later in World War II and in the Korean War.

> Since 1996, a number of World War II and Korean War vets have applied for Purple Hearts on the basis of wounds and injuries received while they were POWs, officials of the Army's Military Awards Branch said. Supporting documentation is required and may include copies of repatriation medical exams, or a witness statement from a cellmate, for example, stating their buddy was abused at hands of captors. The injuries or wounds must be deliberately inflicted by captors, they said. Injuries received while on work detail, for example, probably would not qualify—but if in doubt, apply. (Brocato)

I learn later in reading Ed's letters from Korea that he had hoped to earn an additional decoration. On November 4, 1950, he wrote to Helen, based on his actions that: "I'm not counting on it but rumor says the Col is putting me in for the Silver Star."

He did not receive that decoration or the promotion that he obviously had hoped for while engaging in additional combat. He wrote on October 26, 1950 that he did not think a promotion to major was imminent, as "There are extra majors in the Regt which isn't good." He then returns to reality and his own better interests, when he adds, "Had I gone to the 24th and stayed alive I might have made it but it is better to be alive." Curious, I quickly locate information about the 24th Infantry, to which I assume Ed refers, and discover it was a mainly African-American group that received a Presidential citation for its meritorious action from the Republic of Korea in defense of the Pusan perimeter. I recall that Ed trained an all-black unit during his time in California, for which he received much praise. I will later find in one of his early letters from Korea that he was originally assigned to that Division but was reassigned to the 17th. Two of the 24th's members received posthumous Congressional Medals of Honor. Disorganization among leadership was blamed for heavy losses incurred by the 24th in November of 1950 during Korean combat. Its website reads:

> We are known as "the First to Fight Division," which has been borne out by our record. We were the first to take arms against Imperial Japanese forces at Pearl Harbor, and we were the first to engage the North Korean aggressors with Task Force Smith at Osan, SK on July 5, 1950. Of the 24th, Japanese Army General Yamashita said "It broke the back of the Japanese Army at Breakneck Ridge" on Leyte. And the liberated people of The Philippines called us "Victory."

I locate the bronze star case—I know now that Ed's WWII exploits earned that medal—in which I locate other medals as well. I have always been impressed by how much my husband can tell about military personnel based on the iconography inherent to the decorations and insignia they wear, and I study all of my father's decorations closely. Each medal bears engraved figures on the front sides. Two depict women surrounded by various symbolic items, such as weapons, a helmet, and the sun, its beams shining forth in rays behind the female figure. The third is an eagle. The smaller medal bearing the woman's form reads on the back, "for service during the limited emergency proclaimed by the President on September 8, 1939 or during the unlimited emergency proclaimed by the President on May 27, 1941." The "ribbon" with the clasp that holds the medal to the uniform is yellow with two groups of three stripes: red, white, and blue on either side. The larger medal with a female figure bears the phrase on the front, "World War II." Words engraved in a circular figure on the back read "United States of America 1941 1945." Inside the circle are four lines. The first two read "Freedom from fear and want." What appears to be a feather separates those lines from lines three and four: "Freedom of Speech and Religion." The broad red midsection is flanked by stripes on both sides—white, purple, blue, green, yellow, orange, yellow, green, blue, purple. An eagle appears on the front of the final medal, accompanied by the inscription "United States of America" and the dates "1941" and "1945." On its reverse is a small landing craft surrounded by men in military garb with words engraved above: "European African Middle Eastern Campaign." Two wide stripes of green on the ribbon are separated by thin red, white, and blue stripes, with additional stripes of white, black, and brown. On the other side, the stripe colors are red, white, green, and brown, the two brown stripes being the widest. I know that I can find explanations of the meaning of each item on each medal, but for now, I simply admire what at first seems a simple design for each, but on further inspection elaborate and complicated, the colors making up what would have been referred to on my father's uniform, along with the various accompanying ribbon badges as "fruit salad." A well-informed colleague later lists for me the following explanation:

Purple & White – Purple Heart
Green & White – Army commendation Medal
Yellow – American Defense (prior to Pearl Harbor)
Red w/Rainbow – WW2 Victory Medal
Bronze Star – For valor or achievement in a combat zone
Green & multicolor stripes – Europe, Africa, MidEast campaign
Yellow Ribbon w/star – Asiatic-Pacific Campaign
Coffin box – specifically for decoration
Red ribbon w/white stripes – Good Conduct Medal

When I read "good conduct," I flash back to the summer between seventh and eighth grades, defined in part by my attending Girl Scout Camp, my last summer to do so. I brought home the "Miss Congeniality" title, voted on by the entire camp. When my mother asked how I knew the girls outside of my assigned area, I told her that we talked at the latrine. She wondered aloud how I might have behaved in a "congenial" manner in that particular context.

Glued onto a page removed from a scrapbook in one of the several boxes of family materials I find an article titled "Ike's Aids Offer Differing Views on Bulge Fight." Written by Chesly Manly for the Chicago Tribune Press Service, it features information from a series of articles in the *Saturday Evening Post*, no doubt the series to which I've found previous references. In it, Eisenhower's chief of staff, General Walter B. (Beetle) Smith notes that Ike, like his fellow commanders, had never thought of the Ardennes as a problem previous to the Bulge. He had once admitted "a little ruefully" that he hadn't realized the danger for American troops "until he read it in the newspaper." At that moment I experience a sense of painful irony imagining one of the most powerful and informed individuals in the world as sharing a fragile emotional boat with my mother and other riveted bystanders, dependent upon print and wire for news of the fate of the most important people in their lives. The article concludes with the statement that Smith had written "with all the advantage afforded by hindsight. Sometimes hindsight is of dubious value, especially when it is refuted by contemporary evidence."

A small newspaper blurb glued above summarizes the decorations received by "Edmund C. Roberts, Captain" who "served June 27, 1941 and was released November 8, 1945." His service in "Central Europe, Rhineland, Aleutians, and Ardennes" is noted, followed by a list of awards: "the Asiatic-Pacific ribbon, with one battle star, EAME [Europe Africa Middle East] with three stars, American defense ribbon, Combat Infantry badge and the Bronze Star medal, MOS [Military Occupational Specialty], infantry unit commander, army." I remember my husband commenting after seeing Ed's decorations that the award of the Bronze Star was quite meaningful at that time. Later, the decorations were awarded at a higher rate. I read that when awarded for acts of heroism, the medal can be worn with a "V" device or "combat V" for heroism; I don't find anything resembling a "V" in the small wooden cedar chest that holds Ed's decorations. The Bronze Star Award was established by executive order on February 4, 1944 to be given to those meeting criteria after December 6, 1941 (the day of the Pearl Harbor attack). A quick online search reveals the decorations available to purchase in 2019 for $21.95, with free shipping.

Ed would receive later certificates and commendations. One certificate dated 11 September 1945 from The Infantry School at Fort Benning, Georgia, presents the Combat Infantryman Badge to 1st Lt. Edmund C. Roberts, Jr "for exemplary conduct in action against the enemy in St. Vith Area in Germany from 10 December to 19 December 1944."

Such decorations memorialized actions, some deserved and others not. Many awards were based on the testimony of others. All were presented with ceremony and ritual. Veterans would honor one another at private ceremonies. Among the materials that Frank sent to me, I find a program from a Memorial Service held during the gathering of the 106th in New Orleans in September 2005. It includes a call and refrain by the poet Joyce Kilmer, best known for his poem "Trees."

Chaplain and members:

> CHAPLAIN: Comrades true, born anew, peace to you;
> RESPONSE: Your souls shall be where the heroes are.
> CHAPLAIN: Your memories shine like the morning star.
> RESPONSE: Brave and dear, shield us here . . .
> ALL: Farewell!
> Sgt Joyce Kilmer, KIA 1918

A list of 49 members who have died since the previous reunion is printed on the last page of the program.

When I read about Kilmer at the Poetry Foundation's website, I am reminded that he was among the best-known American poets during his era, his work generally focusing on the natural beauty of the world. He did not have to serve. However, after graduating from Rutgers College and Columbia University and writing as a journalist for *The New York Times*, he enlisted in the New York National Guard in 1917. The following year, he requested to serve in Europe, where he worked mainly to gather intelligence. But "On July 30, 1918, he joined in the battle of Ourcq and was killed by a sniper's bullet" ("Joyce Kilmer"). The military honored him when it later founded Camp Kilmer, an enormous staging site located on 1500 acres between Edison and Piscataway, New Jersey. It opened in 1942, functioning as a holding area for troops where they enjoyed entertainment by performers including Red Skelton, who made many unannounced visits. Baseball great Joe DiMaggio also visited and offered lessons in batting and fielding. After serving as a processing site for millions of servicemen, the camp closed briefly in 1949 but was reopened in 1950 at the beginning of the Korean conflict. In the sixties it was parceled and sold; Rutgers University placed a college on some of the acreage.

Among Helen's scrapbook pages is a large article with the headline "Kilmer Stresses Services for Returnees." I know that Ed went first to New Jersey before coming home, and I assume that Camp Kilmer was the location. It features "Best of chow, no details, short stay" for returnees, as well as "8-hr service at laundry" and "Bright Spots" including "five theatres each seating 1000 and showing the latest film fare" and "shows" in "Kilmer Bowl which seats 8,500" during the summer. Service clubs provide the opportunity to dance "with the 400 WACS in camp." In addition, servicemen may visit twelve different PXs, a barber shop, libraries, and athletic facilities and equipment. Unlike the men like my husband, who fought in a later highly unpopular war, the WWII veterans returned to a robust welcome. I'm reminded of the many that did not return, as I see a photo of a young man in a clipping in Mom's scrapbook that died of malnutrition in a German prison camp. I turn back to my father's prison notebook and scan the list of names on the last two pages, but I don't find that of this Rockford, Missouri private, so I'm unsure why it is in the book. He was 35, older than Ed, and I wonder whether he might have been a friend of one of my uncles.

Ed Roberts would share the private's and Kilmer's fate in yet another "military action" cum "war," two wars beyond "the war to end all wars" in which Kilmer died. During those years following his POW experience, Ed would return to his wife and son, at first consider, and then reject a civilian position as director of the new student center at Knox College, re-enlist in the military, and father two daughters. Before he left the states again for the final time, he would participate with dogged energy to help those who had not served better understand what happened to those who had, as well as to encourage veterans to share their experiences. I add another parental trait to the list that grows as I better value what I might have inherited from my father and mother—an appreciation for the events of the past.

> I don't remember much about our officers—I was in the motor pool and he was an officer in the heavy weapons unit. They rebuilt the 106th after the Battle of the Bulge in about March 1945. Nobody was left from the original. [Today] there are 7 people left in Company D, 422nd Regiment. I never did get to talk with any of them . . . I had someone watching over me. I had a little voice with me—I never got to meet him, but I was glad he was there.
> 10-8-2006 Virginia Brackett, telephone conversation with Willis Bouma

A July 1, 1945 scrapbook article titled "106th Acts as Warden" tells of the function of Ed's reconstituted Battalion being:

> up to their necks in war prisoners—prisoners of 29 nationalities—and they are discharging their huge hordes of captives at the rate of 9,000 each day. The prisoners range from boys of six and eight years old to men of 70. Some women, as well as 77 German and Hungarian field marshals and generals are included.

The name of Staff Sgt. Roy Sharp is noted as among a group of 33 officers and enlisted men who "will serve as instructors in the broad program of vocational and academic courses which is to be opened to men of the Lion Division in the near future." The purpose of the courses was to offer the men "a worth-while method of using leisure time."

On August 20, 1945, the members of the 422d Infantry Regiment received another letter regarding decorations from Colonel Descheneaux, written from Fitzsimmons General Hospital in Denver Colorado. Additionally, the bulletin helps clarify events during the Bulge, after the Regiment had been cut off from others, ordered to leave Schnee-Eiffel and "to attack and destroy a German Panzer Combat Team on the Schonberg St. Vith Road." By this time, I assume everyone captured at the Battle of the Bulge would have read accounts of their surrender that might have questioned the wisdom of that tactic. Perhaps such accounts had spurred Descheneaux to write to his men. He continued:

> By the afternoon it became evident that the accomplishment of our mission was impossible. It became further evident that there was little we could do to help any operation. The paramount question became that of saving the lives of as many of you men as possible, and every possible action to accomplish this was discussed. Our situation was rendered hopeless by our great distance behind our lines, the weather, our ammunition supply, and many other factors. And so, though my spirit revolted against such a decision, surrender seemed to be the only solution to avoid needless loss of life and further suffering.

He wishes all the men "the best of luck" and thanks them "from the bottom of my heart for having made it possible for me to be as proud of his officers, men, and regiment as any commander could be."

A small brochure among the scrapbook pages titled "The Heroic 106th" bears a colorful reproduction of the lion patch and the motto beneath it, "To Make History is Our Aim." It represents "Reprints from The Indianapolis Star," whose reporters would have taken a great interest in the 106th, as many of its servicemen hailed from Indiana and Illinois. The brochure begins with an excerpt from a January 18, 1945 article. It opens with vivid imagery of the natural forces the battalion faced: "From the shell-swept, icy mud of northern France, where it crouched beaten to its knees by the might of Rundstedt's mechanized charge, the battle-broken but unbeaten 106th United States Infantry Division has risen anew to spearhead the Yankee armies at Malmedy." A few lines later, the attack on the 106th is described as "the white-hot charge of the German panzers." According to the articles, two-thirds of the battalion members were under the age of 22, "a tight-belted, clean-cut out-fit of kids who knew their way around." That description contradicts the truth that the "kids" were, for the most part, under-trained and without battle experience. However, the positive light cast on their efforts is understandable, and the perseverance and courage of the individual troops have been honored by later accounts.

This article places total losses at the Battle of the Bulge at almost 75,000. Whatever the final number—and history may never attain that "true" number—great sacrifice occurred. Ed's regiment is specifically mentioned with high praise, with an article noting that after an attack that left only 300 men remaining, "This little group . . . pitched in and helped the remaining regiment, the 424th, to make gallant delaying stands before and behind St. Vith." An article from January 21 includes the detail that for many weeks, "censorship has forbidden transmission of these details."

As I write this page, the 70-year anniversary of the German surrender is marked with fanfare in the contemporary press, and by many observable activities. With the historical perspective of seven decades, we know many more details, "facts" that continue to reveal themselves. However, the memories of the men with whom I spoke have not undergone revision in search of the truth. Their stories are exchanged and compared, regrouped and collected to best advantage at various geographic locations, in an action that might be compared to military maneuvers.

I am delighted to discover a fascinating personal letter to my father dated March 14 [1945], which offers a welcome break from a review of formal printed documents. It originated in Stepanovićevo, a town in Serbia. I recall a name from my father's prison notebook and check to discover the last name, Savcósky, but I find no clear connection to the correspondent. The letter's signature, a first name, is difficult to decipher. The letter is typewritten, lengthy, and the writer's motives heartfelt. He responds to a letter from Ed and tells him that he received one at almost the same time from Bruce (Ed's friend). I read the letter several times, focusing first on its tone—actually several times on the tone—and then on the facts and what I know of Serbia's history, which is admittedly little. I make no changes to the original spelling or grammar:

I injoyed in a couple of minutes a double joy—in a concentrated form, so to say. You can imagine what a pleasure it was for me to see that all of my friends survived all that went on, after having sought them in the PWs graveyard at Hammelburg. Really I did it on April the 6th, on the day of our final liberation. After realizing that the tanks, in spite of their admiring courage, failed, and not seeing you among the recaptured Americans, the only reasonable thing seemed to be to go to the cemetery with the flowers in my hands and to take care for your graves. Luckily I didn't find them there and still more luckily I am able now to make jokes of it. For it could easily happen that I lost ability for making jokes—and for breathing too—for ever during the last couple of the days in the captivity. Namely, our liberation was pretty hot and noisy and some of our men—fortunately not so many—were killed on the very day of the liberation. The Germans, damned (excuse me) as they are and will be for ever, have made our camp a battlefield and so the fighting went over our heads. But really everything terminated with good luck at least for me and for my friends you are acquainted with . . .

You said in your letter that none of you would ever forget our men because of our treating you helpfully in your worst days. I asure you that the Americans have rewarded it well during the three months we were under their protection. We were treated by the corresponding American authorities like sick children and very loved children too. It is impossible to express all the good the Americans made to us. No one nation could have such a human understanding for us. To illustrate this, I think it enough to give only the following fact: In order to remove our psychological depression, your soldiers removed in the first days all the barbed wire out of our sight. It is only one of the deeds of your soldiers, which touched me immensely, not to speak of many other

> kindnesses, apparently more important, the Americans met us with. We cannot forget it for ever.

As I have done daily since beginning this project, I again think of the enormous contradictions borne in the condition of war. To engage in this most uncivilized, but most common, of hostilities, we attempt to civilize it by adopting "conventions," rules of order, rites of passage, definitions, words on a page that determine the fate of "hostiles," "prisoners," "allies," and "friendlies."

As the author of the letter continues to write, his heart open along with his mind, he describes the near-unbearable aftermath of the war, in the same breath as that which made existence more bearable. Those details include that, at least in his area of Serbia:

> everything was during the war destroyed; the means of transportation, the industry, the agriculture, etc. You can imagine how looks it like for my father, as a farmer, to start working again on the destroyed farm without utensils and everything what a farmer needs. We suffer enormously on the lack of industrial products. The cloths, leather, the shoes are still a rarity here.

And yet he recalls with gratitude a few simple compassionate actions by individuals that served to ameliorate against the broad destruction inflicted by an industry—that of war—whose business is annihilation. I will learn after sifting through more correspondence that this individual met Ed in Hammelburg where he had been imprisoned for four years. He would also have been an officer, serving in the Serbian army. Theirs would have been a brief acquaintance, but obviously an intense one. As with so many of my father's fellow-travelers, I can only muse about his life story and eventual fate.

The Serbian mentions that he is in contact with Brana, now living in Belgrave; "he lives as all others do, i.e. pretty hard." I find three letters to Ed from that individual, signed simply "Brana." In an undated first letter, Brana notes that he has received Ed's letter and the message that Ed is sending him a package, which has not yet arrived. He hopes to advance from his job as a clerk with plans to "study high commerce School" in Belgrade, his hopes of attending college in the U.S. relegated to mere fantasy. He praises the assistance of the U.N.R.R.A.—the United Nations Relief and Rehabilitation Administration—for its rebuilding efforts in Europe and the fact that "it has saved many lives". His remarks indicate that he knows that Helen is pregnant, and he hopes for a girl to join Ed's son Bruce. In a March 2nd letter, he writes, "You can imagine how I was merry when the package came. It is not only a gift, but also a remembrance at the friend soon in after wartime." The package was damaged, so he lists its contents in order for Ed to determine that everything safely reached him. He also writes that his Serbian friends were intrigued and "have asked very much of you and how I know you." In the final letter dated March 18, Brana wrote how glad he felt to learn that Ed is well. He thinks of him often and,

> Sometimes I was very sorry that I didn't follow you when tanks came in the camp . . . You know I didn't see you that evening and tomorrow morning. Kolar gave me a fountain pen and a pencil for remembrance of you . . . we saw many Americans returning—they were recaptured. I was looking at fence to see you and call you on me, but you were more clever and happier. You have finished this war just like hero of Lion Head Division even you were decorated by General Patton. Your escaping seems me as a story . . . and you can mention it very proud everywhere.

I understand Brana's statement, as Ed's life has been a story for me as well. Ed must have discussed the importance of freedom with his new comrades, because Brana states, "I shall never forget your prognostication in the camp when you said me about our liberation." He adds details of his return home through repatriation and having found his mother and sister. He references his four years in prison prior to the arrival of the officers of the 106th and writes about Ed's package.

> As for box you didn't forget it. It is very kind of you, but you know I shall never ask for any recompense. I think it was my duty to help you at first days of your prison's life. You could see all people in our camp (who speak and don't speak English) how help and like you. Do you remember the hours when we were together, both thin and hungry how we divide the last thing from package. I didn't know you before and perhaps I shall never meet again but, you know, to give you something meant in our camp to repay a part of American's love for Serbian people.

He writes of his work as a private clerk and how little he earns, hoping he will find a better job soon. Apparently, Ed had asked what he needed, and he replies with some hesitancy, stating Ed has no debt to repay, but that he can offer help simply "as an old war friend."

I must turn to my imagination to conjure the possible conversations between Helen and Ed, Ed and his family, Ed and his friends, during those first few months at home. However, I find Ed's voice clearly represented in a Cedric Foster broadcast transcript at the end of 1945. The program presented what we might label a "first anniversary" report about the battle, complete with first-person accounts. Ed's was among those accounts, and I will be able to read some of the few details about his POW experience that I possess in his own words in that printed broadcast version.

Ed wrote to Foster relating briefly his experience following his capture. My mother saved Foster's reply to Ed's account in a letter dated December 28, 1945. Foster thanked Ed for his letter and enclosed a transcript of the broadcast in which he referenced Ed "and which I hope you happened to hear." Foster's December 20 broadcast begins with a foreshadowing of Ed's future service, as he summarizes,

> rumblings from the Japanese theater of occupation. There were reports that General MacArthur and the Russians had crossed swords regarding Russian participation in the occupation . . . very strongly in this matter. While General MacArthur has never said so in as many words, there is every reason to believe that MacArthur would hand in his resignation if the Russians were allowed by the allies to come into the Japanese home islands with a strong occupational force.

He then reminds listeners that:

> a year ago at this time, hundreds of thousands of American soldiers were locked in mortal combat with the German army of Gerd von Rundstadt in the Battle of the Bulge. Lest our memories are short, it seems to me appropriate today to recall some of the happenings of a year ago.

Foster first reads entries from the diary of a U.S. Army Private in the 590th Field Artillery Battalion of the 106th Division, which includes much detail about his life as a prisoner. An entry that begins December 12 [1944] describes the first food received as "hard crackers and one can of cheese for seven men." On December 21, all boarded an uncomfortable "smell awful" train, with 60 men per cattle car. They experience a "frightening" air raid in which a fellow prisoner was killed. December 24 they were still in the car with no food, but religious services were held "for both denominations. Whitehead sang the Lord's Prayer and then led us in Christmas Carols." December 25 proved a "very sad Christmas," despite services and one man's telling of the Christmas story. By December 27, dysentery increased, and on December 29, they at last receive some "hot soup" and the "first water in forty-eight hours." They are unloaded, marched to a camp, "very, very cold," where they are "deloused, showered, painted and vaccinated. Then given hot soup. Registered, finger-printed, photographed, and questioned." The Private's parents did not receive his communication until May. Foster doesn't comment on whether they knew prior to that time that he was no longer an MIA, but instead a POW. The Private lost 60 pounds during confinement and was in Dresden during air raids, daily fearing for his life.

Foster then turns to the letter written by Ed. He supplies Ed's name and address in Galesburg and continues by stating that he:

> was on that box-car train which started out about a year ago with American prisoners of war. He was the executive officer of Company D of the 422nd Infantry. He was captured on the 19th of December, but some of the units managed to hold out for two days longer. He said to me in a letter only today:
>
> > 'How well I remember sitting up on Schnee-Eifel a year ago tomorrow watching the Germans stream down the Prum highway only four thousand yards away from us. We were powerless to do anything about it. Our artillery was all gone, and we had nothing that could reach the enemy. But that is all over and done. Let us now rejoice that this Christmas will be spent here in Galesburg, Illinois, in a nice, warm home, instead of in a German box car, being bombed by our planes.

I have learned by now that my parents did focus on rejoicing as often as possible. As in many households, my mother's calendar remained prominent. She recorded not only her plans but dates important to all of us. She even stuck separate lists on the calendar margins. She nurtured the seed of joy planted early in her own upbringing through the ritual of family gatherings, both formal and informal. In researching my father's primary documents, his comments further validate my inheritance of the natural tendency to gather the clan. Over the years, my own printed calendars reflect birthdays, anniversaries, and deaths. A part of my own ritual in moving into each New Year has been to copy that important information from the previous year's calendar into the new one. My husband

and I take great care in selecting calendars for their artistic appearance and the connections to our own lives that their accompanying photos evoke—connections that clever marketers learned to exploit long ago.

I glance at my contemporary calendar, now also available in electronic form, a poor substitute, in my opinion, for the printed ones, on which we can flip pages—such satisfaction in that activity. I see that during the first three weeks of May, various members of our family will be together to celebrate Mother's Day; two dance recital performances featuring three granddaughters; and two birthdays; those are the official gatherings. During the first weekend in June, we will have a Roberts family reunion when we'll have fun, but also remember those no longer with us. The family will want to know how my book project about Ed and Helen fares. We'll remember Ginny and Don and our step-father Bob, along with our half-sister, Nan, who we had lost to breast cancer. We remember by playing games, a passion of the members of the previous generation. Word games, including Boggle (an all-inclusive team activity) and Scrabble (for those preferring the *mano-a-mano* approach) occupied our group for many hours. At one recent gathering, I worked a puzzle at the kitchen table with two of my young grand-daughters. They learned the art through abstraction on their iPads but are no less pleased to apply it to the material. Despite our losses, we know well the art of rejoicing.

As I research, I continue to receive responses from WWII veterans or their family members. One wife writes that her 87-year-old husband Edward Olecki suffers from Alzheimer's and can't recall my father. She tells me he was in the 106th, Co. D 422 and was captured on December 16, 1944 and "held prisoner at Stalags 9A and B, Bad Orb, and Zigenkeim, Germany." She refers me to Frank Trautman and concludes, "We wish you the very best of luck in finding the information you are seeking as the World War II Veterans are dying off at a fast rate. Just so sorry we can't help you any further but thank you for your beautiful letter." I find Mr. Olecki's name heading the list my father wrote while imprisoned. One daughter writes that her family just lost their father Lawrence Williams; at age 84 he fell, broke a hip, and died 4 days later. She shares that as a POW, he had frozen feet and received a Purple Heart. I later check the list and see a "Williams" on it. She will pass my name along to a fellow from Birmingham who attended the funeral. "Was that Mr. Temple?" I ask. She replies, "Yes."

I had just spoken with Mr. Temple who explained that he joined the military late, in March or April of 1944, and didn't know Ed Roberts. However, he shared with me, another fellow who knew Ed said that he actually ran the company. Remembering that description from a previous conversation, I asked Mr. Temple, "Was that Mr. Trautman?" He tells me that it was.

I review the notes I made following these conversations. I have written, "I already feel a part, however slight, of this rapidly shrinking community. I've swelled its fragile ranks by one."

I finally discover my father's first connection to the 106th Infantry Division Association, in a letter dated September 18, 1946. I'm delighted to see that the individual who signed the letter is among those with whom I've become familiar during my research, Herbert B. Livesey, Jr. He writes to thank Ed for his membership application, as well as for a clipping that Ed had sent. He regrets that the clipping is too long to print in the newsletter. He adds,

> D. Co. was really very hard hit in many ways. Descheneaux is flat on his back and completely in the dumps. Every single recommendation he sent in for honors and awards for men has been turned down. He has T. B. in both lungs . . . Colonel Matthews, the Regimental Exec Officer has written me several times and feels pretty badly about a good many things.One of the things I never bargained for as secretary were the letters from the next of kin of the KIA's. They are heart rending. Anything we can do to help we should.

I remember the message from Descheneaux that focused on attempts to gain commendations for his men. This letter is dated much later and makes clear that Descheneaux's health has been poor and even deteriorating since his hospitalization following the Battle of the Bulge.

Ed continued his correspondence with various figures regarding the details of the battle, including R. Ernest Dupuy, by that time a retired Colonel. Dupuy responds to Ed on November 11, 1946, "answering your letter of 4 November," writing, "I would be delighted to receive your history of D Co., 422nd Inf." Dupuy writes that he would be,

> particularly interested in the original dispositions, the move from the pill-box positions towards Schonberg, with all the detail you can gather—were routes reconnoitered, was your battalion handled as a unit or piecemeal, how was the attack of the morning of 19 Dec carried off on the company level, did D Co take part in any coordinated attack that morning or was it separated from the rest of the outfit??? I would like to get the "feel" of the move, up to the end. Am writing this from an entirely impartial attitude, calling the thing as I see it from the evidence presented, hence every little detail and incident is of interest.

Clearly, unearthing the "truth" about the Battle of the Bulge remained a passionate focus for many during the years following the German surrender. Ed actively involved himself in the discussion, reading the various accounts, to which he felt obligated to respond on several occasions. During this time, he ostensibly should have been working at Knox College in the position promised him, but my mother's phrase "it didn't work out" makes me wonder whether he began the position, but left due to some challenge, or whether he began at all.

Whatever else occupied Ed's energy and focus, the 106th Infantry Division Association began to play a larger part. He was one of the earliest subscribers to *The Cub*. I have a copy of an entry that he wrote in perhaps the first issue in a section titled "What They are Saying":

> Capt E. C. Roberts Jr. former Exec. Officer and CO of D Co 422 writes: "I received in the mail yesterday the literature concerning the 106th Div. Ass'n and was certainly

> happy to receive it. I have always been extremely proud to have been a member of the Div. even tho one of the many that were forced to accept capture thru no fault of my own. I am enclosing on the form which you sent out the names and addresses of the men KIA in Co D 422nd Inf. As far as I know our company (of which I was Exec. Officer and later CO during the first part of the Bulge) suffered the least casualties in killed of any company in the Regt. All of the names enclosed died after they were captured which I believe is a great tribute to the men of the company during what was their first action. We fired every round of what little ammunition we had and took a few Krauts with us. I'm enclosing a newspaper clipping which, after you filter out the junk put in by a local reporter, will tell you of the experiences of myself and three other officers of the 422, Lt Bruce M. Fisher and Lt John Mason Co D and Lt Joseph Hoerth of Co K. We four were part of a handful who succeeded in effecting our escape in that fracas. It gave us personal satisfaction because even tho the Krauts got us they couldn't keep us. The best of luck to the organization and be sure and keep me on the mailing list for anything else that may come out.

In 1948, he not only attended the group's second annual convention in Indianapolis, but he also spoke there. As I would soon confirm, he had re-enlisted in the Army and was a Master Sergeant by 1948. Within two years he would be stationed at Ft. Riley, Kansas, where I was born. A few months later, he was ordered to fly to California, and then to Japan, leaving his family behind until I became old enough to fly. How odd it must have been to think of living in Japan, its enemy status during WWII still fresh on many minds.

Ed would go to Japan, but only as a stop on the way to Korea when the conflict broke. Plans for the family would radically alter. Helen would later face the difficult and ultimately fateful decision to remain with her sister or to return to Illinois, or to Manhattan, Kansas where she and Ed owned a house. He would mention in a September 29, 1950 letter that while he hoped for a quick end to the fighting, he still had "30 months to do," and perhaps she could still join him in Japan. By that point, Helen had to be used to change and to surprise, the fare of the military wife.

I think back to the day—were I engaged in purple prose, I might write that fateful day—that the letter from Robert E. Merriam to my father dropped from the book titled *Dark December*. If I turn from my desk where I sit at my computer, I can see its dark spine where it stands on my bookcase today. Its discovery prompted one of the most satisfying chapters in my research for this project. Information at the top of the letter indicated it had been typed onto formal stationery, and I assumed my father had written to counter the author's opinion of the activities of Ed's battalion at the Bulge (Merriam, personal correspondence).

I recall sitting on our new library floor after discovering and reading the letter, various questions tripping through my thoughts. A few moments on the computer provided an easy answer to the question, who was Robert E. Merriam? An article written after his death at 69 contains the story of Mr. Merriam's life. After earning a masters degree at the University of Chicago, he served in the Army from 1942–45 and fought at the Battle of the Bulge. He left the service as a captain and earned a Bronze Star, as had my father. It mentions his later "popular book," *Dark December: The Full Account of the Battle of the Bulge*. "Bob was one of a group of guys who came out of World War II and ran for city government as part of a reform bloc," serving from 1946–47 as director of Chicago's Metropolitan Housing Council. After becoming alderman of the 5th ward in 1947, he worked to eliminate housing discrimination and introduced "the idea of one-way streets, civilian crossing guards and parking meters in the neighborhoods."

As chairman of the Emergency Commission on Crime, he fought to end ties between organized crime and city politics. He left his alderman position, resigning from the Democratic Party to run as a Republican against Mayor Richard Daley in 1954; he lost by a few more than

127,000 votes. According to an associate, volunteers ran his office and his campaign. He later published the book, *Going into Politics: A Guide for Citizens*, and "brought a lot of young people into politics." From 1958–61 he held the position of deputy director of the budget and deputy assistant to President Dwight Eisenhower and from 1969–78 chaired the Presidential Commission on Intergovernmental Relations. He became a full-time businessman in various ventures from 1969–76, resigning as a partner in Alexander Proudfoot Co., a management consulting firm, to create a land management business (Heise).

I discover the guide to the Merriam papers, 1918–1984 at the University of Chicago website. The papers occupy 73 linear feet (131 boxes) in the special collections of the University's Research collection. I wonder whether those papers might contain Ed's original letter to Merriam. I send an e-mail message to Julia Gardner, Reference/Instruction Librarian in July 2007, asking whether she might search for Ed's letter. I also mention the original letter that I have from Mr. Merriam. She responds that the archivist would very much like to have the Merriam letter, but that she has not been able to locate my father's letter. Several months pass before I inquire again, letting the librarian know that I'll travel soon to Chicago and would like to visit the Special Collections if she has discovered the letter. She responds, thanking me for my patience, and writes:

> As it turns out, this collection was recently reboxed, a process just finished by our archivists. I went through Box 5, which contains the Dark December correspondence, and found a letter from your father, E.C. Roberts, to Merriam, in folder 5 of that box. The letter is dated November 14, 1947. You are welcome to read this letter . . . during your visit here . . . Do you plan to visit in the next two weeks? If so I can just keep the box on hold for you.

I plan the trip to Illinois with great care and, of course, with several lists. In addition to visiting the University of Chicago, we will travel to

Galesburg. My memories of my parents' early homes remain generally vague, with the exception of certain vivid details from my own childhood—the frightening claw foot tub in the Kost house, the wide porch of the Roberts residence. I revisit various photos to remind me of people and locations. I'll also speak with Mr. Lindstrom while in Galesburg and visit the Knox alumni office to find any materials about my parents that I don't have among my mother's possessions. The alumni office personnel will gladly pull materials on both of my parents and make copies for me of any items I request. My parents would be pleased, as both remained dedicated alumni of Knox College. I find in one box a "Living Endowment Certificate," indicating that my father, Capt. E. C. Roberts contributed "an amount equal to an annual three percentum return on invested endowment of $83.33." That certificate is dated May 1, 1950, about eight weeks before he would depart for Japan and then Korea.

As my husband and I walk across the University of Chicago campus a few weeks later, we admire its beauty and the sense of history that inhabits all such established campuses. As the extremely helpful rare books librarian promised, the materials are ready for me to peruse. Ed Roberts' letter is typed with a handwritten signature, below which he has typed his Galesburg address and added in parentheses, "Formerly Captain Inf Co D 422nd Inf 106th Div." I stare at the paper for some time before reading the letter. I'm again enthralled at the capabilities of institutions like this university to preserve our public past, and personal stories, through the respectful collection and chronicling of personal documents. Though the costs remain high, both for storage and for the energies required for such preservation. I offer a quick academic's prayer of gratitude to those who still believe such activities worth the necessary investment.

I include Ed's letter in full:

> Dear Mr. Merriam:
> No doubt you have received many letters like this but I feel that I should spring to the defense of my unit so vividly described by you in your book "Dark December". I am taking it for granted that I have the right Merriam.

First may I say that I enjoyed the book immensely and feel that you handled a very difficult subject very well. However being a loyal and true member of the 106th Div and of one of the regiments which you described as giving up without a fight it hurt me very much as it did other members of the units. I don't know of course whom you may have talked to from our units but there are a few things that you should know about Col Deschaneaux and the surrender. In the first place the part of the regiment that he surrendered was only a small part, the unit was so broken up and separated. Parts of the regiment were still fighting on the 21st of Dec. The feeble attempt as you put it in the book on the 19th to break out of the ring was one of the best coordinated attacks I have seen considering the fact that we had no artillery, no anti-tank guns, poor communications, almost no ammunition and hadn't eaten for three days. The minute we started toward the Schonberg St Vith road on the morning of the 19th we were immediately subjected to terrific attacks by tanks infantry and artillery from every direction but down. We took some of them with us but you can't fight tanks with your bare hands. If you disagree try it sometime. In my company we had 60 rounds of mortar ammunition when we moved into the line for six guns and 3000 rounds per machine gun. You can imagine how long that lasted. Our artillery was gone after the first six hours on the 16th also. We had plenty of grenade launchers but no grenades. Bazooka ammunition was almost nonexistent. All in all I feel you were very unfair to say what you did. I have had veterans from many divisions tell me that the same thing would have happened to any outfit in the same position. In your zeal to tell all about the 7th Armored you failed to mention the fact that a large number of the troops conducting the defense of St Vith were the units left of the 106th. The 81st Engineer Bn of the 106th got the Presidential Citation as did some units of the 424th Inf. You didn't even mention General Perrin our Div Exec who conducted the defense with General Hasbrouck. He later got the Distinguished Service Cross. Major Parker of Parkers Crossroads was a member of the 106th and you didn't mention that either. Seems that the 106th must be a sore point with you or something.

One thing which I feel you were justified in talking about was the division staff. They were pretty poor in general. I will always remember what Col Mathews the 422 Exec said the G-2 said to him over the phone when he reported that there was a tremendous concentration of vehicles opposite us. The G-2 said "Don't worry about it. The Germans are playing phonograph records for you." All I can say is then deliver me from ever facing such phonograph records again. We also captured in front of our position an officer with a copy of the corps attack plan in our particular area and according to regt they never even got confirmation of its receipt from Div. We knew something was going on but division thought we were just jittery. We were jittery but then we tried to be on the ball at the same time. The lst thing the units of the 2d Inf Div told us as they pulled out was "take it easy and relax this is a quiet sector." That is not conducive to making troops alert.

I hope you try to get a copy of the Div history and read a little more about the 422 and 423. I think you will find that what the regt Cos did should not reflect on the rest of the regt. There are many things I could tell you about them but space does not permit. Possibly you may be acquainted already. I have reenlisted in the army as a M/Sgt and all this is done and past but the memory of the men that I was privileged to lead in the 422 makes me write this letter. We were attacking when we were captured and believe me the devotion to duty of the group I was with was superb. Col

Descheneux did as he saw fit and I guess those higher didn't agree. Wish some of them had been in his place. I'm not defending him I'm merely making a statement.

Well I have said my piece now and will close. Again let me repeat that I enjoyed the book immensely but felt that the 106th didn't deserve to be the only unit that you made deriding remarks about. I would like to get together with you sometime and talk the whole thing over but I guess the chances of that are rather slim. Best of luck in your political career and if you have time let me hear from you on the reaction of what I have said.

Yours very truly,
E.C. Roberts, Jr. [handwritten signature]
E.C. Roberts Jr.
[Home address in Galesburg, IL]
(Formerly Captain Inf Co D
422nd Inf 106th Div)

The effect upon me proved profound. I was fortunate enough to hold pieces of paper that my father, and perhaps my mother as well, held, carefully folded and inserted into the addressed envelope. The experience also proved interesting simply from a research point of view. The fact that such a personal family artifact belongs to the collection and must remain was, I knew, to be a general rule, although I had never encountered it first-hand. However, as I learned, because the letter did originate from my family, I would not be required to request permission to formally cite it in any writing. I complete a photocopy request for the items from Merriam's file that I wish to copy.

I discover from the letter that Ed had "re-upped" in the Army by November of 1947. Neither of my siblings know details about why the promised job managing the Knox College student center did "not work out," as our mother wrote. I think of how well plans for that center occupied Ed's time and energies while in prison camp. As my brother speculated, "After years in the war, and prison camp, his world view changed, and perhaps the Student Union did not appeal anymore." In Phil Klay's book, *Redeployment*, he writes of the impossible act of reintegration into civilian life following his service in Iraq. Upon his return home, he must face polite questions from others who can't find Fallujah on a map. He compares movement through city streets during wartime— "your Marine on point went down the side of the road, checking ahead and scanning the roofs . . . The Marine behind him checks the windows . . . the Marine behind him gets the windows a little lower, and so on down . . . In a city there's a million places they can kill you from"—to his wife's drive through town toward a mall. In the first situation, he's on "orange." In the second, he's expected to come down to "white" immediately, which is not possible. He simply can't relate to civilian surroundings. He re-ups and suffers the loss of his marriage and other civilian relationships.

Also on hand in the Merriam collection I find an excerpt from a copy of *The Cub* column, "What They Are Saying," where I had earlier found Ed's letter to the editor. Of the three blurbs on the page, all of which are comments by *The Cub* readers in response to a previous publication, two are crossed through. The one of interest to the collection refers specifically to Merriam's book, its title reading "Condemns Dark December." Ed Roberts had served as a book reviewer for *The Cub*, and the statement appears in reaction to his review of *Dark December*, which had appeared earlier in the publication. From Salem, Ohio, one reader "writes to take a few swings at Robert Merriam's book 'Dark December,' and at Ed Roberts' review of it on pages 51-52 of the February–March 1949 CUB" (Hiltbrand). The reader's comments provide additional evidence of the immediate emotional response that reports characterizing actions during the Battle of the Bulge would continue to elicit, long after the event.

One sweeping generalization that even I can make about military action is that not all wars are created equal. My research efforts are hardly necessary to support that point, but they have secured it as a fact for me. The Korean Conflict, later War, would affect members of the military and the U.S. civilians learning about their involvement differently than did matters relating to the world wars. The act of engagement in traditional patriotism lost its appeal, and the unity that resulted from former acts of patriotism wore thin. Some citizens may have experienced more annoyance than enthusiasm for a distant, localized conflict like that in Korea. Not only was its relationship to, and effect on, the U.S. unclear, it interrupted a long-anticipated return to "normalcy" following a world war. It also seemed to disturb the subsequent economic upturn that many, although not all veterans, enjoyed. The return home from Korea would also not be the celebrated event that members of the military experienced following the previous wars. I think of the iconic Alfred Eisenstaedt photo, "VJ Day in Times Square," of sailor George Mendonsa kissing Greta Zimmer Friedman, a dental assistant who he believed to be a nurse; what better representation of the national jubilance that welcomed home those who fought in WWII (Callahan)? Such jubilance stands in stark contrast to the public reaction that greeted Korean veterans upon their return. The subdued national reaction to the Korean War could later be viewed as a type of preparation for the sharp change in public reaction to U.S. military forces and their efforts abroad, brought into focus by the next war. That attitude, varying from indifference to vilification, resulted in relative silence on the part of military personnel who returned from Korea and Vietnam to a largely unsympathetic public. Their wars were not celebrated, and neither were their efforts for many decades to come. The suffering of all affected by personal loss and injuries in war, however, remains equally debilitating. Suffering is relatively unaltered by the geographic location or political environment that serves as a backdrop for any international dispute.

- CHAPTER EIGHT -

"THE UNHAPPY PENINSULA"

I belong to a military funeral detail and have been in quite a few parades along with Korean War veterans. They think they're isolated and that there's no reason talking about the war, nobody cares. They don't want to be friendly with other veterans.

Personal Correspondence – Virginia Brackett

How is it, then, that the other great mid-twentieth-century conflict with communism, Korea, remains so neglected? Popular awareness of the Korean war today centers upon the television comedy show *M.A.S.H.*, which dismays most veterans because it projects an image of the struggle infinitely less savage than that which they recall. The United Nations suffered 142,000 casualties . . . Many Westerners were happy to forget Korea for a generation after the war ended, soured by the taste of costly stalemate, robbed of any hint of glory . . . Above all, perhaps, Korea merits close consideration as a military rehearsal for the subsequent disaster in Vietnam" (Max Hastings. *The Korean War*. 9-10).

I am blessed by the abundance of Ed's letters from Korea that my mother saved. For years, I had access to a group of about 15 letters, the ones transcribed by my daughter and on which she would base a college essay. As I moved into the latter stages of writing this account, I found many more, so that I had a total of 31 letters—30 written to Helen and one to her parents. Those additional letters deeply affected me. Written during his later months in Korea, they brim with information and expressions that allow me to come to know Ed Roberts far better than I felt I had before. He freely expresses his opinions and shares information about his locations, allowing me to use his accounts and a map sent to me decades later by Lieutenant Carrig to follow his route. He mentions in one letter that he can share so much information because his letters aren't censored, unlike during WWII. As I gain more intimacy with my father, I truly grieve his loss and the loss of the Helen Roberts that I would never know. I take from his replies that she was warm, sexy, sentimental—barely resembling the rational-to-a-fault individual with whom I matured. My mother once told me that I would not have recognized her while married to Ed, a time when she was glad to allow him to plan and arrange everything, to let someone else lead and direct. That description flabbergasted me. I had known her as an independent, headstrong woman with little time for emotion and sentimentality, causing clashes with my sisters and me. I later understood that like any creature threatened, she had to engage survival instincts and morph into a different being, developing new coping mechanisms and strategies.

Finally, as I transcribe letter excerpts written throughout the month of November 1950 and into December, I'm haunted by my knowledge of how little time remained to my father. I would note while reading of his hopes and plans that he would have only three more weeks to live, then ten days, and by the final letter of December 18, only five more days. Often I had to stop writing, ambushed by unanticipated waves of nausea.

As I research, I begin to feel that I am, in a metaphoric sense, losing skin, a layer of emotional protection from my environment. The sluffing of that barrier to the assault of the elements leaves my nerves exposed. That new sensitivity may be what allows my recognition of multiple intersections between my writing of this narrative and various occurrences in my own restricted universe. In the past, I labeled such intersections ironies, but over time have come to understand that they are simply the result of shared interests and interactions with my environment. They surface only when I stand ready to accommodate them, as my vulnerability will permit at any given moment. They form a web that supports my frustration not just over the loss of my father, but over the broader losses that so many military families and civilians touched by war experience—of lives, certainly, but also of dignity, security, and hope.

An example of such interweaving was my random decision to read Jeff Talarigo's novel *The Ginseng Hunter* just before I began writing this chapter. My choice to read the novel at this random moment coincided with my retirement, which gave me the time to engage in reading for pleasure. By pleasure, I mean reading not toward a goal, such as use in the classroom or in research, but then, as I was to discover, Talarigo's book closely connects in subject matter and thematic concerns to this research project. Set in 1960s China, a decade following the Korean War, the novel focuses on a character of Korean descent. His ancestors had along with many other Koreans been brought into China by the Japanese Army. I read elsewhere that the more than two million Koreans living in China still constitute the largest population outside of their country. My mind jumps again to recall a Chinese student that my husband and I mentored at the University. During our third meeting, he explained that although he was a Chinese citizen, he descended from Koreans, a fact he generally did not reveal to his community. His family's treatment upon revelation of their ancestry had not been kind. *The Ginseng Hunter* supports that fact and makes clear a point about which my father worried—what did the war effort mean to the inhabitants of the country that he and others from an international community sought to protect?

Talarigo's protagonist lived the isolated existence of a ginseng hunter. He becomes exposed through monthly brothel visits to the horrors experienced by those trapped in North Korea after WWII and the subsequent Korean War. Talarigo effectively renders those horrors by alternating the protagonist's narrative with the tale of a North Korean mother and child.

Talarigo's introduction of a child turns a fictional terror into a realistic tragedy. What human can watch a child suffer, even a fictional one, without feeling as they witness her trust broken, her promise never realized, knowing this figure represents a multitude of real individuals?

The tiny family struggles daily, not only to eat but to survive the ever-present scrutiny of those representing "the Great Leader" Kim Jong Il. In one horrific scene, while searching for food and wood to heat her home, the mother finds the bodies of soldiers killed by a sniper, their hands permanently cupped by death, holding precious rice rations where they fell. Acute hunger drives her to lick the rice from the filthy frozen hands, quickly swallowing the only food she's had for many hours. She does so realizing that she will have no food for her child upon her return; even that recognition can't empower her to stop consuming the rice. After cleaning the corpses' hands, she licks up grains where they have fallen on the frozen ground. The narrator tells us, "Hiding in some thick bushes, she knows that this day-to-day humiliation will be with her forever. She realizes that in this country even the living are dead" (Talarigo 70).

The woman staggers home without food or fuel to find a government agent inside her house. He grabs the back of her neck and forces her face against a picture of the "Great Leader" that hangs in every hovel via edict. While reprimanding the woman for not dusting the picture, he chokes her. Prior to the famine and the end of national aid, her daughter had practiced as a first-grader singing praises to the Great Leader. Now she lays on the floor in an early starvation coma.

A few days later, Agents return to the house, inspect the photo and seize the woman to "parade" through her village. "She sees no one," yet she knows that the villagers observe her sorrow, neither to celebrate nor empathize (72). They simply wait until her captors have taken her away. Then they will rush to her house, "searching for food or something that they can burn. No one will take in her daughter; she is just another mouth to feed. She thinks, as she is forced onto a truck, that her daughter will die. The realization bludgeons her fear" (Talarigo 72).

As I read my father's letters from Korea, I will think often of this passage and others, proof that for those in North Korea, the results of the country's post-WWII division would be bleak and long-lasting. In addition to Ed's statements, formal reports note that UN troops seemed unprepared for the national internal conflict they encountered when they invaded Korea. One would think they might be better prepared for the hostility and/or ambivalence on part of the Koreans. It was the post-WWII Allies that neatly split the country into two pieces with little to no regard for its effect on Korean citizens.

The differences between the World Wars and the Korean War challenged the U.S. armed forces, as well as U.S. civilians. The United States would enter WWII with "boots on the ground" only after provocation at Pearl Harbor, the reason for engagement simple and clear. Constant newspaper and radio reports of events in the theater of war mesmerized those at home. They felt intimately a part of war efforts through U.S. food and other resource rationing, as well as through the change in need for women to take up the work vacated by men called to serve. U.S. citizens followed the bidding of posters to remain vigilant for spies and to buy war bonds, feeling patriotic in the process. Civilians traveled without spare tires, surrendering theirs to reduce the shortage of rubber, sorely needed by the military. People gathered to listen to radio reports, to talk about the war, the country's gains and their own losses and found themselves united by shared events.

But the Korean War, one begun for reasons unclear to many, did not produce the same reaction for those at home. It was fought in an exotic location, seemingly without provocation or national threat. Retaining civilian interest in war proves difficult without direct involvement through sacrifice, victory campaigns, or a marshaling of industry, none of which occurred in response to the Communist challenge to the 38th parallel.

Even when involved, over time people suffer war fatigue and grow weary of thinking of others, fighting to protect what may incorrectly be viewed as only the rights of strangers on the other side of the world.

Late into the Iraq war, I heard one veteran comment that in order to force a war-weary populace to care about the fighting, one dead body per night should be shown on television. Even then, we who have never served know too little of the actual formal demands of war and the vital nature of national support for those abroad. In the first of two letters from Ed dated July 25, 1950 to Helen from Korea, he wrote of such issues. He noted the misunderstanding those at home might experience and wrote with disgust of the sub-quality military equipment. The men on foreign ground were expected to protect UN interests in South Korea using World War II "left overs":

> We have a big job because men are badly needed in Korea. It may not seem like much of a war to people in the states but there are lots of dependents in Sasebo that don't have any fathers & husbands now and others that are missing in action. You can't imagine how rough it has been on the units that first went in. And yet they have put up a wonderful fight. We destroyed the best army the world has ever seen in 1945 and because of a few penny pinchers in Congress good Americans are going thru hell because of too little. Guess I better get off the soap box but you know what I mean.

The conflict in Korea did not at first even rate the label "war." In early stages, it was labeled a police action, undertaken by President Harry Truman and the United States in reaction to Soviet-promoted Chinese activity. In a document that is part of the George M. Elsey papers, located at the Harry S. Truman Presidential Library in Independence, Missouri, I can access Truman's statement of June 27, 1950. It reads, in part, "communism [*sic*] has passed beyond the use of subversion to conquer independent nations and will now use armed invasion and war." Truman avoids direct accusations against what was then Soviet Russia by blaming the ideals of Communism, rather than any specific entity, possibly making any threat less real to U.S. citizens (Truman). As for the equipment, historian Max Hastings writes in *The Korean War* that the first push against the invading Chinese by occupation troops moved into Korea from Japan proved disastrous. He bases his claim on the stark evidence of early retreats and withdrawal: "The Americans were softened by years of inadequate training and military neglect, bewildered by the shock of combat, dismayed by the readiness with which the communists had overwhelmed them, and the isolation in which they found themselves" (20).

Perhaps the "unknown" factor of the Korean War affected my father's attitude toward his possible return from Korea. My mother included a note with some of Ed's letters that she sent to me referencing that attitude:

> I know there was one letter that's not in this box, written probably in November 1950, in which he seemed to doubt if he'd make it back to us and told me he wanted me to get married again, if he didn't. [I later locate this letter.] During WWII neither of us ever doubted that he'd be back. In Korea, he wavered between pessimism and optimism, but the latter was much more often expressed. He was very much an optimist all of his life.

She adds, "These letters should be kept for posterity." Such urging suggests that not only might Ed's words enlighten his children about his service and death, but perhaps others as well. I feel the weight of that charge as I write.

As I peruse Ed's letters, I find a number of references to his insecurity regarding his future. On July 19 Ed reminded Helen that, "My orders were changed from the 7th Div to the 24th Div which is the one that is carrying the brunt of the fighting in Korea. They are issuing us field equipment this afternoon and no doubt by the time you read this I will be in the fight. I'm more scared this time than I was before but I guess that's good because it puts you on the alert." He would, fortunately, be reassigned yet again to the 17th Infantry, which would not face the challenges encountered by the 24th. On July 21, he wrote of a reunion of sorts in Yokohama with several men he knew from Ft. Riley and home.

However, his focus remains firmly on the task at hand, as the troops prepare to enter Korea. On September 10 he instructed Helen:

> Let's don't talk about me coming back to the states until it happens. Doesn't look very promising now. Just hope the Chinese don't come into this thing . . . I think of you a lot and wonder if I will be lucky enough to return to you and the kids again . . . Keep your fingers crossed but remember they ain't going to take me prisoner again as long as I have legs and arms left.

His October 16 letter, distinguished by battle detail, but also by several romantic comments, closes, "I love you much and think we will be together again before too long." By November 6, he wrote to Helen, "Keep your fingers crossed and I will make it I hope." He concluded his December 7 letter with, "I love you very much and keep hoping we will see each other again." I detect the optimism that Helen referenced in Ed's constantly looking toward the future. In the end, crossed fingers, redundant hope, prayers, and thoughts would not be enough.

Ed could not foresee his fate absolutely, of course, but he could distinguish between his attitude in WWII and that in Korea. Now intimately familiar with his enthusiasm for service and the military, I detect the contrast between negativity and positivity in his tone and the conflict between his love for military ideals and the reality he faced. Like all feelings, intuitions, insights, and hunches, such "ways of knowing" lack rational explanation and prove those foolish who attempt one.

The collection of letters from Korea offers me an intimate view of its landscape and early war-time events that would prove impossible without the first-hand reports. I can track not only the military progress—and lack thereof—during the first few months of combat, but also Ed's reactions to the maneuvers, matching that information to newspaper articles and other sources. Many of the articles clipped by my mother, an arduous task I might guess while caring for three young children, bear her markings. She circles names of cities referenced by Ed on maps, and collects articles that focus on the U.S. Seventh Division and its 17th Infantry, sometimes in reaction to direct requests by Ed.

Ed remarks in the July 25th letters that he enjoyed an unanticipated "reprieve." It resulted from the fact that he had impressed Major Curl with his organizational skills within his own group at Sasebo, prompting the Major to put Ed to work assisting to organize the entire Battalion. I believe this may be when he moved from the 24th Infantry to the 17th, particularly as he describes being 12 miles from Pusan where the scenery is beautiful, and he can see the ocean. While grateful for the notice and the activity, his concern is for the poorly-supported troops, as expressed in an excerpt from the same letter quoted above. In the second July 25th letter, he clearly states that he is "very happy" about having been given command "of Co A [also known as Able Company] 17th Inf 7th Inf Div," which removed him from the Replacement Battalion. While the change means that he will most certainly go from Japan to Korea, he will have time to train "and get acquainted with my own unit" in the Japanese naval camp that he describes as "better than the buildings we had at [Ft.] Riley." He's enjoyed little sleep but describes the ocean-side assignment as beautiful. He writes of his interest in the history of his regiment, which dates back to the Civil War and explains what joy he feels "to be working with men who are trained for a change. Beats working with recruits." He describes the Regiment CO as "a Col Powell and I have seen him a coupla [*sic*] times and he sure is a fireball. Just as good as some of the others I have had are bad."

Like others of my generation, I know a few details about the Korean War, but not as much as I should, particularly in my situation as one whose father died there. I refresh my memory not through an in-depth study, as a detailed understanding and rendition of military action is not the purpose of this project. I delve into research to bolster the information that I find in articles saved by my mother and complimented by facts contained in Ed's communications. Ed Roberts served in Korea from near the war's beginning, arriving in mid-July 1950 only until he died the following January 3. Naturally, the articles in my family archives focus only on those early months of combat. Letters of condolence and military documentation and information received by my mother following Ed's death constitute the largest number of artifacts related to his Korea service.

As I seek to bolster my knowledge about the logistics of the Korean War, I read on a history website that on June 25th, 1950, 75,000 North Korean People's Army troops crossed the 38th parallel ("Korean War"). The action was perceived as a threat because that particular parallel marked the division of the former nation of Korea into the post-WWII settlements of North and South Korea. In 1945, Russia received control of North Korea as its war prize; the additional Allies received control of South Korea as theirs. Thus, North Korea became part of the Communist hold. The Truman Doctrine, created in 1947, ushered in a policy of post-war "U.S. global leadership" that remained in place for 40 years, meaning that the U.S. would assume the lead to protect against forces such as those crossing the 38th parallel (Gruenberg 26).

In May of 1948, the UN sponsored an election in South Korea, resulting in the inauguration of Syngman Rhee, a well-known political figure, as president of the Republic of Korea (ROK) with Seoul declared its capital. In September, a counter-move by the Russians formally created the Communist regime in the North, declared the Democratic People's Republic of Korea, headed by Kim Il-sung. Kim Il-sung had matured in Manchuria, where his family fled to avoid the 1920s Japanese occupation and became a Korean Freedom Fighter. He eventually moved to the USSR and joined the Communist party. He was active in the Soviet Army during WWII, curried favor among the USSR's politicos, and returned in 1945 to North Korea. He chaired the Communist People's Committee of North Korea, later the Korean Workers' Party. In 1948, with the founding of the Democratic People's Republic of Korea, Kim Il-sung became its premier with Pyongyang established as North Korea's capital. Most accounts about Kim Il-sung, later known as "The Great Leader," noted his regularly perpetrated crimes against humanity, and North Koreans suffered a loss of employment, famine, and a loss of fuel to heat their homes. However, Max Hastings explains that many living under Rhee "were dismayed and disgusted by the corruption and injustice that the old President came to represent. For all the rumors filtering down from the North, about land reform and political education," South Koreans were not convinced that life in the North would be any worse than that under the Rhee regime (89-90). Thus, internal conflict was born along with the two regimes, causing disrupted loyalties and destroying any sense of nationalism former Korean citizens may have felt. Skirmishes between the North Korean dictator Kim Il-sung and the American-supported Rhee led to the deaths of thousands of soldiers before any formal declaration of war.

As I read about the beginning of the conflict, I recall lines from Billy Joel's song "Leningrad": "Stop 'em at the 38th parallel; blast those yellow reds to hell." Joel then sings, "Cold War kids were hard to kill, under their desks in an air raid drill" (Joel). His words fling me back to junior high days when the U.S. was deep into the Cold War with Russia in the early 1960s. Communists were the bogey men of our nightmares, and we were unfortunate in our proximity to the 13,000-acre Pine Bluff Arsenal, established in 1941 as a U.S. Army Installation. As it continues to do today, it boosted the local economy and was favored by Pine Bluff and state officials. Originally named The Chemical Warfare Arsenal, its name was changed four months later, for reasons we may all surmise. It was part of a nine-arsenal system designed during WWII to develop Chemical Warfare and was, not surprisingly, deemed a viable enemy target. I learn online that:

> The arsenal began producing lethal biological pathogens in 1953 at its Production Development Laboratories under the direction of the Army's chief microbiologist, William Capers Patrick. Patrick had perfected the production of anthrax spores that could be dispersed through the air. In 1956, he became the chief architect and production manager of such large-scale operations, called Project X1002, at the arsenal. (Bearden)

Thus, the need for our safety drills, developed in the event of a nuclear attack. I clearly recall those drills, signaled by a school siren. We were instructed by our teachers to crouch under our desks for protection. These practice drills were executed by the same school system that a few years earlier had gathered us in assemblies to show films of the victorious bombing of Hiroshima and Nagasaki, and their results. The films sparked more than a few incineration nightmares for my circle of grade-school friends. Incredibly, we were to believe a few years later that ducking our heads under school desks would save our lives should a nuclear bomb explode eight miles away. Although I couldn't know it at the time, I was exposed early to the ironies of war.

What many U.S. citizens chose to view—if they considered it at all—as a localized Korean border dispute would morph into full-blown aggression, and the powers-that-be interpreted the move by the Communist Chinese to assume power over all of the now-divided Korea. The U.S., self-designated protectors of world peace, needed South Korea, a country strategically positioned to help them react to such Communist threats. Although the Soviet Union had switched loyalties to join the Allies late in WWII in order to defeat Germany, it had again become the enemy, just as hungry for world power as its former partners.

According to all accounts, the division of Korea was made swiftly and without consideration; such accounts differ only in details. Leif A. Gruenberg writes that as the U.S. celebrated "victory over Japan," the Soviets schemed to expand Communism into Korea. He quotes historian Clay Blair to explain that the Pentagon moved quickly to plan the division of Korea, and the resulting selection of the 38th parallel as a dividing point was made by an officer after a brief study of a map used in a school classroom (18-19). Other accounts claim that military aides made the arbitrary division. Little consideration was given to the fact that Korea needed both its industrial north and agricultural south to become a viable economic entity, or to the repercussion of such arbitration on its citizens' survival.

The Soviet regime offered the primary Communist threat to democracy and would support China, and, vicariously, North Korea, although its military contributions to the war in terms of troops proved negligible. While, according to Brian Catchpole, historians still do not unanimously agree that the North Koreans were the aggressors, that version remains the most widely accepted rendition. Assistant Secretary of State, Dean Rusk, stated on June 27 of 1950 that "'a south Korea absorbed by the Communists would be a dagger pointed at the heart of Japan'," leading to American "pressure on the Security Council to act in this emergency according to UN principles" (8). Actions resulting from that pressure drastically altered the fate of my family and a multitude of others.

Ed originally headed to Japan to become part of the post-war forces. However, when he left California by boat on July 6, 1950, he knew he was headed to Korea to support the conflict. His family could not follow as originally planned, and details such as the fact that the family car waited in California to be shipped to Japan, already treated for exposure to seawater, would have to be addressed. Our family would still join him in Japan at the end of the Conflict if the original assignment stood. For a time, Ed believed that would happen fairly quickly, and even when the goal moved months in the future, he still believed it a possibility. After exposure to families that had been assigned to Japan, Ed would optimistically ask Helen whether she wouldn't like to see her youngest—me—learn to speak Japanese, as he was seeing other American children do. However, he tempers his optimism, writing more logically to Helen about their separation in a July 19 letter:

> It's a shame it has to be this way but we can hope it will turn out for the best. I'm thankful that if anything happens to me you will be pretty well off financially. The way things are now I don't see a chance of your coming over very soon if at all.

He counsels her to consider moving back to Manhattan Kansas, close to Ft. Riley, where they still own a house, "unless Don and Ginny really want you." Her eventual decision to sell the Manhattan house and remain in Pine Bluff with her older sister during her separation from Ed would strongly affect our futures.

In that same letter, Ed reflected on his recently-completed journey aboard the USNS *General E. T. Collins*. I learn that the acronym USNS means United States Naval Ship and indicates a de-commissioned ship, one not presently involved in a war, with a civilian crew, although its officers were generally Naval. He mentions a pillow that Helen sent to him, one of many requests he will make of her during his time in Korea. He wrote that:

> The trip over was very smooth and the new pillow worked wonders when it did get rough. I was I & E officer and had to publish the ships [*sic*] newspaper. I never worked so hard in all my life [*sic*] only got about 4 hours sleep at night and couldn't sleep in the daytime cause it was so hot. About 16 of us officers were down in what they called a dormitory on E deck with no portholes and the ventilation poor. The accommodations were worse than during the war. I'm glad it is over.

Ed would receive a commendation from A. Segarra, Col. [Colonel] Inf [Infantry], the ship's commanding officer. The Colonel commended Ed "for the superior manner in which you have performed your duties" during the July 3-19 journey from San Francisco to Yokohama, Japan. The commendation notes that Ed, as an "I & E Officer," was "confronted with many problems of organization, coordination, and discipline, magnified by the unfamiliar surroundings of a troop ship," to which he found a "successful solution," indicating "a high degree of initiative and imagination, and close attention to duty beffiting [*sic*] and [*sic*] officer." Colonel Powell would also recognize Ed's talents, and so his expectation of promotion and decoration while in Korea had a basis in reality. His only medal, however, would be the posthumously awarded Purple Heart.

At first on the offensive to retake South Korean territory from the North Koreans, the UN troops did not fare well. The disciplined North Korean military easily bested disorganized and ill-trained South Korean troops, described as willing to desert at any provocation, a result of diminished nationalism in the wake of the country's division. The heat of the first summer proved as debilitating as the cold that would follow, with many U.S. military falling ill from drinking raw fertilized water from fields. Soon the American troops found themselves on the defensive. In Ed's September 5 letter, he corroborates those claims, as he comments on a wind so strong that "the whole division had to take all their tents down in that driving rain and boy did we spend a miserable night. Luckily the sun came out bright & clear the next day, we got everything dried out and the tents back up. What a time for it to happen as you can imagine." The Korean landscape and elements proved, as Secretary of State Dean Atcheson supposedly stated, the worst place in the world for such a face-off. Ed's descriptions of the terrain and the people they fought would support that judgment. On December 18, having endured several months of conflict and frustration over the actions of those in command, he wrote, "I hope it doesn't change my outlook on life but there is nothing good about the whole country of Korea. We are helping people that have been oppressed for centuries and they support whatever side is winning."

Catchpole writes that from the beginning, General Walter Harris Walker believed that South Koreans supported by the U.S. might be passing intelligence to the North, so efficient were the North's actions. American soldiers often could not distinguish between North and South Koreans and so came under unexpected fire. General William F. Dean, commander of the U.S. Army in Korea managed to hide for five weeks in the mountains after being hurt in July while searching for water for U.S. troops. But he was betrayed by two South Korean peasants to the North Korean People's Army (NKPA). By late July, the U.S. had lost a General, 50 American troops had died in the Battle of Taejon, and 200 had been wounded. Perhaps the most grievous figure was 900 soldiers captured. The NKPA was rumored to execute prisoners on the spot during battle or just after so that many of those captured would remain classified as MIA. On July 21, Ed, still in Japan but anticipating a move to Korea, wrote to Helen, "I have never seen such a deal as this. Same old army. Big rush into Korea and nothing to rush with. Some of the boys were sacrificed needlessly but it always happens that way." I begin to understand why he was unsure that he would return home. This appeared to him a very different war from the one he had experienced six years earlier.

As I return to Talarigo's novel, set during the years following the Korean War, the narrative emphasizes the continuing conflict between the Chinese, the North Koreans, and the South Koreans. It makes clear that the war did little to alleviate any such turmoil. It characterizes not only the Chinese as ready to hand over illegal North Koreans to authorities for a bounty but also the North Koreans as ready to turn against one another, so great is their need for any type of sustenance. The focus on basic survival under the post-Korean War regime results in North Korean inhabitants no longer viewing one another as human. In one of several heart-rending scenes, two starving adult males steal from a young girl that the protagonist has assisted. They lie to her, frightening her across the Tumen River back into North Korea, knowing that Chinese soldiers might kill her as she crosses. That is, indeed, her fate. The protagonist eventually aids the two men, but only as a ruse. She then takes revenge for herself and the lost girl, turning them over to Chinese authorities and earning a bounty. At the beginning of the novel, one would never have predicted the main character would behave in such a manner. The echoes of war and dissent clearly continue to reverberate via historical fiction.

In an early September letter Ed writes, "Lets [*sic*] don't talk about me coming back to the states until it happens. Doesn't look very promising now. Just hope the Chinese don't come into this thing." Perhaps he didn't want to "jinx" his chance of return. Poised to enter the action, Ed clarified, as quoted in an earlier chapter, that he didn't feel he was violent by nature, but circumstances could turn almost any man into a killer. On September 5 he wrote that he was again on a ship but could not share any details about its name or destination. He did remark that "old home week" continued as he met men with whom he previously served. Such focus on community, both within the military and without, surfaced as vital to his survival.

By late July of 1950, General Walker received Sherman medium tanks and additional armored cars that would prove crucial to victory, and at last the Communist offensive was stalled. The American and ROK (Republic of Korea) troops established "a defense line running along the Naktong River," as Catchpole explains, and would be fortified by the arrival of "long-awaited Marines . . . at Pusan" (24). Ed told Helen in a September 10 letter that he wrote from "a cabin on the ship setting in the harbor of Pusan," noting that he was not at liberty to explain why he was there, but that it would be clear to her by the time the letter reached her. With the harbor so quiet, it seemed odd "to think people are killing each other about 35 miles from here." At that point, he was enjoying excellent food and many hours at leisure and for sleep. He was beginning to learn more about his surroundings, having been told by others that "Korea is even a dirtier country than Japan. 100% VD almost in Pusan, also some cholera which we have shots for." The previous night he had enjoyed the movie "On the Town," his first since crossing the ocean on the Collins. He added that casualties were "higher than stated," although he doesn't clarify who did the stating.

Almost two weeks later, Ed's September 22 letter explains that the 7th Division is "still sitting in Pusan harbor. Most of us are pretty disgusted but it is still better than fighting." He reported the "news" about the war as good, other than "the item of troops coming down from Manchuria spearheaded by 40 tanks. If they be Chinese Communists better not count on seeing me for awhile if ever. I'm only kiddin' honey but its goin' to be rough if they come in." I'm aware of his purposefully dropping the final "g" from words, invoking a playful tone to counter his previous serious statements. He writes of his pastimes, which include much reading. He lists *Time*, *Newsweek*, *Red Book*, *True*, and *Coronet*, magazines which he has consumed "cover to cover." Additional movie viewing includes "Bad Boy" with Audie Murphy and "Luck of the Irish" with Tyrone Power. He adds, "nice to see women if they are only movie stars." Such recreational activities had always been important to Ed and Helen, and she no doubt appreciated the ability to picture him enjoying American pop culture, even at a distance of thousands of miles.

Ed would repeatedly write that the U.S. must not go to war against the Chinese, as their numbers and strength were too great. Peace should be attained instead through arbitration. That was President Truman's stance as well, but his own military leaders, famed WWII General Douglas MacArthur, especially, would become embroiled in attempts to escalate and prolong the war, prompting the removal of MacArthur due to insubordination less than a year later. The Chinese contributed thousands of troops and lives to the war, in several instances overwhelming UN forces, as peace talks continued across the globe where more and more families felt the effects of the misunderstood war. A final settlement would be achieved, but not until May of 1953, more than two years following Ed's death. In the end, Korean POWs could choose in which portion of their still-divided country they would settle, South Korea gained more territory, and the de-militarized zone created then would remain in existence decades later. The war exacted steep payment. South Korea suffered the highest number of lives lost and individuals wounded, followed by the U.S., which counted 36,514, in addition to my father, dead; 92,134 wounded; 8,176 missing in action; and 7,245 taken prisoners of war. In addition, losses were suffered by, in order of the largest to the smallest number, The United Kingdom, Turkey, Canada, Australia, France, the Philippines, and South Africa. Losses, injuries, the imprisoned, and those missing in action by both sides (North Korea, China, and the Soviet Union on the "other" side) totaled between 1.1 and 1.5 million, a truly massive, international sacrifice ("Korean War." *Encyclopedia*). That is particularly true when one considers the effects on military families that would reverberate through generations. Later in the war, Ed dropped his normal optimism to write seriously to Helen:

> The US is still too idealistic and these people don't understand that. We should be arming Japan now and our worries about the Chinese would be over. The Japs could take care of them. The 155,000 NK prisoners we have could help the army too but that also is against our principles. Reading some articles in Time and Newsweek make me so mad the way we do things I don't read them anymore. The only really happy thing in my life now is the thoughts of our past happiness together and the hope that God willing we will get back together again in the future.

His voice is that of one who encountered conflict with the idealistic view of warfare and found it in great contrast to the reality he faced in what he described in another letter as a "lousy filthy country."

Ed's letters naturally moved me in many ways. First, I was shocked by the sheer number of them and by how frequently he wrote; then I noted his elegant expression, even under obvious duress. I compared them, not in a judgmental manner, but more via the scientific method, to the letters in Phil Klay's award-winning book, *Redeployment*. In multiple voices, Klay liberally employs brutal imagery and profane rhetoric, perhaps more indicative of his era. Of course, Ed was a single individual writing letters to a single person with whom he shared a rich background and set roles. He had no purpose in mind other than communication with her, certainly never imagining the broad audience they will find in this format. Klay, on the other hand, assumed a readership, his purpose publication for a popular audience. Finally, I followed Ed's shifts in attitude toward not just war, but that particular war, and his chances of survival. As my mother had described, he was pessimistic at times, optimistic more often, but even when negative about the military and the global political decisions that resulted in so many specific and personal deaths, he never grew cynical. In his November 23 letter, for instance, he wrote,

> I can't help thinking if we get to Japan soon, and it can happen, that you will get to come over especially if they only use two Div to occupy Japan as is talked now. The 7th & 1st Cav. That will give lots more quarters. There is no use hurrying back again like we did last time and then have it all to do over again even if it means separation. I know its tough on us and our family but for my money the US has been good to us and somebody has got to believe in it and support it.

The move to Japan would not prove imminent, in part due to the powers-that-be who eventually merited Ed's criticism.

As I attempt to find parallels in the details of Ed's letters to those about the movements during the War, I locate many references to the same localities as those in formal reports. His September 24 letter notes that he is "in the harbor of Inchon . . . We will get on around midnight and go ashore presumably to join the rest of the Division." He describes that portion of the division as "setting up the shooting gallery as the Reds come back north." The battleship Missouri is one among many, as there is "more stuff in this harbor than there was at Pusan." In September, General Almond had agreed with MacArthur, who proposed moving with strength into North Korea by capturing its capital of Pyongyang. I find a map from the first page of *The Pine Bluff Commercial* published on September 27, 1950, on which my mother has circled the location and name of the city of Pusan. The caption beneath the map notes that my father's 7th Division pushed from the north to link with the U.S. 1st Cavalry division from the south, "trapping thousands of North Korean Reds."

As Ed reports activity in September, I am excited to find perfect parallels in my historical references to what I read in Ed's letters. On September 15, Hastings explains that U.S. X Corps launched a "successful amphibious assault on Inchon, enabling UN forces to break out of Pusan and push north to the 18th parallel" (346). U.S. X Corps also circled Seoul on September 19, as the Eighth Army swept north and west, driving Communist forces before them. Filipino troops arrived in

Korea about the same time, and on September 26, Seoul fell to UN forces control. Brian Catchpole writes at length of MacArthur's plan to take Seoul and then stage in grand ceremony a formal restoration of Syngman Rhee to power. He also notes that a "momentous decision" had been made by MacArthur, Truman, and the Joint Chiefs of Staff to determine whether "the United Nations had the moral and constitutional right to advance beyond the 38th Parallel" (51). Catchpole describes a resulting resolution (376V) that would be passed in early October urging that "'all constituent acts' be taken to create a united Korea" (51).

Catchpole notes that on September 26, MacArthur issued a UN communique, based on reports by General Almond that Seoul had been taken. Marine and Army squads continued to engage tough battles as they cleared streets, "constantly under attack from mortars, machine-guns and grenades," confronting suicide bombers who attacked tanks by running beneath them with satchel charges, and additional resistance. On September 27, the Marines and the 7th infantry (Ed's company) cleared enough of the city to accommodate the planned ceremony (48).

Despite the continued conflict following the UN forces' relentless attack on bridges and roadways and the Communist forces' retreat, it proved a heady time for the soldier on the ground. My father makes that clear in his comments on September 27: "We are in Korea right smack in the middle of the enemies [*sic*] country. However, they are badly disorganized and it won't be too long now." By "won't be too long," I presume he means until the end of the conflict. I base my presumption on the rumors he reports, as well as from the misinformation that I learn from formal sources, which proved a constant challenge.

Ed also faced the challenge of disease, but not from his Korean surroundings. While still aboard the ship, he endures a second bout with illness, treated by aureomycin, which made him feel "almost back to normal." When I search the web for information about the drug, I find that it is presently FDA-approved for animal use only. In cattle, it fights, among other things, bacterial enteritis caused by bacteria such as e.coli. E. coli likely proved rampant among soldiers occupying shared quarters for extended periods. According to an advertisement for Manna Pro®

products, it proves effective for swine, lambs, and poultry as well, used for more than 50 years to "protect, prevent, and produce." I smile at the last phrase, one that could almost be lifted from military propaganda.

Ed's enthusiasm for the military again runs high when he writes on September 29:

> This army is terrific. Bitching all the time and doing a terrific job too. I'll bet the Koreans [*sic*] eyes popped when we got to the Nam river in front of Seoul and the Air Force had blown all the bridges, the amphibious tractors began swimming the river with troops, trucks and supplies and about 6 hours later the engineers had a bridge across the Nam that would carry the big tanks and are they dandies. Really give the Russian tanks a fit. Too bad Old George [Patton] isn't here to see the tanks named after him.

Ed had begun his letter by explaining to Helen that "We were within about two miles of Seoul the other night and it was on fire. The original plan was to try to save the city, but the Commies talked the civilians into fighting and so the artillery went to work including the Mighty MO with its 16 in. guns firing from 18 miles away." With what would later prove a chilling irony, he adds, "We have had little action except snipers and they are lousy shots." They've suffered no battalion causalities, and exist on C rations, which he describes as not too bad when warmed. He anticipates little resistance, unless they encounter "fanatics," noting they have had to bury "a lot of dead ones around here," and that the North Koreans seem to be losing "a lot of their fight."

Ed mentions an original plan to take Seoul without destruction, which would have been MacArthur's wish, in preparation for Rhee's "inauguration," a re-staging of the original event for PR reasons. Ed's first-hand account corresponds with that of my historical sources as he describes Seoul hardly in shape for such a celebration following the fighting. Even so, he is delighted to have taken part in a historical moment. He writes on September 29 that Able Company "made a little history today," telling Helen that she probably heard of MacArthur's meeting in Seoul with Rhee "giving him his capitol back." My mother has saved two articles with photos from the event. I envision Ed pacing between passages, hardly able to contain the energy and pride obvious in his words:

> Well your husband was in command of a company that was protecting the palace grounds. I was right next to Macs [*sic*] car when he drove in. There were so many stars there it looked like the night sky. There was still fighting going on in the north part of the city but we have got so much stuff in Seoul there wasn't a chance of the Reds interfering . . . Seoul is a mess. Buildings all blown to hell, wires down, glass all over the place, stiffs lying around and stinking and not a pretty sight.

Catchpole describes the situation as follows:

> General MacArthur . . . was met by General Almond and President Syngman Rhee and they drove across the Han River through the battered streets of Seoul to the shell-pocked National Assembly hall. Despite the distant sound of shellfire and the crackle of machine-guns Almond created the illusion of an orderly atmosphere for the moment of MacArthur's triumph. The podium was draped with flags; immaculate military police were everywhere. At noon precisely, MacArthur turned to Syngman Rhee and with dramatic solemnity intoned, 'I am happy to restore to you, Mr President, the seat of your government . . ." (51)

In MacArthur's grand plan, the Eighth Army would advance north from Seoul to move on Pyongyang from the west, while X Corps would move by sea to land at Wonsan, and attack from the east. Almond had experienced the force of North Korean anti-tank guns when positioned on high ground, causing him to withdraw his X Corps when the 7th Marines unsuccessfully attacked Hill 550 south of Uijongbu on October 2. According to Catchpole, Almond felt his "well-equipped X Corps would effect a surprise landing" that would allow a swift deploy of "both tanks and infantry units," enabling them to "advance in the valley between the menacing mountain peaks rising about 5000 feet in the Taeback Range because the ground and rivers would be frozen" (55). Catchpole adds that at that point, little consideration was given to the "effects of a Manchurian-style winter on men and material." General Walker was not pleased with the plan. He felt an integration of the X Corps with his Eighth Army would be "more sensible," resulting in "a common advance northwards" that promised to rapidly end the war (56). In his estimation, the loss of "time and energy" in a transfer of X Corps could result in a lack of resources for his Eighth Army. He proved correct, as "serious transportation problems" delayed movement of the proposed Eastern campaign. The "very limited capacity" of Inchon harbor, where MacArthur proposed the X Corps embark on limited ease of handling for the 1st Marine Division, would support the Wonson landings. It could not simultaneously bear the brunt of the X Corps' "transport and its huge administrative tail" (56), which would have to travel by road and rail from Seoul to Pusan.

Ed's October 6 letter shares somber news, representative of additional friendly fire tragedies not often included in formal reporting:

> Tragedy struck at A Co yesterday. We were giving a demonstration of a Bn [Battalion] in attack for General Almond the tenth Corps commander. We were attacking two companies on the Line A on the right and C on the left. We were moving under our own artillery and mortar fire and just before we got to the objective the Heavy Mortar company fired the wrong concentration and about ten rounds fell right on top of us. I had two men killed and about 21 wounded. One of the killed was Sgt McLaughlin . . . He is from Ark so I guess I will have to go and see his wife when

> I get back. It just about broke my heart because it was in training. Sgt Abe was hit in both legs and will be lost to us for some time. You must have said the right prayer because it happened right in a small valley and I was right with them. Two rounds fell right behind me and I hit the ground as the rest of them came in. It got every NCO in the 1st Platoon and Lt Carrig. He was hit in the leg but not seriously . . . The total dead is seven and about 40 wounded . . . Everyone was pretty bitter and I almost cried. A lot of the men suffered quite a bit before the medics got to them. Our three medics . . . did a magnificent job. There was no way to save Sgt Mac tho as he had two flares in his belt and they went off when the shell hit and burned him horribly. After I finish this letter I am going to write to his wife. The other boy I lost was named Wright and he was killed instantly.

In addition to my father's rare detailed expression of shock and grief while in the field, this letter is important to me in its reference to Lieutenant John Carrig, who will become an important bridge in my journey to better understand my father's motivations.

Following the lengthiest focus on action found in any of his letters, Ed immediately switches subjects to focus on his family. He writes that he just remembered that it was Kay's birthday and sends her his best wishes. My mother has penciled a note in the letter's margin that contains an address for a Mrs. Arthur E. McLaughlin, presumably the wife of "Sgt Mac." She may have spoken to Mrs. McLaughlin, as she adds a note to herself to "Ask Ed if Sgt. Mac's body could be brought back . . . ask about his belongings." I think ahead to the letter that my mother will receive, advising her that Ed's belongings will be shipped in due time. More important would be the letter informing her that her husband's remains had been temporarily buried in Korea with details about the military's plans to ship them to the states. She would choose the military cemetery in Little Rock, Arkansas, for his burial.

As MacArthur's plan was put into action and Almond prepared for the amphibious operation, he received unexpected news. The "ROK Capitol and the 3rd Divisions had moved north on 9 October and broken through the NKPA defenses in front of Pyonyang" (Catchpole 57), rendering Almond's move to Wonsan unnecessary. Even so, Almond and MacArthur held to the original plan. Almond learned "that Wonsan harbor was virtually unapproachable for it was reputed that 3,000 Soviet manufactured sea mines had been sown in the main approach channels," which would have to be swept before the Marines and equipment constituting the invasion force that had sailed from Inchon (850 miles away) could land (57).

In an October 9, 1950 *Life* editorial, the unidentified writer praises U.S. "warriors" as the North Korean Red Army appears to be in full retreat north of the 38th parallel. However, while praising the strength of U.S. "biceps," he wonders about U.S. "brains," asking "will it be the old story all over again this time? Or can the U.S., with the aid of the rest of the free world in the U.N, prove that it is something more than a giant with big biceps . . . "? ("But What Comes Next" 38). Ironically, an article titled "Seoul and Victory" depicts the war as over. The unidentified author writes of it using past tense: "This was a war offering no threat to American's shores and fought in a country many Americans had not even heard of. Most of the world did not expect the U.S. to fight it. But the U.S. went into it as a matter of principle. And won" (29). One illustration features Chinese dead, "victims of flame throwers" under the bold print caption, "**BURNED REDS**" (31).

Ed's October 13 letter brims with news. As planned, he has returned to Pusan and has engaged in combat, a fact that makes his purpose for choosing the military clear. Perhaps more importantly, it allows him to express that purpose to Helen, the most important person in his life. Consistent with the formal reports I have read, winter threatens, but the UN forces believe they have the upper hand on the North Korean and Chinese troops. That rumor, later proved false, supports his soaring emotions, as he compares maneuvers to a game of cops and robbers in which he clearly assumes the role of the cop:

> We have been in our first real combat. Last Sunday the division was moving from the north to Pusan and they were ambushed in a mountain pass and lost several men killed. So they hollered for someone to come and clean up the pass and it fell to the 1st Bn 17th. We were chasing them around the hills for three days, killed about 20 and lost one of our boys killed. I was proud of the co as they did very well. So they got the Combat Infantry Badge which they all wanted. We are getting ready to hit up north again so right now we are preparing for that. Issuing cold weather clothing . . . I am fine and outside of the general run of hard work nothing much to report. You might as well know that we are slated to be in on the main landing, so there will be some excitement although they are not meeting too much up north so far. I have been careful so far and will continue so. This is nothing but a game of cops and robbers now because there is no organized resistance and everytime you find them they run. They are short on ammunition and have no artillery or mortars. However we are still not under-estimating them and won't until it is over.

Ed's flirtatious next line hints at the romance I notice appearing more often in his letters before he returns to the business of war:

> Yes I have been looking at the moon but it isn't for the same reason as you I'm sorry to say. It was a great help in Seoul and later to spot the gooks running around. We landed at Inchon on the 25th and went into reserve for 10th Corps and were there south of Seoul for about a week until we moved to Yoju. Except for the day and night in Seoul for Gen McArthur.

He does return to the more favorable topic, adding, "All you say about love making makes me very happy," the type of parental declaration that would make most children shudder. He assures Helen that she needn't worry that he will be exposed to VD as he "wouldn't touch one of these dirty women over here even if I was inclined which I'm not." Also in that letter, he explains that "Lt. Carrig my Platoon leader hit in the mortar barrage which killed Sgt. McLaughlin will be with us when we go north," a crucial detail. He then describes his disheveled physical appearance, noting that he and a friend indulged a bath in a nearby river and a change of clothes.

By October 16, Ed is again aboard a ship in Pusan and tells Helen to watch the media for references to "Task Force Whirlaway. We will be leading it." He's not been involved in recent combat and has heard more rumors about a pending return to Japan: "the North Koreans are about thru." He lapses romantic again, writing, "with your compliments you'll give me the big head but I love it and you too incidentally . . . I sure do remember all those things you mentioned about your honeymoon clothes and the things you wanted to do that I didn't. You're not the only one that is going to do a little correcting when I get back." My eyebrows lift as I read these lines and the even more personal lines that follow. Ed's words ring vividly in my mind's ear, and my imagination runs to the crazy, as I try to conjure what Helen might have written to him to elicit such a response. I'm buoyed by the knowledge that my parents knew such passion before he died and feel confident that many people live long—surely emptier—lives without feeling or expressing such thoughts.

On October 20, Ed remains on the ship "while the brass makes up their mind where we go. Latest word is the far north of Korea near the Manchurian border." He emphasizes how much Helen's letters and pictures of us kids mean to him, telling her "Gosh they are swell. Bruce looks so much more grown up and Ginger sure is a fat one. Kay is cute as ever." He compliments Helen as well, adding, "and last but not least I see my Mommy still has her pretty legs."

He notes that when recently in Yoju, troops moved into abandoned homes, although they would not be considered homes by American standards. However, in his October 6 letter, he had noted that "the Koreans invented this radiant heating about 2000 years ago. They build fires under the floors of their house and keep it nice and warm. Kinda smoky some times [*sic*] but not bad," and he remarks often that he is thankful for his warm military clothes. Helen has apparently asked for more details about the Seoul ceremony, which Ed is obviously happy to supply, as he writes, "yes, I got two good looks at Mac as he went by in the car. He was smiling and returned our salutes." I have to think that not only did Ed take pride in being able to claim proximity to a military celebrity, but he was also well aware that his experience gave Helen currency to spend in her discussions with others. He has recently run into men she knows, a fact that he also shares, and then he explains that the troops receive news bulletins daily. He moves on to important matters, with an earnest request for an air mattress. I picture my mother making a list of things to do for him, the activity allowing some outlet for her frustration over their continued separation.

Ed's next letter reminds me of the structure that ritual can provide for one when away from home. On October 21, he anticipates the holidays, requesting a pipe and tobacco; a metal, not plastic, soap dish; pocketbooks on sports and mysteries; a good flashlight; air mail-stamped envelopes and stationery; a big picture of Helen "in a durable folder, not a frame;" lighter flints; and pipe cleaners, as he tells her the available PX is "lousy." I recall that in one letter he described a fellow officer's photograph of his wife, an Arkansas beauty queen, and a "knock-out" like he had never seen. Her photo was kept in a folder like the one he requests from Helen. My mother had to recognize the connection and be happy to oblige.

Ed also looks ahead to an uncomfortable winter that he improves through fantasy: "It will be a cold one for sure. I think I would rather have a double sleeping bag somewhere with you if it is going to be winter but guess the U.S. Army won't permit that. So I'll just dream." In contrast to his typically well-organized letters, at this moment his emotions seem to produce a string of topics without warning or transition, which he recognizes. He labels his writing "kinda mixed up."

Ed quickly returns to the topic of war as he explains—with obvious disgust—that "We docked in Pusan this morning and got off for a hike. What a stinking, lousy country this is. I agree with the principle we fight for but not the country or the people." I pause to consider these words, their meaning one that many could apply to any era in our country's history, each marked by war. His description of the South Koreans leaps from the page, so strong is his hostile tone: "They will steal the clothes off your back if they get the chance. The little kids are bare from the waist down so they don't need diapers. That is only a sample of the sanitation. The average life expectancy of a Korean is 29 years longevity." He's unconcerned with the political correctness that we might expect today. Instead, he considers the military's goals and clearly assumes it is not Korean community values that have brought him there.

A few days later Ed expresses his concern that something might be wrong with Helen, as he hasn't received mail for a time. As I look at his next letter, I see that he will mention, with relief, having received her first letter in five days. I pause to consider my father, surrounded by men, a member of a community that he obviously respected and loved, and yet craving word as well from home. Then I consider Helen and, having been a mother of three small children myself, empathize with her situation in the midst of constant demand from us, having just rented a house of her own a block away from the Sperrys' home, our transitional housing as she waited to move to Japan. Such insecurity, the unbearable weight of the unknown, had to be borne by both. I feel a deep compassion for Helen and Ed, caught in a situation that neither of them remotely desired.

My parents search for common ground during a time when they should without thinking share so much. Instead, each must endure a reality that the other can only imagine. Ed suggests that Helen find a map and "Locate Iwon on the far northeastern coast of Korea and you will see where the 17th will be." He mentions her sorority, the Pi Phis, at one point, based on an article he is sending her from *The Stars and Stripes* that includes information about various golfing teams.

My review of their correspondence moves me closer to my goal of discovering what I gained from each in an inherent, even biological sense. I discover my father's ability to inhabit two roles simultaneously as he writes, his command of metaphor, and his ability to communicate all perhaps a part of my rich inheritance. He concludes his October 26 correspondence writing a passage in which he manages to combine desire, humor, pathos, longing for his wife, yet also pride in the very role that separates them physically, and, no doubt, emotionally as well:

> Well its [*sic*] nice to hear from you and I sure hope you have heard from me by now. You speak of lying on your tummy and writing to me. I wonder if that bed sheet knows just how lucky it is. Wish I could change places with it. A bedsheet would look kinda funny commanding A Co 17th Inf wouldn't it. I love you honey and miss you twice as much as you miss me.

He closes with his normal "All my love, Ed," but in this instance underlines the term "All."

I continue to marvel at rhetoric so clear, distinctive, and refined. It reflects Helen's words and emotions back to her; she knows that he carefully absorbed and considered her concerns. Even when supplying the advice about practical matters that she may have requested, he remains solicitous, mostly careful to consider her reaction. To the news that she has found a house in Pine Bluff, he responds that her description sounds nice, and he retains a balance between his feelings and what he can only perceive as her reality. He clearly recalls their house in Manhattan, Kansas, with some longing as he writes that it "is nicer probably but its [*sic*] true it would be more expensive." Then he adds support for his own preference: "you could still rent the basement. If space bothered you, you could buy one of those pre-fab garages from Wards and use it for storage. They cost about $500 and it would make our property worth just that much more." Regardless of the advice he offers, he never fails to return to his longing and love for Helen before he closes. I find such rhetorical strategy startling and realize that—revealing my own prejudice—I'm stunned in no small part because these writings come from the pen of a 1950s American male.

As I return to my historical sources, I read that although the Inchon sweep cost casualties and the loss of one minesweeper on October 19, "the 1st Marine Division . . . land(ed) safely on October 26" (Catchpole 57). Almond had to change some plans due to the delay. I continue to read of botched plans but also some success and am interested to note the involvement of Australian infantry, which performed admirably. I read that on October 28 they helped occupy a city called Chanju, which they found deserted. Meanwhile, the U.S. 21st Regimental Combat Team led north toward the Yalu River, "where elements of the 7th ROK Division were now encamped," close to Chanju (60). This passage catches my eye, as I remember the Yalu River figuring importantly in my father's later activities. An unattributed column my mother clipped re-emphasizes the Koreans' confusion as to what their part in this conflict should be. It is dated October 31, the conclusion to the lengthy article reading:

> It had been believed generally that if Red China had intended to intervene in the Korean War it would have done so in September, when allied forces still were south of parallel 38 dividing the peninsula. (Unconfirmed reports to Formosa, Chinese nationalist island stronghold, said the Chinese Red 118th and 119 divisions of Red Ge. Lin Piao's Fourth Army corps were fighting in Korea. Nationalist officials said the reports probably were true.) AP Correspondent Ben Price reported that Chinese prisoners taken northwest of Hamhung told him they were rushed into battle a week ago—without rifles, but each with two hand grenades. The prisoners said they were former Nationalists who were put to farming by the Chinese Communists, and then rushed into the army and sent to defend North Korea against "American imperialists."

The U.S. 1st Cavalry Division moved northward from Pyongyang. On November 1, Catchpole describes the temperature as falling below zero, "rendering life inside the foxholes almost unbearable and freezing the nearby paddy fields so that the enemy had endless opportunities to attack this isolated American force" (61). On November 4, Ed writes that his letter will be short,

> because we are right in it as you can tell by the news. I'm so proud of my outfit I don't know what to do. We got put in the line just before a big attack by the 71st North Korean Rgt which was about 900 strong according to prisoners. We threw them back with very heavy losses and saved the entire bn. I lost 8 killed and about 17 wounded but the NKs lost about 200–300 . . . It was rough but we took em.

He explains in a letter written two days later:

> I'm writing this sitting on a base hillside on the front line. It is very cold here but we do have plenty of clothes. The water in our canteens is frozen most of the time. We have been firing a lot of artillery at small groups of N Koreans but the last two days haven't been much. Don't know when we will go on now. We are 36 air line miles from Manchuria. We are all waiting to see what the Chinese do. They are not in our area but further to the west. I hope an agreement can be made on the power plants. Seems funny to all of us here to get letters saying the war is over and we will be in Japan by Thanksgiving. Doesn't look much like it now . . . Between lines I'm watching the artillery fire at 8 of the enemy up high in the hills. Think they just got em.

Chinese assault troops moved on November 8 to target two Eighth Cavalry battalions at Unsan and to block any retreat by American troops.

Catchpole's description of the ensuing ambush of the Americans is horrifying:

> The Cavalry decided to break out using their vehicles under cover of darkness. A full moon thwarted their hopes of a surprise escape and revealed that they were driving into a Chinese ambush. The leading truck, its radiator and windshield shattered by Chinese machine-gun fire, swerved and crashed into a ditch. Behind the truck the driver of a towed howitzer braked, jack-knifed and blocked the entire road. Trapped, the rest of the convoy halted. Soldiers jumped out, returning the enemy fire while a US tank tried to bulldoze the stalled vehicles from the roadway . . . Chinese soldiers dashed to the tank, wrecked its tracks with a satchel charge and set it on fire. (61)

Following much fierce combat, Almond revised his plans on the recommendation of Generals Kim, Barr, and Smith. The Chinese pulled back and Almond again advanced X Corps toward the Yalu River. Although he failed to link up with the Eighth Army as planned, Almond ordered X Corps toward the Yalu. Supported by Marines, on November 14 Colonel Powell's 17th Infantry, my father's own, "struggled across the Ungi River" (Catchpole 61).

This proved an exciting time for Captain Ed Roberts. On November 18, he wrote to Helen "at the end of our 17 mile dash," explaining they were 14 miles from the border:

> Two weeks ago the 71st NK regiment tried to stop us in the first attack I wrote you about and today we cleared up the rest of them. We really shot hell out of them this morning killing about 30 and capturing about 50. They haven't a chance. We think there is a good chance of us getting relieved after we get to the border and maybe back to Japan. <u>All</u> the stuff you have read about the 7th Div around

> Pungsan, Kapsan etc has been the 17th Inf and the 1st Bn has been in the lead all the time. As we were hiking along the road today Gen Barr stopped his jeep beside me, shook my hand, threw his arm around my shoulder and said what a wonderful job we were doing. Boy is he ever proud of his outfit. I'm pretty proud myself. It is bitter cold with snow on the ground but so far no foot trouble [Ed refers to his being forced to stand barefoot in the snow in the WWII German prison camp, a condition doctors later told POWs would lead to pain in the future with exposure to cold]. Since leaving Camp Fuji I have lost about 100 men from all causes [*sic*] lots from sickness.

He is particularly proud of the Yalu River arrival on November 21, completed without opposition. The next day, Ed would write with jubilation to Helen,

> Well as you have seen by the papers and radio we rolled into Hysanjin yesterday morn about 0930 with the 1st Bn 17th Inf leading. This is one time the 1st Cav wasn't 1st. You may see my name in the papers as nite before last I took two tanks on ahead with 10 men from the company and was the 1st American Officer to see Hysanjin and the Yalu River from the bluffs above them. The best news of all is that I think we are done. The 32nd is coming up on our left and the 31st is right behind us so I think the 17th will occupy here until relieved. Seems funny to have Manchuria lying about 300 yds from the house you live in but there it is.

His tone turns more serious as he adds,

> The last three days were rough as we made about 40 miles but the NKs never had a chance to get set so we had no fight the last two. In a final burst of anger they killed 100 civilians here and tried to burn the town. They are

> surrendering in droves to the rest of the Div behind us now that we are on the border.

Ed's excitement is echoed by the 7th Infantry Division's Headquarters, evident in the content of the typed communique dated also November 22, 1950 from David G. Barr, Major General, U.S., Commanding. It reads:

> It with a deep sense of pride that I pass on to you, Officers and men of the fighting 7th Infantry Division the following commendations:
> FROM CG X CORPS TO CG 7TH INF DIV:
> "As commander of the Tenth corps I extend my heartiest congratulations and deep appreciation to the officers and men of the 7th Infantry Division for their courageous efforts and magnificent achievement in being the first American unit to reach the Yalu River.
> The fact that only twenty days ago this Division landed amphibiously over the beaches at Iwon and advanced two hundred miles over torturous mountain terrain and fought successfully against a determined foe in subzero weather will be recorded in history as an outstanding military achievement. The 7th Division has reached its objective and I am confident that you will hold it."
> Extract of Message Fr General MacArthur to CG X Corps:
> "*** Tell Dave Barr the 7th Division Hit the Jackpot. MacArthur."

I will see this exact message re-printed for the public in one of the many articles saved by my mother. The article that featured Ed had appeared in the *Chicago Tribune*. The copy of that article which I find in the box of clippings has a hand-written note from Ed: "Save this."

I share Ed's sense of pride and joy in a job well done. I can only imagine the thrill of receiving such a message from one's commanders. I find a small article in my many files dated November 23 with the headline,

"GIs on the Border Thank Protecting Airmen." In it, Barr, as Seventh Division Commander, offers credit to the First Marine Air Wing for the air support that allowed the Division to reach the Manchurian Border.

The conclusion to Ed's letter is as heartbreaking as the previous contents are uplifting: "There are all kinds of rumors out about the 3rd Div relieving us. Sure hope it is true. Tell Bruce I hope he had a nice birthday and tell his mommy that I love her and it may not be too long before we can get off paper and back together."

I stare at the paper with full knowledge that they would never move off that medium, never hear one another's voices again in the traditional sense. Then I pull from my collection the time-darkened lenses of Ed's tank goggles and hold them in my hands.

- CHAPTER NINE -

COME IN STRENGTH

Ed and Helen's hometown newspaper featured Ed and his accomplishments in a full article titled "Tank Drive Through Korea." It begins by noting that Ed had been "quoted in an Associated Press dispatch concerning the army's advance to the Manchurian Border." I feel confident that such national, even international, attention centered on a home-town boy would have engendered much pride in the Galesburg community. Two paragraphs yield details that I had heard most of my life:

> Being in the thick of the fighting is not a novelty for Capt. Roberts who saw plenty of war in Europe during the previous conflict. He, then a lieutenant, was captured by the Germans in the Battle of the Bulge, but later escaped from the enemy and safely returned to American lines.

The article recounts Ed's meeting with Patton and subsequent decoration at the airport by a Patton courier. A subtitle to the second half of the article captures the situation well in reference to Ed's re-entering of the Armed Services: "Longed to Return."

Ed's brief, terse summary of complicated movements reminds me that due to the insular nature of fighting, individual units, perhaps blessedly, have little knowledge of what happens around them. Delighted with the outcome of Iwon and the ensuing combat, Almond found, with the enemy all but vanished, that his main problem would be the sustenance of his troops and avoiding ambush by NKPA troops that roamed nearby mountain ranges. Still, in the first week of November, in the face of the Chinese withdrawal, Catchpole notes that some considered the time appropriate "to seek a cease-fire" and end the Korean War (68). Although estimates of the Chinese troops were 30,000–60,000 strong, the Eighth Army outnumbered them and was receiving reinforcements. On November 10, Britain's Foreign Secretary, Ernest Bevin contacted the British Ambassador in Washington, Sir Oliver Franks. Bevin told Franks he "was prepared to state in a secret memorandum . . . that he believed the time was appropriate to complete the UN operations in Korea, withdraw the troops and leave to UNCURK [UN Commission for the Unification and Rehabilitation of Korea] the task of carrying out the 'political and economic rehabilitation' of Korea." Some sort of buffer zone would be established in order "to placate the Chinese" (69). In another round of confusion, MacArthur compared the leaked plans to "Chamberlain's appeasement of Germany in 1938" (69), unaware of Dean Acheson's having himself suggested the buffer zone before the Cabinet memorandum had been received. As circumstances developed, Acheson eventually changed his mind and supported MacArthur's plan for a full troop advance to the Yalu.

The Americans had no idea of the Chinese objectives, so before executing additional military plans, a Chinese delegation was invited to visit the UN Security Council. The delegation arrived in Washington D.C. on November 24, which was to have been the day that MacArthur began a new offensive. Ambassador Wu Xiquan addressed the UN just as Chinese forces in Korea "were suffering new defeats at the hands of the Chinese People's Volunteers" (Catchpole 70). Predictably, Wu's resolutions were voted down on November 30. The following week, the General Assembly condemned Chinese involvement in North Korea. The Chinese delegation walked out not to return to the UN Assembly, as Catchpole emphasizes, for 21 years (70). In a passage that bears personal significance to me, Catchpole concludes his chapter by writing that the development of a demilitarized zone would not occur until July 1953. The failure of the British proposal and "peace effort during October–November 1950 meant that the war would continue and that many thousands, servicemen and civilians alike, would lose their lives in the unhappy peninsula of Korea" (71).

Many of my father's letters contain remarks about concerns more appropriate to a civilian than to a soldier in the field. He begins his September 27 letter with what seems to me a ludicrous focus considering his situation, referencing a deed postmarked on September 5. I assume it must refer to the sale of property in St. Joseph, Missouri, where Ed's predecessors had settled. Ed regards it as a nuisance but promises to return it with an attorney's letter "right away." Later, he references a deed that he had to sign and continues to focus his energy on what seems to me unimportant details. He makes clear his frustration in his November 27 letter, writing,

> Well I received your letter last nite with the deed in it again and will do again that which I have already done. I'm getting rather disgusted about the whole deal because here it isn't as simple as you might think to sit down and do things like the law requires. We are at the end of a very long supply line which means mail takes as long as a month to get here. I know the money means so much to those people in St. Joe but money to me right now doesn't mean a damn thing. All I'm worried about now is keeping alive and trying to keep warm. You should have the other deed back by now but I'll do this one too. The fact that I mail the letter to the lawyer ten days after I sign the deed doesn't mean it will get there when he wants it. Excuse me for blowing my top but things like this leave me very cold at this point.

However, my mother could not complete such transactions on her own, and the ability of the U.S. forces to conduct and encourage such communication leaves me in awe. One reason for Ed's annoyance may be news he received in "a surprise letter" from a Sgt. O'Donnell, previously a part of the Seventh Division, now injured and on his way to the states. He informed Ed that "Porubsky was killed . . . in addition to Capt Milleson." Ed reminds Helen that Porubsky "was the one in the training aids shop with the four children. I tried to keep him at Sasebo in the Repl Depot but he was eager to get to Korea." Such news had to weigh heavily on Ed, as he considered his own chances of survival.

As the war continued, U.S. forces faced the Chinese in both open, predicted attacks, as well as in the form of individuals who "took to the mountains, moving cross-country at night, hiding by day on the hillsides in skillfully camouflaged tents or tucked away in innocent-looking villages," moving quickly and nimbly, "unimpeded by heavy equipment" (Catchpole 75). As Catchpole notes, the "greatest strength of the Chinese lay in their tactics: concealment and surprise" (75). In a description that resembles that of a whack-a-mole game, he describes the enemy as popping up at will and then disappearing, offering shaky targets for the Americans. Without a "tangible front line" and engaging in "inexplicable tactics," the Chinese offered a glimpse for the U.S. military of the enemy in wars to come. Men described the "endless columns" of Chinese as part of the November 1950 offensive as operating without warning, without the artillery bombardments that had signaled the NKPA's move earlier at the 38th parallel. American divisions forced to move south away from the Yalu River clogged the roads, their commanders "unable to gauge the best form of resistance" (78), due to poor information. Later the Chinese offensive plan became clear. They saw Kunu-ri as "key," due to the two roads from that city that would accommodate an American southern retreat. They would cross the Chongchon River and trap the American transport in the many valleys crossed by the mountain roads (79). Max Hastings describes the beginning of the Chinese offensive as having "a bizarre kid-glove quality of a drawing-room game" (142). That was not to last, as "the most savage American experience of the Korean War" soon began (142).

My father wrote on November 23 that he had little news and described a Thanksgiving meal. His battalion was assigned to defenses in the city, while the Second and Third Battalions were on perimeter patrol.

Ed notes that arrangement seems fair based on his Battalion's recent excellent showing in leading "all the way from Iwon . . . we deserve the rest." He again is thankful that his feet "are no worse than usual" and was pleased to learn about Helen's trip to California. She must have expressed the pain of the separation as being more trying of late, as he writes "I'm sorry you are down in the dumps but now things look rosier at least for the 17th and the 1st Bn." He writes of his regret that "stuff got in the LR [Little Rock, Arkansas] paper about Sgt. Mac but it can't be helped now I guess." I wonder whether some details had been included from which he had hoped to shield his dead friend's family. Toward the end of the letter, he poignantly writes, "I'm glad the kids still remember me and I hope you won't let them forget."

On November 26, a date that formally marks the beginning of the fierce combat known as the Battle of Chosin Reservoir, the British 27th Brigade took position north of Sunchon, on one of the roads to Kunu-ri. Lack of transport then caused the Brigade to reverse their movement and back-track 22 miles in icy wind for the first ten miles. At that point, transport trucks at last arrived, and they gratefully climbed aboard. At 4 AM, they tried to briefly sleep in a frozen paddy. The next morning the Brigade arrived at a valley through which they had passed without incident the day before. As Hastings describes, "A few miles up the road, they met an American jeep coming the other way, a colonel hanging dead over the side of the vehicle, two other corpses lying in the back" (143). While the British deployed, a number of white-clothed figures leapt up from the ground and raced away. When the Chinese attacked, the Middlesex Brigade suffered 30 casualties, some accidentally inflicted by American troops (143).

Ed wrote on November 29:

> Day before yesterday it was 24 below and yesterday morn it was 17 below so you can see it is really cold. When it gets that cold fighting is pretty much out of the question because if you're out you spend most of your time keeping warm. Naturally we were perturbed last night by

> MacArthur's announcement about the 200,000 Chinese in the west stopping the 8th Army Drive. That isn't too many more men then [*sic*] the 8th Army has considering the quality of our weapons but it seems to block any chance of getting back to Japan by Xmas. I feel that it would be foolish to become involved in a war with China because we can very effectively neutralize targets in China by air and forget about the ground. I hope MacArthur looks at it that way as he said before but whether he will pull us out is another question. We are still scheduled to go into Div[ision] reserve as soon as a ROK outfit gets here to relieve us but we are afraid the Chinese will hit them and then we will have to come back again. So far there has been nothing doing here since we got here but that doesn't mean there won't be any. We have a good open view of Manchuria from our positions and I don't believe they can come across without being seen. The only bad feature is that we are not permitted to fire across the river now. In view of the present situation I'm sure that will be changed.

He looks forward to receiving holiday packages from home with the various items he has requested and tells Helen he'd liked to receive monthly packages, if possible:

> We get a PX ration about every two or three days which usually consists of Life Savers, cigarettes, soap, toilet articles etc but only the bare necessities. Some big plumbers candles would be good because light is a problem. I could use some kind of a gasoline lantern too (not Kerosene because we don't have any) made by Coleman (Don has them I think) they are very handy. I could also use a couple size 40 sweat suits as they make better underwear than long johns and are warmer. I have one pair now that one of the officers gave me.

I still find it odd that men in the field were not supplied certain items and had to request them from home. I understand why my father so looked forward to receiving such supplies, in addition to newsy letters from Helen and other members of the family. He comments on having received a letter from his parents and one from hers as well. Neither contained much news, but he will respond to his in-laws' letter on December 10; I have that letter in our family collection.

Hastings relates that in the afternoon of November 30, a 2nd Division convoy drove from Kunu-ri directly into Communist bombardment from mortar and machine-gun. The so-called "death ride" became one of the grimmest of the Korean War, "as American vehicles tried to smash through six miles of enemy fire, having to avoid the many vehicles set ablaze, infantry men running alongside" (144). Hastings then writes that "A dreadful paralysis of command and discipline overtook the division" (144). The loss of 3,000 men and almost all of the Second Division's transport vehicles dealt a stunning blow to American forces, in terms of life, equipment, and morale. Along the road to Pyongyang, according to Hastings, "a growing element of panic was overtaking the whole of the Eighth Army, with rumors flying about the number of Chinese that had gathered to block progress, many of which proved unfounded" (145). Echoing my father's comments about rumors of the end of the war, one participant stated, "We had believed that it was all over. Yet now we knew the war would be over no time soon" (145).

By December 5, American troops left Pyongyang, abandoning "vast quantities of stores and equipment," on the heels of "11,000 casualties dead, wounded, and missing" during the first few days of the Chinese offensive (Hastings 146). The website "Military History" totals losses as follows:

> Marine losses in the campaign numbered 836 killed and 12,000 wounded. Most of the latter were frostbite injuries inflicted by the severe cold and winter weather. U.S. Army losses numbered around 2,000 killed and 1,000 wounded.

> Precise casualties for the Chinese are not known but are estimated at 35,000 killed. (Hickman)

Both Generals Almond and Walker saw their formations separated, enduring "entirely separate nightmares, divided by the central spine of North Korean mountains" (Hastings 147), although they shared "the horrors of weather, isolation, Chinese attack," and the threat of continuing disaster. In the opinion of O.P. Smith, Almond's "lust for glory" led to an impatience that Smith feared would inflict yet another disaster on his 1st Marine Division. Hastings tells of angry exchanges via men in all forces, their leaders included. Sources agree that the Marines and other UN Troops successfully conquered overwhelming odds at the Chosin Reservoir (148). As I view a video account of that horror, I'm thankful my father was not there. However, he was not having an easy time of it.

In the first of two letters that Ed wrote dated December 7, he spares no details regarding the difficult terrain:

> Well here we are in Hamhung on the east coast of Korea after a fast move south from Hysanjin. We haven't hit the Chinese yet but the 31st has and has been hit hard. Luckily the 1st Bn which Moel [/Moll] is in is OK . . . Got your letters of 21st & 23rd today and was surprised about my name in paper although some correspondent did ask my name and address. We hated to pull back but we were out on a limb. The Chinese made no move while we were there tho we watched for them all the time. We patrolled and occupied positions around Hysanjin with part of the outfit while the rest stayed inside. Due to icy roads etc we lost a lot of equipment coming down. We made a 24 hour train ride in an open gondola with snow which was almost as miserable as the prison camp train ride. However we are back in houses again and all dried out. We also made an 18 mile march on icy roads which was a bitch too.

I'm unsure about the reference to his name in the paper and have been unable to locate a copy of any such article. He adds in another intriguing passage, "Dad said Trevor showed your letter all over the campus to show true loyalty even tho overseas which makes me feel good." Whatever the details, it makes clear that the two continued to be viewed as an important couple at Knox and in Galesburg. He returns to focus on the situation in Korea, adding,

> I feel this thing will be straightened out by arbitration [*sic*] if not we have a powerful force here (7th, 3rd, 2 ROK divs) and they [Chinese and NK forces] will lose many getting here if they can get here at all. We have naval gunfire, lots of artillery and plenty of tanks & ammo. As I have said before we should not fight the Chinese.

In a second letter that he "forgot to mail," he thanks Helen first for receipt of several items: a clipping and a picture, a letter from her parents, a Knox College alum magazine, and a box of gumdrops. About the candy, he writes, "Gee honey they were wonderful. I sure thank you." I recall his list of candy made in the German Prison Camp, and I also think of Helen's gumdrop tree, which made its annual appearance at family Christmas gatherings. One has now become a part of my own holiday ritual, Ed's grandchildren and great-grandchildren alike eager to decorate it.

My father adds what he knows about the combat taking place around and near his position:

> The 7th has gotten together all right and we are setting up a defense around Hamhung here. There are fairly substantial rumors that we will evacuate by sea but nothing definite yet. The harbor is full of ships and it all seems to hinge on whether the Marines and what is left of our 31st Regt can be bailed out. The Air Force is attacking all out trying to

> blast open the road and are doing a pretty good job I guess. They are killing hundreds of Chinese but as you know there are thousands. The situation isn't good but it isn't hopeless yet. The Navy has the big MO here and many cruisers which adds [*sic*] to our firepower. We are getting a lot of our wounded back which is slowly bringing the co. back up to strength. If we have to leave we will abandon all of our vehicles & equipment which will be a staggering loss. However it could be replaced. The troops we have here will be needed to train the big army building at home.

Historic accounts of the war support Ed's description of the weather, which continued to delay progress by UN Forces. When the Marines occupied the town of Hagaru for a few weeks at the end of 1950, photos show that it resembled an Arctic mining camp that might have existed during the previous century. Hastings writes that snow covered the peasant houses and the military tents and all of its equipment, while "the local saw mill was kept in perpetual motion by the engineers," as they cut timber to use to shore positions and assist with airfield construction (151). While the men at first "marveled" at the low temperatures they could tolerate, watching the thermometer sink to minus 20 degrees Fahrenheit on some nights, they described not only slowed physical but also mental, capacity (152). Rumors of the Chinese bayoneting enemy troops in their sleeping bags made some unwilling to seek relief in a zipped bag. "Warming tents" were introduced to warm freezing arms and legs every few hours, encouraging the return of blood circulation. In addition, as Catchpole explains, the equipment was also affected by frost, ice, and winds: "At 15 degrees tank and truck radiators freeze, as did the 1950 issue anti-freeze! M-1 rifles, carbines and Browning machine-guns froze up and wouldn't fire on automatic while shells stored in the open gun limbers would solidify and even crack" (93).

One positive note about the briefly successful occupation of Hagaru was that the Americans became good friends with the small British 41 Commonwealth group, celebrating their differences. While many

Americans preferred whiskers, the British shaved regularly, believing the activity important to discipline and morale. Over time, survivors of the Seventh Division's "Task Force Faith" arrived at Hagaru, "handfuls of men stumbling, limping, even crawling. Some were without weapons. Most had lost their equipment. Many were at the extremities of frostbite" (Hastings 154), some simply walking in circles, needing to be led into the town. On November 27, General Almond had flown by helicopter to encourage the Seventh Division by telling them, "'We're going all the way to the Yalu . . . Don't let a bunch of Chinese laundrymen stop you'" (154). His staff didn't realize the extent of the losses until the remainder of the Division emerged.

Before the retreat from Chosin, General Smith's will prevailed over Almond's when he insisted on withdrawal. The 10,000 Marines of the Fifth and Seventh Divisions were said to have leapfrogged each other as they moved southward toward Hagaru, making progress a scant one yard at a time. The first units arrived at Hagaru on December 3rd, and Almond and Smith would continue to clash over plans for their troops.

General Almond flew north as far as Koto-ri on December 10, inspecting "Hungnam's port facilities and calculated that he could evacuate X Corps plus its 17,500 vehicles by December 22" (Catchpole 91). The Seventh Marines headed the evacuation and would garner ten Medals of Honor for their efforts, followed by "the heroes" of the Seventh Infantry Division and others. Almond informed refugees who wanted to join the evacuation that they would first have to "tow barrels of fuel behind their rowing boats" to deliver to the ships. According to many reports, "the evacuation was a triumph of organization and a tribute to the US Navy" (93).

Helen's collection includes an article from *Life Magazine* titled "Once More 'We Got A Hell Of A Beating'," quoting from "the late General Joe Stilwell . . . as he said of Burma in 1942." Attempting to answer the question "What had happened," the article states that "The versions became as confused as the battle-front," then summarizes activities by the U.S. Eighth Army, the X Corps, the "magnificent and battle-hardened U.S. 1st Marine Division," and the Army's 7th Division, noting that the UN troops retreated through Pyongyang. Hasting's Timeline clarifies activities during the month of December: the Eighth Army and X Corps withdrew on the first, and on the fifth, U.S./UN troops withdrew from Pyongyang, that capital city later occupied by the Chinese. By December 9, X Corps withdrew by sea from Wonsan and evacuated Hungnam on December 11 ("Once More" 347).

At first, the rest of the world paid the crisis little attention, although the article recounts British Prime Minister Attlee's plan to meet with Truman in D.C. Americans looked to Russia as the primary cause of the war, and "some took too much comfort in the knowledge of U.S. superiority in atomic weapons" (Once More 33). After seeing the overwhelmed U.S. forces, "they looked also to the home front and, with a sinking feeling, began to see that the unpreparedness of 1941 was again a threat to free America's survival" (33). As I read on, Mom's reason to clip and save this particular article becomes clear: it features the "small task force . . . with some tanks, artillery and mortars in support" and an interview with Major Carroll Cooper. Cooper's task force was from my father's U.S. 7th Division, the first to reach the Yalu at Hyesanjin on November 21. As I scan the photos, I find a Sergeant Cox holding up frozen long-johns in demonstration of the Korean frigid weather. They stand rigidly in Cox's hands, with the effect that he appears to be part of a tumbling duo.

As troops struggled in North Korea, back in the U.S., President Truman remarked during a press conference on November 20 that he would consider all military weapons in order to end the war in response to a reporter's question about the possibility of use of the atom bomb. In the wake of the media translation of his off-the-cuff reply to threaten the use of the bomb, the British House of Commons was in "uproar" and France "disquieted" as they considered the possibility of a third world war (Catchpole 97). When Prime Minister Atlee flew to the U.S. to begin a series of meetings with Truman, he quickly discovered that the Americans under no circumstances "would recognize the People's Republic of China; that it would defend the Chinese Nationalist claim to Taiwan; and would use the Seventh Fleet as a powerful deterrent in the Far East" . . . and they were not interested in "a positive, constructive approach to Chairman Mao Zedong" (97).

According to Catchpole, the Americans found an uncomfortable echo in the British proposal for "an unconditional ceasefire" of Neville Chamberlain's willingness to appease Axis forces prior to WWII (98). However, Truman and Atlee struck a "gentleman's agreement" that the U.S. would not employ the Atom bomb without first consulting with the British Prime Minister, an agreement that held when Eisenhower took office two years later. In a radio broadcast on December 15, Truman made clear to the American people, still largely ignorant as to reasons for the Korean War, the seriousness of the situation, defining "the forces of Chinese and Soviet Communism as a threat to the future of civilization" (98). He would declare a national emergency on December 16. Diplomatic exchanges heated up during the next several weeks, as Truman and his embattled Secretary of State, Dean Acheson, worked to convince members of the UN to condemn the People's Republic of China as "an 'aggressor state'" (100). Among UN members a belief in a cease-fire remained. They also believed that the Chinese People's Volunteers might withdraw "without making a settlement of the crucial questions surrounding the future of Taiwan and Korea a pre-condition of withdrawal" (100). However, neither side in Korea agreed to a cease-fire, and "on January 30, 1951 the General Assembly formally condemned China as an aggressor state" (100).

As the failed negotiations were underway, fierce engagement continued in Korea. General Walker died in a jeep accident on December 23 and would be replaced by Lieutenant General Matthew Ridgway on December 27. Ed's final letter would be dated one day later. His six December letters discuss many topics. He swings from a tone of confidence to one of insecurity regarding the military action of which he remained a part. While in Hamhung on the ninth, he wrote:

> We moved yesterday over nearer our defensive positions so that we can move out to them in a moment's notice . . . There are still lots of rumors about us leaving but nothing

> concrete yet. Think the Chinese will have a rough time getting in here. Right now a small group is reported about 20 miles away and we are watching them. Today was a clear day and the planes were out in force. We counted about 100 in an hour and a half. Yesterday we had about a foot of snow so everything is white. It is very cold and windy out tonight and I'm glad to be inside.

By December 18, his tone turns cynical:

> We were supposed to load on the ship yesterday but they postponed it 72 hrs. so I don't know what goes on. We are in a tight perimeter around Hungnam now which is the port for Hamhung. The Chinese were reported to have patrols in Hamhung yesterday. The artillery was really pouring it on them all night . . . and since we are not in Corps reserve we're right back with the artillery. We have been moving around like crazy the last few days and so far haven't fired a shot or had one fired at us. Guess the Chinese slowed down considerably due to icy roads, our air and the wild weather. I get despondent sometimes because of the way things are going. None of us feel there is any sense in fighting these people until we can get enough stuff to do some good. We are losing a lot of equipment in the evacuation and retreat and I doubt if there is much more in the states until the factories get going. The plan is to hold Pusan again and if we do, so what. Saving face I guess.

By the time he wrote again on December 21, conditions had changed for the positive. He writes that he is "in heaven," if only for a short time, aboard ship and traveling to Pusan:

> A hot shower, wash [*sic*] clothes, PX, sit down toilet etc are with us again. The ship is the Breckinridge and its [*sic*] a

> dandy. Has a snack bar, PX wonderful chow etc. It was a Navy dependent ship and thats [*sic*] why it is so nice. We are terrifically crowded with the whole 17th Inf. the 49th FA Bn and the division command group, a total of 6,000. Two men assigned to one bunk in the troop compartments. Not so good for the GIs. You would get a kick out of watching me wash my clothes in the wash bowl with Lux Flakes. Boy they were filthy. I drowned my lice in the hot shower. Boy was that wonderful. And yesterday we had strawberry shortcake for lunch and ice cream for supper. That was out of this world too.

He sobers as he adds, "I hope this rumor about the 17th being wiped out never got to you. It was out in Japan and the Red Cross was swamped with inquiries. We are still in good shape and ready to go." He spends several days on the ship, but in his final letter of December 28, conditions have changed, as he explains:

> Dad sent me a little clipping out of the Tribune about the 17th being surrounded and cut off and its [*sic*] no wonder you people were worried. We had to move like hell, a hard march, and train ride in an open gondola and snow but Able company got to Hamhung with all men and vehicles. The Chinese army doesn't even compare with ours but they do have numbers. They will pay dearly to take Korea and I'm not sure they can do it. We need a little more stuff here but we can hold I think. I sure hope we don't have to go clear back to the Yalu again. This could be another forgotten front like Italy.

As for family matters, throughout that final month, Helen continued to keep him as informed as possible, and he liberally shares his thoughts and emotions. On December 9, he wrote, "Ginger must be a dandy. Guess she is just like her mother. Glad to hear your folks are coming down for Xmas. Sure will be nice for them. Sorry you are having such a time with Kay. It will get better I'm sure." He regularly updates her on his living conditions, thanking her in that letter for sending the air mattress, adding that his group was fairly comfortable in Hamhung houses. On December 18, their anniversary, he writes to celebrate that occasion and to let her know that the ingoing and outgoing mail services stopped temporarily, but he wanted to write on that date so she would know he was thinking of her.

> Nine years ago we didn't realize what was in store for us but they have been happy years [*sic*] those that we have spent together. You have had to put up with a lot with having the kids and taking care of them by yourself a lot of the time. I wonder sometimes if I made a mistake getting in the army for your sake but I know I wouldn't be satisfied doing anything else.

This is the closest I will come to identifying a reason for my father's return to the military following WWII, stated in his own words. Introspection tells him that his decision may have been selfish in its effect on others. However, his statement that he couldn't have been satisfied in a different occupation suggests that he knew such dissatisfaction would negatively affect family and friends. By this point, his idealistic view of the military had fallen away. He could now more clearly see that the goals of the Korean War were not ones he particularly supported. Yet the larger goal of preserving liberty from the threat of Communism for those he loved, he supported whole-heartedly.

On December 21, Ed noted that he must send his happy holiday wishes from the ship, the U.S.S. *Breckinridge*, writing "hope you and the kids have a wonderful Xmas and think of pappy who would like to be with you." His December 23 letter lets Helen know that while other officers were "in town letting off steam," he preferred to indulge in writing another letter to her, a hot shower, and many hours of sleep. In Pusan, he had run into an "old golfing buddy" who was heading north as an advisor to a Dutch unit, and he also sees daily the friend he has referred to often as Voseipka. I'm struck again by how frequently my father was pulled by ties to the past while having to remain very much in the present on active duty.

Ed brags a bit about a "small" poker game in which he won the money that Helen can "salt away" for use in "the spree when we get home." His tone is tender when he writes that he hopes she received the anniversary flowers on the 18th. Then he adds, "If I get home at the end of my time here I guess I'll be lucky. I don't care for myself but I sure did want you to have that vacation in Japan while Ginger was little." He describes enjoying the best physical condition of his life, his legs especially strong from all of the mountain climbing. He adds in a particularly flirtatious mood that,

> with good arms and legs both, you would have a hard time getting away if you know what I mean. If you feel like I do I don't think you would try very hard to get away. Every night in bed I recall some of our 'best' nights together and then I hurt worse than ever.

He wishes everyone a wonderful holiday, asking Helen to "tell the kids I wish I could be there playing with them." He signs off, "I love you darling with all my heart. Your old man, Ed." I read the ominous P.S.: "moved out in hurry money order later. Love, Ed." My mother received a telegram from Ed of which I have a copy dated December 26th. It reads "Happy Christmas and New Year. Love to all the family. All well and safe. EC Roberts Jr." On the 27th of December, he writes that he spent the entire previous day picturing the kids with their toys.

I force myself to read his last letter slowly, paying particular care to its tone and information; it is the final morsel in what has served as a feast for me. Dated 28 December, it's written on U.S.S. *Breckinridge* stationery. He has received a letter from Helen letting him know that the roses—I know now they are her last to receive on an anniversary—had arrived. He writes, "I would like so much to get you lots of things but we'll wait until later. I appreciate the offer of a kiss for the roses and will take a rain check. You wouldn't get off with one kiss tho. My presents come high as you no doubt are fully aware by now . . ." Helen would receive the letter and read these words following his death. Ed then lapses into the mundane, writing about topics all couples discuss, such as insurance and a new car purchase. He closes with "My love to you and the kids and keep your chin up. Your [*sic*] wonderful and I'm proud and happy to call you my wife."

At the end of December, the Chinese Field Armies had settled on Seoul as a major objective, and when they assaulted the city in January, American troops offered little to no resistance. Ridgway's attempts to intervene "and halt the 'bug-out'" (Catchpole 101) proved ineffectual. He did succeed in organizing roadblocks as a weak resistance. MacArthur's post-Inchon-landings government fled, and South Korean President Syngman Rhee shocked UN troops by ordering the brutal murders of all his government's critics. British and Commonwealth brigades guarded roads in and out of Seoul for two days while portions "of the U.S. 1 Corps and IX Corps plus 29 Brigade passed through" (101). A January 3 Chinese attack, named Chaegunghyon after the village around which Chinese troops appeared, was met with strength by the 19th Brigade and the Royal Northumberland Fusiliers, who "held three hilltop positions just north" of the village. The Chinese proved no match for "the Northumberland's 'Fighting Fifth'," causing the British to question why "the Americans and ROKs had been unwilling to stand and fight" (102).

My father was killed on January 3, 1951. I did not learn any details about the day my father died until a few years into my research when I discovered John Carrig and the article he had written about that day. I learned from the article details that my mother never knew. In the notebook he prepared for me, Lt. Carrig included an introduction with the following paragraph:

> I found no magic or enchantment during those many months of my Korean War combat service. I did find much terror, danger, suffering, hunger, pain and death.

> My responsibility as the leader of my small platoon was both 'rudder and keel' keeping me on course during our firefights, our patrols and yes, during the inevitable periods of boredom. The readiness of my men to follow orders without question still amazes me to this day . . . My entire world during most of the Korean War was the First Rifle Platoon of Company A, 17th Infantry Regiment. I counted on them and they never let me down.
> John Thomas Carrig, Jr., Malverne, New York, 1992.

The collection includes comments about the Inchon Landings and the secret mission for Able Company to help provide security for MacArthur's staged transfer of power in Seoul to Syngman Rhee. It also includes photos of my father that I've never seen. Carrig supplies a "Synopsis of: His Last Command," published in *Army Magazine* in January 1995.

Carrig's summary relates that Company A was the last of the 1st Battalion, 17th Infantry Regiment to leave "a battalion objective in South Korea," and the final unit to join Hq, 1st Battalion at Tanyang, South Korea. They hoped to enjoy a brief rest but instead were ordered to retrace their recent route and travel back through Tanyang Pass. Captain Roberts passed the news, encouraging the battalion to remain positive. They took little comfort in the "icy cold" of some "small shacks," "firing up the under-the-floor 'central heating' system." They heard distant fire, making sleep difficult, rising "at the usual 0500 hours on 3 Jan 51." At 0800 hours, Captain Roberts and WOJG [Warrant Officer Junior Grade] Marvin Petersen left to investigate the fire, telling Carrig they would not go far. "Roberts put me in charge and told me to send out patrols as directed in our assigned mission." So later, Carrig sent a mess truck and a jeep to follow Roberts with Sgt Allen and Pfc Dillenburg. Carrig reconstructed events based on Allen's and Dillenburg's accounts:

> The C[ommanding] O[fficer]'s jeep was first and as they rounded a curve, it was taken under fire by North Korean guerrillas. Capt Roberts was wounded in his neck but I

> have no knowledge of what happened to Petersen (his body later recovered). Apparently, attackers fell back and Roberts, alone now and badly wounded, was able to start up the road toward CP.
>
> Dillenburg said that rounding a curve he saw a staggering Capt Roberts waving for him to turn the truck around. Almost immediately, there appeared several enemy who sprayed the windshield wounding Dillenburg. Sgt Allen, not hurt, jumped out and ran behind the mess truck. The enemy withdrew, probably thinking that this huge 2-1/2 ton truck might be the first of an American convoy. Dillenburg told me that he and Capt Roberts then staggered up the road trying to return to our CP. Finally, the Captain, unable to go farther, told Dillenburg to try and make it back on his own. It was then that Roberts issued his last command telling Dillenburg to "Tell Carrig to come in strength." Too late, our patrol found Roberts dead (Carrig "Captain").

As noted earlier in this account, I found online a contradictory statement that my father was returned to camp alive. I also found a note in my mother's handwriting attached to an official letter that noted Ed's instant death upon attack. She wrote that a major who later visited her told her Ed did survive for a time following his wounding. The confusion of the moment, lack of information and additional reports, makes impossible for me to know which account was true. I know that everyone making reports believed in the truth of their accounts.

I am tremendously moved by Lieutenant Carrig's efforts in assembling the notebook and in paying homage on a number of occasions to my father's memory. He includes a letter that he wrote to Ed Roberts as part of a 2006 Korean War Project. Veterans were asked to contribute to a Memorial Service by writing a letter to "a friend you can't forget" lost in battle. The letter would update that individual about "how you have lived your life." Lieutenant Carrig concludes his letter to my father, then deceased for 56 years, by writing, "Will try to touch base with you again very soon. With a sad farewell salute: to one of my best combat leaders!" (Carrig "Letters").

I return briefly to the facts of the Korean War. By January 13, the Chinese had advanced further in South Korea heading for Suwon, Osan, Ichon, and Wonju, struggling through snow and under constant fire. Catchpole describes the action as follows:

> The US 2nd Infantry Division had withdrawn across the road bridge over the Wonju River where the 3rd Platoon of Company C, the 2nd Engineer Combat Battalion, devised the most complicated destruction imaginable. Its task was to blow two substantial bridges, one road and one rail, 16 boxcars filled with high explosives and ammunition and the valuable airstrip facilities nearby. Nothing could be left for the Chinese. There were enemy troops . . . who fired at the engineers as they worked. Vast quantities of Composition C3 explosive were fitted round the piers, log cribbings and concrete supports that held up the two bridges. Fuses were set and everything exploded when the 3rd Platoon was six miles away. For several minutes night turned into day and Wonju was left as a barren shell for the Chinese 120th Division to occupy . . . the Americans fought back and did not bug out. The war was not over after all . . . (103)

By February 1951, my mother would read in *The Emporia Gazette Newspaper* about the confusion that defined UN and American troop movements in Korea during the first and second retreats. Not only was communication within the country difficult and agreement among military leaders lacking, but reporter Drew Pearson clarifies that the American public did not realize "both retreats have had an extremely bad reaction in other parts of the world. Furthermore, war stories published in Europe are frequently quite different from those published in this country—especially when it comes to the reasons for retreating and the size of the Chinese Communist army." As other reports have shown, the size of the Chinese army remained unknown. Most striking in the article is a description of "General MacArthur's own confidential dispatches to the Pentagon," which somewhat support British reports that as the Eighth Army in the first retreat "raced 120 miles southward, along with UN forces . . . the enemy had not been sighted for a week." Pearson explains that,

> During one point in the retreat of the 8th Army shortly before Christmas, MacArthur actually sent his field commander, the late Lieut. Gen. Walton Walker, a blistering cable ordering him to make contact with the enemy and be 'aggressive' about it. MacArthur even used the command 'I direct' in his message to Walker: also ordered him to 'give high priority to bringing in prisoners.'
>
> It is most unusual for a headquarters commander to give such blunt orders as 'I direct' to a field commander . . . Another significant point . . . in MacArthur's reports to Washington is that during the evacuation of the Hungnam beachhead, never were the U.N. forces attacked by any Chinese force stronger than a company.

While the Tenth Corps did fight valiantly during the withdrawal . . . "the real story of the 8th Army's retreat is not so glorious. Its difficulties were due in part to poor liaison, poor command, and to the inevitable problems which arise when troops of different nationalities are fighting side by side." Within the Second Division of the Eighth Army, "friction developed between the South Koreans and the Americans, including fist fights." The Americans were told to keep away from the South Koreans, lost contact, and did not know that the South Koreans had pulled back, exposing the Division's flank. Men panicked and ran, and suffered casualties that "amounted to over 50 per cent and caused MacArthur to cable Washington that the 2nd Division was 'unfit for duty.'" Pearson writes that the message likely carried a "double meaning—namely, that the 2nd Division was not only decimated by battle casualties but unfit for further combat duty because of bad morale."

I can only imagine the horrifying effect such information had on my mother, freshly widowed, as she wondered whether her husband fell victim to poor leadership. In light of others' characterization of Ed as an excellent and accomplished leader, such musing would have carried with it a strong and painful irony. The Korean War had ended for Captain Edmund C. Roberts, Jr. The long-term effect of his loss on his family had just begun.

- CHAPTER TEN -

"FINAL DISPOSITION"

Captian roberts was my C.O. from 1949 in Japan until his death. He was loved by all his men. He was the perfect soldier. He was killed in a ambush , along with about 15 or 20 others. They put up a very strong fight but were greatly outnumbered. It was my unpleasent task to recover the dead. Capitan Roberts lived for a few more hours after we got him back. He has remained my roll modle ever since i first met him. I was underage and received a minority discharge after the goverment found out. I have a letter from capitan Roberts mailed to my mother about my being underage. Please email me.
Sincerly Pvt John Okeefe
Korean War Project Remembrance posting (unaltered)

Capt Roberts was an excellent commander. He had Co A, 17th from about September 1950 until his death. I served as his 1st Rifle Platoon leader. On the morning of his death, the captain took WOJG [Warrant Officer Junior Grade] Marvin Petersen, his jeep driver and one KATUSA [Korean Augmentation to the United States Army] and drove from our position in Tanyang Pass going north toward the Town of Tanyang. He went to investigate probable guerrilla activity and told me that they would not drive as far as

> Tanyang. Roberts put me, the senior lieutenant, in charge with instructions to carry out the company mission: "Patrol vigorously along the ridges of Tanyang Pass." Thus, I had dispatched the three rifle platoons on that mission and had limited resources to attempt a rescue when we got the word that Roberts was pinned down. He and Petersen were dead when we found them later.
> Submitted by John Carrig
> *Korean War Project Remembrance posting* (unaltered)

> Last Thanksgiving we were talking with my grandpa about how nobody remembers Korea, and he said the only way to do it right wasn't to do a film about the war. Do a film about a kid, growing up. About the girl he falls in love with and breaks his heart and how he joins the Army . . . Then he starts a family and his first kid is born and it teaches him what it means to value life and to have something to live for and how to care for other people. And then Korea happens and he's sent over there and he's excited and scared and he wonders if he'll be courageous and he's kind of proud and then in the last sixty seconds of the film they put them in boats to go to Inchon and he's shot in the water and drowns in three feet of surf and the movie doesn't even give him a close-up, it just ends. That'd be a war film.
> From *Redeployment* by Phil Klay

My mother supplied a few details for me about the evening when she learned of my father's death. As is the traditional approach, specially appointed members of the military appeared at her house to deliver the news. My brother recalled that evening as follows:

> I turned 8 in November 1950, so in January I was 2 months into my 8th year.

> We had bunk beds in the room where I slept, down a hall from the main living room. I slept on the top bunk.
>
> Sometime late enough that we had all been put to bed and were sleeping, I woke up and heard several voices in the living room, and Mom crying. I leaned out of the bed and peered around the door jam. Mom was seated in a chair and there were about 5 people with her. I am sure Don and Ginny were there, and it is likely that Dr. Macouglin the minister from the Presbyterian Church was also, but I can't be sure.
>
> I asked, "Mommy what's wrong?"
>
> She answered, "Your Daddy is dead," and continued crying.
>
> I don't know what I felt; it wasn't sorrow—perhaps more confusion. I had not seen Ed since I was not quite 7.
>
> I probably just went back to bed and dealt with it in the morning.

Helen recalled that some friends were there playing cards, and their support proved helpful. The unfortunate truth, however, was that nothing could help her or her children in that moment. I think again of my asking how she could bear up, especially with three children to raise and of her reply that "So many women were going through it." What a terrible realization that would be, to know one had been inducted into that community, initiation achieved in such a distressing fashion.

I learn of another exclusive community that one can enter only via the military death of a loved one when I come across the term "Gold Star Mothers," a title that indicates a mother has lost a child during that child's military service. I visit the group's website and learn:

The organization was named after the Gold Star that families hung in their windows in honor of the deceased veteran. After years of planning, June 4, 1928, twenty-five mothers met in Washington, DC to establish the national organization, American Gold Star Mothers, Inc. The success of our organization continues because of the bond of mutual love, sympathy, and support of the many loyal, capable, and patriotic mothers who while sharing their grief and their pride, have channeled their time, efforts and gifts to lessening the pain of others ("Our History").

I realize that my grandmother, Muzz Roberts, had gained instant membership in this restricted group on January 3, 1951. Family shared with me that she and her husband, Dee, never fully recovered from Ed's loss. When writing to my mother shortly after Ed had been killed, she shared news and some logistical information, but in a one-line paragraph wrote, "I can't talk about Ed." The title of Gold Star Mother must be among the least coveted in existence.

The Gold Star Mother icon is impressive, the equal of any military insignia, representing a medal of loss, but also honor. The circular icon's exterior is wreathed by double-oak leaves, like the ancient corona awarded to Olympic athletes. The wreath is composed of 16 symmetric leaf pairs, suggesting the balance in life and death. The top pair slightly overlaps the one beneath. The open portion of the wreath crowns the circle; at the midpoint of its arc below the circle, a chevron appears, juxtaposed against the leaves. On a thick golden inner border appear the upper-case letters, GOLD STAR MOTHERS INC. In the middle of the circle sits a gold, patterned five-pointed star on a white background, suggesting the stars that distinguish almost all military insignia. The group's motto is "Perpetuating the Noble Principles for which They Fought and Died." Gold Star Mothers "honor through service." I doubt that my grandmother ever participated in any such service, although I could be mistaken.

On February 6, 1951, my mother received the following letter, posted to her Manhattan, Kansas address:

> My Dear Mrs. Roberts:
>
> The President has requested me to inform you that the Purple Heart has been awarded posthumously to your

husband, Captain Edmund C. Roberts Jr., Infantry, who sacrificed his life in Korea.

The medal, which you will receive in a short time, is of slight intrinsic value, but rich with the tradition for which Americans have so gallantly given their lives ever since the days of George Washington, whose profile and coat of arms adorn the medal.

Little that we can do or say will console you for the loss of your loved one. He has gone, however, in honor and in the company of patriots. Let me, in communicating to you the country's gratitude, also express to you its admiration for his valor and devotion.

Sincerely yours, Frank Pace, Jr., Secretary of the Army

The phrase "rich with the tradition" may be a comforting phrase to some readers, in its suggestion that their loved ones are not alone.

My mother would be unable to bury Ed for several months. Having been informed that his body would be temporarily interred in a Korean cemetery, she inquired a few months later about the receipt of his remains. A letter dated 8 May 1951 from the Army's Quartermaster reminds her that the Army's policy is "to comply with the wishes of the next of kin in making final disposition of remains." I won't discover until reading a personal condolence later that she considered for a time not requesting the return of Ed's remains. The letter informs her that he may be buried at any national cemetery, identifying three in the state of Arkansas. Schedules "for the return of the remains of our Korean dead are set up by the Far East Command," and when the Army receives notice that remains are ready for shipment, she will receive a telegram. "Ample time is given for the next of kin to complete any necessary personal arrangements . . . Please be assured that every effort is being made to return the remains . . . expeditiously." Helen is reminded to include in all correspondence Ed's name, rank, and serial number.

Helen selected the Little Rock National Cemetery, the closest to Pine Bluff, where she had decided to stay in the house on 25th Avenue close to Ginny and Don. The promised notice of the funeral date and time arrived by telegram on August 18. It confirmed the date as August 30 at 2 PM. She was to advise "whether or not you will attend and particular denominational services desired if you have a preference." Attendees were to cover their own travel expenses, flowers were permitted.

As I look through the florist cards in her collection, I recognize many names and groups, including the Pi Phi Alumni and the Officers and Members of the American Legion Auxiliary, Hearin-Connolly Unit No. 32. On a card from Jesse and Jane Donovan (Jesse was Ed's cousin) and Augusta (perhaps their child), Helen penciled the notation "12 roses." Another dozen roses and a spray of white carnations came from John and Louise Burns, Dean and Anne Lindstrom, Bob & Mary Mariner, Bob and Roy Howell, and John and Betty Barnstead. My mother dutifully recorded the gifts and their senders, as she would send each a handwritten thank you note. Following the funeral, an article appeared in the Galesburg paper titled "Roberts Rites Held Recently." It notes the burial was with full military honors and includes information that Ed's parents attended, along with his half-brother who traveled from New Jersey. Presiding over the service was Reverend Macouglin, pastor of Pine Bluff's First Presbyterian Church. He would soon gain tremendous importance in our lives as "Dr. Mac," along with the church community we would love and that would love us.

The reason for Helen's decision to remain in Pine Bluff rather than return to Illinois is a story that has become family mythology. It begins at a First Presbyterian Church picnic. My mother had been grappling with whether to return to Galesburg, as many of her acquaintances urged her to do. But as she explained to me later, an odd attitude toward war widows had developed. The prevailing attitude was that military wives should not have multiple children, knowing that their husbands might never return from war. I have my own opinion about the possible causes of this attitude. First, the Korean War was unpopular. Second, the need for financial support of widows and children following WWII may have turned some attitudes from compassion for those who lost a loved one to disdain for their need of public assistance. The community attitude toward Helen's children remained tantamount for my mother, as, no doubt, did her thoughts of how relationships with both sets of grandparents might develop if she relocated to Galesburg.

Tension in her story escalated. I could picture Helen on a clear day, no doubt also humid, finding a piece of shade to stand in with us, her three kids. Church picnics always supplied paper fans, but she wouldn't have had a free hand to use one. Still, she was one of those people who had the ability to fix a pleasant expression on her face. She could appear neutral, committing to neither smile nor frown. It's the type of expression that appears easy and natural but requires effort to cultivate, as I would later learn.

She would next explain to us that she had become used to hearing the inevitable inquiry about her background and her "folks"—family connections remained crucial in the South. They dictated the social level into which one might be accepted and afforded an instant boon or burden, depending upon the family's reputation. At this picnic, a woman approached her with that question and heard my mother explain the death of her husband and that she was in Pine Bluff due to her sister, Ginny Sperry. The woman paused, unhurried, gazing at me in my mother's arms and Kay and Bruce playing nearby. Reportedly, she replied, "How wonderful for you that you have your children." Our future was in large part determined by this single woman's remark, or so the satisfying tale goes. Like most stories not 100% factual, truth lingers in the details. It remains a treasured story and a simple explanation as to why I grew up in Arkansas, rather than Illinois.

In reality, my mother considered many factors in making such a momentous decision, most equally-weighted. What she needed to hear or see, from stranger or friend, was that one phrase or action that would serve as a beacon. Fate at times inflicts itself like a tornado, twisting and changing lives in an instant. But at other times, it may creep softly upon our consciousness, making its presence known in a simple and thoughtful declaration. The picnic moment would not be the last to deeply affect my mother as she sought a way forward.

I struggle to best write about the many letters of condolence and printed notices that my mother received, or retained copies of, following Ed's death. I'll cite a few of—hopefully—the most interest to readers, but also of the greatest weight in helping my mother. I'll begin with one Ed would have appreciated as a passionate golfer. He continued playing following graduation from Knox and its competitive team, competing in the Army and receiving certificates of appreciation. I refer to a copy of a brief sports column that appeared in the *Galesburg Register* titled "On the Rebound by 'Swick.'" Swick writes "with deep regret" of Ed Roberts' death in action and offers "deepest sympathy" to his family. He continues, "Ed was extremely popular at Galesburg High and Knox College, where he was golf captain in his senior year. He loved golf, and the last time the Rebound saw Ed before he went overseas was at Soangetaha [Country Club] hitting the little white ball around on the practice green . . . Ed wouldn't want any tears splashed over a paper for him. He wasn't that kind of fellow . . . He was a soldiers [*sic*] soldier."

I sort the condolences into two groups: personal and formal. Helen saved more than 60 personal notes that include repeated themes. Naturally, friends of my mother, Ed, and their parents write of shock, sorrow, an inability to find the correct words to express their grief, and also of their belief that Ed is in a better place, that perhaps there is some mistake, that the world will be safer due to sacrifices such as Ed's, regret that Helen lives so far away, a desire for her to return to Galesburg (What are your future plans? I can't imagine Galesburg without you. I know it would be a comfort to have some Galesburg friends near) and include multiple invitations for Helen to let her know how they can help.

Some refer to Ed as "Bud," his childhood nickname, and tell her of their husbands, sons, and brothers lost in WWII, lost in Korea, still in Korea. Just as her friends beckon her home to Illinois, members of Pine Bluff's First Presbyterian Church remind her of their support. For example, a woman I remember well sends her sympathy and adds, "If you plan to stay in Pine Bluff, please remember that you're among a host of friends." Ginny and Don received a similar card, declaring support for

Helen. At my vantage point decades later, I can see a community already forming to comfort Helen and her children, at that point still unknown to her. The warmth of sincerity frames all the expressions. Ed's father Dee tells her that "Each of us knows how the other feels," leaving little to say about their shared grief and its partner, exhaustion. He adds, referring to the effect of Ed's death on Galesburg, "I do know that there has never been anything that has been the shock to the community or has been more widely discussed." Another person writes, "I think you'd have to be here in Galesburg to see how it shook everyone."

Many condolences include details about Ed, such as when one woman writes, "I have remarked so many times that he was an unusual dad and seemed to have such a happy time being with his family. He was a grand fellow." Another reveals that Ed was kind to her in high school, at a time when other boys were cruel. A third writes that upon learning of Ed's death, her husband said, "Well—it would be some one [*sic*] like Ed. Ed would always be out front, showing a good example to his men, always doing his job regardless of danger or hardship. He was one of the best." That same writer then describes her belief in a parallel reality, departing from other mourners who claim relief from the knowledge of a heavenly existence for Ed. The friend references what I assume must be a member of her family who has died, as she explains, "Ed and Byron are part of that unseen world now, and one day you and I shall go to greet them, and home, and life, and death, shall dawn upon our consciousness with a far greater degree of understanding than we can now grasp."

Those who know Helen more intimately offer words of encouragement and/or concern. A friend named Fran writes of her shock over the news, adding, "Hardly a day has passed since we have been in the Army that I haven't thought of you . . . And, Helen, you are such a plucky person and have always been able to adjust yourself to any condition that I know how bravely you must be enduring your great loss." Another reminds her to "keep your chin up," one of Ed's favorite admonitions in his letters to her. One friend reminds her of a conversation in which they had agreed on their good fortune to have "such wonderful guys to love. That is something . . . no one can ever take away. I read an article one time that said a separation is like two persons going home to meet after a long parting but one of you takes one route and the other takes another. It may take a while but you can still be together in thought . . . Nothing can destroy love." Yet another begins, "You know what? I remember a Helen Kost who had a terrific will, and a true zest for living. She is a gal who will show this tough old world what courage really is. Can you keep saying to yourself, 'How am I doing Ed' and make him proud of you?" From another friend in a Valentine's Day card, I'm surprised to discover that my mother must have debated on whether to bring Ed's body to the states for burial, apparently based on information Ed must have shared with her separate from any correspondence that I discovered. The letter contains stronger advice than others, as her friend writes that she was glad to receive Helen's letter:

> However, it didn't sound like you. I know you feel cynical about circumstances—so does everyone when adversity strikes them. But don't let it leave you cold, as your letter sounds. You've all the right and cause in the world to be broken hearted . . . I know the insiduousness [*sic*] of grief—you don't need to pretend, to me, you know. I remembered that you said Ed had said he would not want to be brought back—but I thought his mother would want it. The final word would rest with you and I didn't want you to be persuaded to agree to something that would hurt you all over again. It would upset the kids too. As it is, it will be realized by them so gradually that it will all be like a dream.

One letter is from her insurance agent making clear that he will take care of filing Ed's life insurance claim. A second is on stationery bearing the embossed words "HOWE-ANDERSON BAKERY," dated February 21, 1951. The Howes write, "We took care of the birthday cake for your dad. Tiny delivered it yesterday. Please accept the cake this time as a present from me. Next year you can pay. But this time it's on me." They had wanted to express their sympathy but "were at a loss for words." This gesture allowed the Howes to assist Helen and her family from afar, as so many wished they could.

The most painful letter to read is dated January 23. It begins, "Was surely glad to get your note, and relieved to hear that Ed got to Hamhung all right—do you know where he is now?" She then adds detail about her own husband's experience in Korea and the hope the men will be home soon. She continues, "Now let me hear all about you all, and your latest news from Ed," closing with, "Wish we could get together—I need a shoulder to cry on once in a while with someone who understands." I find a later note from her in which she expresses with obvious regret "how badly my letter must have made you feel." She adds that she's never known a "finer person than Ed." Her husband, still in Korea, "respected him and sought his advice on many occasions as you well know. I dread writing Miles of Ed's death—he will be more bitter than ever, and for good reason."

My mother understood her friend's point about the helpful nature of sharing with those immersed in a similar experience. She would later do just that, as evidenced by a letter dated April 25, 1952 from James A. Van Fleet, General, U.S. Army Commanding (commander of the Eighth Army). He informs her that her "kind letter of sympathetic understanding and hope for my son missing in action is deeply appreciated. It brings tears of grief, both for your husband and my boy, and then comfort. We both comprehend and stand together. Your message helps Mrs. Van Fleet and me to bear up and keep our hopes high for our boy's safe return." My research of General Van Fleet reveals that after a highly-decorated military career, he continued service to his country as a diplomat, retired to ranching, and lived to be more than 100 years old. I read that his only son, a bomber pilot, was killed in Korea. I also carefully preserve another item in the collection, the envelope returned to Helen, a slash over Ed's name and address, with the hand-stamp "deceased" across it. Tears, then comfort—two linked reactions suffered by many during wartime.

Life happens, as it were, out of sync with human awareness. Time and space bind tightly our limits to understanding, but we eventually adjust as we must. If fortunate, we have assistance along the way to that adjustment. Time grows telescopic, or it may contract, producing a microscopic perspective, resulting from each individual's chosen point of view. It is in that choice of perspective that we gain a modicum of power over our environment.

I read a stack of letters from my maternal grandfather, John Kost and grandmother Elsie Kost to Helen. During her time of grief and thought about her transition, Helen carefully preserved a *Galesburg Register* blurb about her parents' golden anniversary. As it notes details of the lengthy marriage of the Kosts, the brief article includes Helen's war-widow status, placing Ed's name again before its readers, and not for the last time. The Kost anniversary was not celebrated publicly in the traditional manner, due to "a recent death in the family." Helen's father, every inch the attorney, covers all legal matters for his baby daughter, no doubt of immense help to her, his technical knowledge bridging one gap between emotion and reality for my mother. He is tender and commanding by turns, and to my surprise, much more expressive than my Grandmother Elsie.

As I consider this rhetorical tendency and recall what I learned about my grandmother from the years I was able to know her following her husband's death, my surprise is tempered. Unlike her husband, Elsie did not enjoy an extensive formal education, which may have worked to my benefit as a child. Never verbose, stern but not taciturn, my grandmother allowed me an escape from the adult direction and pronouncements to which I was accustomed. Thus, I often pedaled my bicycle to her small Pine Bluff duplex; she had relocated from Galesburg following her husband's death. In addition to her lack of judgment on my character flaws, many rewards awaited me, from the soft cookies she always kept on hand to what seemed at the time an enormously high bed, ready-made for my short legs to clamber up. Her silence spoke strength and something else, perhaps a tenderness not obvious to a quick glance that beheld her German forbearance. In the correspondence to my mother, I find a poem dedicated to Elsie, written by her husband three years after Ed's death. The poem's first line makes the occasion clear: "Fifty three years we have trod together." The final lines of the untitled poem's three verses read: "Basking in the twilight of life / With our children and loved ones dear, / Ever remembering to follow the right / We have nothing whatever to fear."

My mother could not choose a long life for her husband. What she could choose was whether to look forward or backward following his death. One view would propel her through her own long life, while the other would certainly have paralyzed her, rendering impossible the life her children would be able to enjoy. Fortunately, she had support from two excellent fronts in making that choice. The first was the example of her parents and their determination to "follow the right." However, in a world where we mostly take for granted all that is exceptional about our parents, Helen likely adapted them as role models in a manner more unconscious than conscious. The second was a letter of condolence striking in its simplicity and its heart, written by the doctor who had delivered her first child, my brother Bruce. Excitement replaced my sorrow as I read his words and understood that they may have provided her a flight plan. And as is often true regarding parental experience, I immediately find application to my own circumstances.

Helen has stapled a note to the letter explaining that Ralph Bell stood "6 ft 7 ins," a fact I'd heard multiple times during the story of Bruce's birth. The note tells me that he was a civilian obstetrician but served as the medical officer in Ed's battalion at Camp Roberts. Dr. Bell's letter reveals that he and his wife had a close relationship with Helen and Ed; for whatever reason, the young couple had captured their attention. Dated June 4, 1951, the letter opens with the remark that "Betty Jo and I have given a great deal of thought to your letter," and as in so many instances, I'm left to imagine the contents of my mother's letter to which he refers. This one would have contained the news of Ed's death. I don't know whether Dr. Bell reacted to her specific remarks or simply instinctively knew what to tell her. His next paragraph is practical, reflecting that they knew Ed "might not have been entirely safe" and that "we knew enough about him to feel that his personal safety might be disregarded if the moment seemed to him to call for direct exposure, and I'm quite able to understand just how it happened." He refers to the "unfortunate" timing that led Ed to that specific situation in North Korea, comparing it to the timing of his being stationed directly where the Battle of the Bulge would occur during the previous war.

I am stunned by what follows and feel compelled to include verbatim the majority of the message. I feel confident that Dr. Bell's words, written at a distance now of more than 60 years, could help others during any era as they face a choice vital to their futures. He made clear that Helen *could* move forward, tentatively test the unknown, and assemble a firm foundation—action as hard as hell with success not guaranteed—or she could structure her future on insubstantial yearnings yoked to her past—a simple and mindless activity, leading to sure failure. Dr. Bell wrote:

> Just recently I heard a lecturer say that it was unfortunate indeed, that we looked at the end of the road as we did. He mentioned a number of races, primitive ones for the most part, who looked at death as the opening to a better life, one in which all the troubles of this world are forgotten and everlasting joy is life. And when we come right down to it, we do really know that Ed is not suffering and that most of our grief, in fact practically all of it, stems from the fact that we who are left hated for him to leave us behind. That's the selfish part of love, the part we exact from those who love us and are loved in return. A few months ago, you were a fortunate girl with a lovely family and a devoted husband; now you are one of a group of war widows with a family to look after. If you keep the plans you had when Ed was alive you are sure to run into frustration and misery. But look back a moment and see how you used to handle problems.
>
> At one time you would not have been overwhelmed by the necessity of a change in your entire future outlook, and now, whether or not you wish it to be so, you have to change or fail to see facts. To live with Ed, you have to live in memories—the past—and that is good only for moments. You are young and must look ahead, not backwards. Having a bunch of kids makes your problem no easier, but neither does it

preclude a satisfactory solution. Time is one of the dimensions of life, and actually, Ed is as available to you right this minute as he was six months ago. The main difference is that you know that he will not return. But knowing that your lives together were happy, there should be no regrets for the past, and I'm pretty sure that it is the things the future cannot bring that troubles you now.

It's relatively easy for someone to sit a thousand miles away and tell you what to do, or how to feel. I don't mean to do that exactly, but I feel that I should urge you to accept the inevitable and resolve to make a good future out of what is trying to cloud every view you have. Because you can't ever have a home with Ed again, doesn't mean that you can never have a home of your own. It may not happen—you may remain a widow the rest of your life, but that is not a certain event by any means. If you think the thought of a home with someone else in place of Ed is a horrible thought, just reflect for a moment and ask yourself, "What would Ed have wanted me to do, or what did he tell me he wanted me to do in such a case?" Please don't think I'm trying to be the silver lining to your dark cloud, for I know something about the futility of reaching the depth of sorrow under these circumstances.

And like a person surveying his loss after a fire or storm, you've got to take stock of what's left—not what you lost. Time or energy spent in mourning is lost to everyone. The things you said and did are the things that count. When the accounts are closed, nothing new can be added, it's only a matter of adding up the score. And in your case, I think you'll agree that you have a good deal to be happy about.

Ed died in his chosen profession, doing the things he believed in and fought for. We have no reason to be sorry for that. We think he could have been with us a lot longer, but just as we had nothing to do with his appearance on

> this earth; so we have not been consulted in his leaving. It is only his stay here that we were permitted to influence. I think you did a lot to make him happy, and more than that no one can expect to do. We shall miss him, not like you do, but he will be missed by many people, most of whom you and I shall never know.
>
> So, it is up to you, and those who are always left behind, to rise again to new heights, unhampered by memories that impede progress or spoil the present and future. If love and confidence in you will help, then you should feel noticeably better after reading this.

I can, as in so many instances, not comprehend the precise effect these words had on my mother. However, because I know her well, I surmise that after the hundreds, probably thousands, of words of condolence, sympathy, loving advice and admonishment that follow such a loss as Helen's, Dr. Bell's words would have keyed a different reception. They supplied a lifeline to rationality, gave her permission to get on with things, indeed, *directed* her to do so.

I clearly recall my mother's frequent "visits" to me shortly after her death, experiences that many in recent bereavement have described. In one vivid dream, I told my mother in a perhaps clichéd but earnest declaration, "I can't do all that I need to without you." Then I heard her response as clearly as if she were standing beside my bed. "Yes you can, because that's the way I raised you."

Helen lived decades beyond Ed. She raised his children to "follow the right" and taught me that we can at the most influence only the moment at hand through our reaction to life's challenges. Despite my parents' shared love of lists and planning and dreaming of what might be, they knew those pleasurable exercises occupy an important, but not resolute, position in the messy business of life.

I know now that what I have missed all these years are memories of Ed Roberts. I hadn't known him to miss him, I instead take a moment each day to call up a remembrance, to hold in my mind the treasure he gifted to others. And he *had* been known—as Dr. Bell remarked, by many people of whom my mother would never even be aware. That included not only those who shared a close relationship with him, but also those lightly touched by his presence. No doubt Ed Roberts appears in photos that exist in treasured personal collections; some in possession of the photos can identify him, others cannot. He abides, with or without a name, in stories told around holiday tables in various U.S. states, in war mythology in Belgrade, or St. Vith, or Hammelburg, or Pusan, Seoul, or Hamhung, stories emerging at odd, unpredictable moments. People note his name while walking a cemetery, in the Knox College and other Korean War exhibits, and more generally in the bronze faces of the Korean War Memorial in Washington D. C. Like all of us, he is a spark in history's light, shining brighter than some, less bright than others. And if I must spend time thinking about how he died, I can think with some confidence, not about whether or for how long he lived beyond his wound, whether he was in pain, felt sorrow or anger, had thoughts of me and others in his family, but rather that he believed that because he died, another person would not.

Thus, I face the end of my project, my metaphorical suitcase more filled than when I began, the original possessions liberally replaced. Where I began with questions—some admittedly petulant and naive, some divisive, most with rational intent—I depart with few definitive answers. However, I now possess a long list of recognized gifts from both of my parents. Although I thought I did not know my father when I began this journey, I realize many years and hundreds of pages later that I knew him all along. I may have lacked a specific memory to call to mind, but I knew him through my talents, my strengths, and weaknesses, and through his influence on my mother, an influence that surely must be strong within his daughter, as Helen passed along much to me. I have always had access to Ed Roberts, as he is a real and intimate presence in my biological being, my DNA coding, of course, but also deep in my psyche. Like sound waves that broadly warp through space from a single cry, his story and its effect ripple through time. I echo his cry, as do my grandchildren, as will their own. That inheritance is what I claim at last in gratitude, with clear recognition of its value.

- EPILOGUE -

BY SHANDRA MEREDITH

HELEN'S LEGS

SEPTEMBER 27, 1950

Captain Edmund C. Roberts wrote to his wife from Korea, "We have had little action except snipers and they are lousy shots."

Helen Roberts, encouraged by the letter and several others that outlined dreams and plans for Ed's return home, continued raising their three children and waiting for the time when she could join him on base. After all, he'd escaped a World War II prison camp.

JANUARY 3, 1951

Captain Roberts was shot and killed by snipers. His wife, Helen, heard the news seven days later. Later, the thirty-year-old widow accepted a job in a physician's office, working for free in exchange for healthcare for her 8 year old, 4 year old, and 8 month old children. Desperate for control within her devastation, she assembled a steely realism and unflinching logic that harbored her for the rest of her life.

APRIL 7, 1961

Helen's third child celebrated her eleventh birthday. The young girl's birthday party included her older sister, who'd once been tied to a wagon full of bricks by her mother, so that she couldn't run away again, her older brother, who was already showing signs of his mother's logic and reason, her stepfather Bob, who'd assumed the role of "dad" six years before, and a new half-sister, who sported the flaming red hair that her siblings managed not to inherit from their grandmother.

MAY 23, 1978

Helen's daughter looked down at her own newborn daughter and told her, "you may not be a pretty girl, but we'll love you anyway." My mother regretted reporting this to that particular daughter, me, twenty-three years later when she, through squinty eyes and pursed lips recalled the saga of Jimmy Duffs. Jimmy Duffs was my mother's strange little fat adoring nemesis throughout high school. He ran into her step-dad, Bob, outside Pine Bluff Arkansas' Presbyterian Church one day. "Aren't you Ginger Roberts' dad? . . . She was so beautiful." Bob reported this to his wife Helen with a chuckle. She looked at him matter-of-factly and said, "Oh . . . no . . . she was never beautiful . . . cute and full of pep, though!" I couldn't resist facing my mother's hot dignity with a friendly reminder of the little speech she'd delivered over my first few breaths. "Oh silly, "she sputtered, "it was only because your sister was so beautiful and then you just looked like a regular baby . . ."

NOVEMBER 15, 1988

In . . . Joplin magazine's essay winner, Ginger Meredith, my mother, saw her essay in print for the first time. The essay was titled "Uncommon Heroes" and told the story of her mother and father, Helen and Edmund Roberts, as told to her through her father's war correspondence and her mother's memories. She followed the win with a successful writing career as Virginia Brackett—her given first name and second husband's last name. When my mother gave me a copy of the magazine, I kept it, boasted to all of my friends about it, then proudly displayed it on the coffee table when I moved into my first apartment, but I don't remember ever reading it. I didn't know it was important. Several years later I would realize that it was important for nothing more than the fact that my mother wrote it, and a few years after that I would realize all the other reasons it was important.

JANUARY 10, 1995

I remember five very distinct scenes about my grandmother; playing Boggle in her kitchen; sitting at her Thanksgiving table with her china cabinet on the opposite wall; her telling my mortified sister that we don't wrap maxi pads in toilet paper because it is wasteful ("we wrap them in old newspaper"); attending her summer water aerobics class; and looking at the living room of the assisted-living home she checked herself into. She didn't want her children to have to sell her house.

Most of my memories of my grandmother are like those I attach to a favorite childhood book. The memory is a feeling, one big general awareness; I know I am fond of it and I recognize the space it occupied in my life, but if someone asks about a certain page featuring a particular character, I keep just seeing the cover of the book.

JUNE 14, 1996

After outliving the oncologist's prediction by eleven years, my grandmother Helen died. I wasn't there, nor did I go to her funeral. My parents had an ugly divorce and my father wouldn't let me take his car, "to go see your mother." I'm sure he regrets that as much as I regret not stealing the car.

I didn't cry when my mom called and told me my grandmother died. I didn't know her well enough to cry. I did get out an old thank-you letter I'd written her after Christmas one year, but forgot to send; I don't know why I keep these things. I was sad, looking at it then, but the memory of the unsent note wretchedly clogged my chest later when my mother told me how much joy Grandma took in "first class" mail, what she called letters with real stamps. I probably wrote my grandmother fifteen letters in my whole life, including the one she never got. I didn't know she needed them.

OCTOBER 20, 2000

I wrote a poem about my memories of my mother reaching back from the front seat to squeeze my hand every time we were both in the car. Her small gesture remains in the back of my mind. She told me once that her mother didn't show affection or need and wasn't very romantic with her second husband. I nodded as she spoke, thinking, "yep that sounds like Grandma."

Later, my mother decided to do another project centered on the letters that her father, who she had never known, Edmund, wrote to her mother, and asked me to type them out for her, so they could be more easily handled. When I came across one letter where Ed hinted to his wife that he couldn't wait to get back and get her into bed, my jaw dropped and I gasped, "Grandma!" It only then occurred to me that Edmund's Helen, and my mother's mother, and my grandmother might exist separate from each other.

An Internet blurb about Degas, said of the painter's work, "On the one hand, he's trying to capture the fleeting impression of movement. On the other, he's systematically arranging images and creating things from his memory—not directly from the impression."

FEBRUARY 4, 2002

Six years after my grandmother died, I read the chapter of my mother's book describing the night she succumbed to cancer. It was titled, "Putting the Flowers In." I paused when I read the seventh paragraph on page 141. "When I reply, she lifts herself up on her elbows, leaning toward me. Thinking she wants the ice, I place a hand behind her head for support, and move close. But she doesn't put her lips to the glass rim. She lays her head, just for a moment, on my chest." I stopped reading two paragraphs later, when Grandma's fluttering breath stopped, and I cried longer than I've ever cried before. Suddenly she didn't have her own space in life; her space enveloped mine, and I wished I wrapped it around myself while she still breathed there.

FEBRUARY 5, 2002

I read "Putting the Flowers In" again. I recognized my grandmother in the passage describing her response to a nurse's inquiry about the intensity level of her pain. The nurse asked her to rate the pain on a scale of one to ten and my grandmother, suffering from unidentified liver cancer, while she was vomiting tissue, replied, "seven," because she was, "raised not to complain." The chapter closes with my mother's description of a dream she had after her mother died. My mother told her that she musn't die because she couldn't do what she needed to do without her. She heard my grandmother reply, "Oh yes you will, because that's how I raised you." My mother heard the words so clearly that they jerked her from a deep sleep. I can't even remember my grandmother's voice. But I'm learning what she did with it; my mother and my grandfather are teaching me.

OCTOBER 20, 1950

My grandfather, Captain Edmund C. Roberts wrote to my grandmother, his wife, in response to recently mailed family pictures, "I see my girl's still got her pretty legs." I had a boyfriend who always liked to talk about my "hot little stems." I think I must have Helen's legs.

BIBLIOGRAPHY

CHAPTER ONE: "SUCH FINE MEN"

Carrig, John. "His Last Command." *Army*, January 1995, 45-47.

———."I Knew Him." *Korean War Project Remembrance*, 2017, www.koreanwar.org/html/korean_war_project_remembrance_2011.html. Accessed 15 June 2006.

Magner, James E., Jr. "Repository." *Poems of the Korean War: the Hermit Kingdom.* Edited by Paul M. Edwards, Center for the Study of the Korean War, 1995. 43.

O'Brien, Tim. *The Things They Carried.* 1990. Mariner, 2009.

"Organization, Equipment and Tactical Employment of Separate Tank Battalions." *Xenophon Group International*, n.d. www.xenophon-mil.org/milhist/usarmy/boardreports/generalboardtankbattalions.htm. Accessed 15 Sept 2016.

Rasmus, Robert. "A Chance Encounter." *The Good War: an Oral History of World War Two*. Studs Terkel, editor. Pantheon, 1984.

Trueman, Duncan, Dr. Chaplain. "Chaplain's Message." *The Cub of the Golden Lion*, Jan-Feb-Mar 2007, vol. 63, no.2, p2.

CHAPTER TWO: "A THOUSAND DELIGHTS"

"Alma Archer Fox; Former Fashion, Style Columnist." *LA Times*, 24 Mar 1988, 2017, articles.latimes.com/1988-03-24/news/mn-55_1_alma-archer-fox. Accessed 20 September 2006.

"Camp Highlands." www.camphighlands.com/. Accessed 13 April 2009.

Dickinson, Emily. "Tell all the Truth." *Poetry Foundation*, 2017, www.poetryfoundation.org/poems/56824/tell-all-the-truth-but-tell-it-slant-1263. Accessed 15 October 2014.

"New York Times." *New York Times Archive.* 22 June 1941, www.nytimes.com/search?query=Archives. Accessed 12 July 2012.

"Pollyanna." *Revolvy*, 2013, www.revolvy.com/topic/Pollyanna. Accessed 15 May 2013.

CHAPTER THREE: AN APPRECIATION OF PARTICULARS

"November 1941." *Ibiblio*, www.ibiblio.org/pha/timeline/4111int.html.

"No Place Like Home." *Steppenwolf Theater*, 2017, https://www.steppenwolf.org/tickets--events/seasons/200203/no-place-like-home/. Accessed 10 April 2009.

CHAPTER FIVE: THEIR OWN STORIES

Carver, Dale. *The Cub of the Golden Lion*, Jan-Feb-Mar 2002, vol. 58, no. 2, p. 6.

Dailey, Hampton J. "How My Marriage Came About Because of the Battle of the Bulge." *The Cub of the Golden Lion*, Oct-Nov-Dec 1990, vol. 47, no. 1, p. 36.

Hogan, Terry. "Those Were the Days." *The Zephyr Online*, 4 Apr. 2001, www.thezephyr.com/backtrack/TWTD.htm. Accessed 15 February 2012.

"Kenneth Albert Koyen." *Thewesterlysun.com.* 25 July 2007, www.legacy.com/obituaries/thewesterlysun/obituary.aspx?n=kenneth-albert-koyen&pid=91398677&#sthash.T71SPpyi.dpuf. Accessed 15 Oct. 2010.

Koyen, Kenneth. "General Patton's Mistake." *Saturday Evening Post*, 1 May 1948, vol. 220, no. 44, p18.

"Lt. E.C. ROBERTS is missing in European War." *Daily Register-Mail*, 12 Jan. 1945, 2.

Schaffner, John R. *The Cub of the Golden Lion*, May-August 2011, vol. 67, no. 2, p 10.

Sheaner, Herb. "Memorial to 'The Last Five Hundred Men'." *The Cub of the Golden Lion*, Jan - Apr 2012, vol. 68, no. 2, pp. 27-28.

Strand, William. "Bulge Battle – Proud Chapter in U.S. History; GI Courage Routs Hitler Bid for Victory." *Chicago Tribune*, 14 Jan. 1947, archives.chicagotribune.com/1947/01/1947/01/10/page/4/article/bulge-battle-proud-chapter-in-u-s-history. Accessed 15 June 2009.

CHAPTER SIX: "THE REAL DIRTY BUSINESS"

Bell, Anne Olivier, ed. *The Diary of Virginia Woolf: Volume Five, 1936–41.* New York: Harcourt Brace Jovanovich, 1984.

"Ruined St. Vith Regained at Low Cost to Yanks." *Chicago Daily Tribune*, 25 Jan 1945, n.p.

CHAPTER SEVEN: "ALL THE ADVANTAGE AFFORDED BY HINDSIGHT"

Brocato, Joseph E. "An Array of the Medals." *The Military Order of the World Wars*, Mar. 2011, www.mowwvandenberg.org/MedalsPage.htm. Accessed 22 Oct. 2012.

Callahan, Maureen. "The true story behind the iconic V-J Day sailor and 'nurse' smooch." *NYPost*, 17 June 2012, nypost.com/2012/06/17/the-true-story-behind-the-iconic-v-j-day-sailor-and-nurse-smooch/. Accessed 20 Dec. 2015.

Hiltbrand, Walter. "Condemns Dark December." *The Cub of the Golden Lion*, vol. 5, no.2, April-May 1949, np.

"Joyce Kilmer." *The Poetry Foundation*, www.poetryfoundation.org/poets/joyce-kilmer. Accessed 20 Dec. 2015.

"List Yanks Released From Nazis." *Chicago Daily News*, 7 May 1945, n.p.

Merriam, Robert E. *Dark December: The Full Account of the Battle of the Bulge*. New York: Ziff Davis, 1947.

Personal Correspondence. 1 Dec. 1947.

"Robert E. Merriam." *Chicago Tribune*, 26 Aug. 1988, www.chicagotribune.com/news/ct-xpm-1988-08-27-8801250908-story.html. Accessed 20 June 2012.

Walker, Jack Dixon. Letter to the Author. 2006.

"What They Are Saying." *The Cub of the Golden Lion*, vol.3, no.3, Oct. 1946, n.p.

CHAPTER EIGHT: "THE UNHAPPY PENNISULA"

Bearden, Russel E. "Pine Bluff Arsenal." *CALS Encyclopedia of Arkansas*, 2006, encyclopediaofarkansas.net/entries/pine-bluff-arsenal-2927/. Accessed 23 Feb. 2011.

"But What Comes Next in Korea?" *Life Magazine*, 9 Oct. 1950, p.38.

Catchpole, Brian. *The Korean War: 1950-53*. New York: Carroll & Graf Publishers, Inc., 2000

Gruenberg, Leif A. *Defining Moments: The Korean War.* Detroit: Omnigraphics Inc., 2012.

Hastings, Max. *The Korean War*. New York: Simon and Schuster, 1987.

Joel, Billy. "Leningrad." *Storm Front*, Universal Music Publishing Group, 1989, www.billyjoel.com/song/leningrad-5/.

Klay, Phil. *Redeployment*. Penguin, 2014.

"Korean War." *Encyclopedia Britannica*, www.britannica.com/event/Korean-War/media/1/322419/70868. Accessed 17 May 2015.

"Korean War." *History.com*, 9 Nov 2009, www.history.com/topics/korea/korean-war. Accessed 23 Jul. 2011.

"Seoul and Victory: Record of How South Korea Was Retaken By U.S. Marines." *Life Magazine*, 9 Oct. 1950, pp.29-31.

Truman, Harry S., President. George M. Elsey papers, Harry S. Truman Presidential Library, 27 June 1950.

CHAPTER NINE: COME IN STRENGTH

Carrig, John. "Captain Edmund Condon Roberts." Received by Virginia Brackett. 25 Nov. 2006.

———. "His Last Command." *Army*, Jan. 1995, 45-47.

———. "Letters to the Lost." *Korean War Project*, 11 Nov. 2006, www.koreanwar.org/html/letters_to_the_lost_from_korea.html?letters=125. Accessed 1 Dec. 2007.

Catchpole, Brian. *The Korean War: 1950-53*. New York: Carroll & Graf Publishers, Inc., 2000

Gruenberg, Leif. *The Korean War*. Detroit, MI: Omnigraphics, Inc., 2004.

Hastings, Max. *The Korean War*. New York: Simon and Schuster, 1987.

Hickman, Kennedy. "Korean War: Battle of Chosin Reservoir," *Thought Co.*, 28 April 2017, militaryhistory.about.com/od/battleswars1900s/p/chosin.htm. Accessed 1 June 2017.

"Once More 'We Got A Hell Of A Beating'." *Life Magazine*, 11 Dec. 1950, p. 347.

Pearson, Drew. "Washington Merry-Go-Round." *The Emporia Gazette*, 11 Jan. 1951, p.4. newspaperarchive.com/emporia-gazette-jan-11-1951-p-3/. Accessed 15 Feb. 2012.

CHAPTER TEN: "FINAL DISPOSITION"

Carrig, John. *Korean War Project Remembrance*, 2007, www.koreanwar.org/html/korean_war_project_remembrance_2011.html. Accessed 15 June 2006.

Klay, Phil. *Redeployment*. New York: Penguin, 2014.

O'Keefe, John. *Korean War Project Remembrance*. 2012. www.koreanwar.org/html/korean_war_project_remembrance_2011.html. Accessed 10 October 2012.

"Our History: Then and Now . . ." *American Gold Star Mothers, Inc.*, www.goldstarmoms.com/our-history.html. Accessed 15 Mar. 2015.

ACKNOWLEDGEMENTS

Many individuals deserve acknowledgement for their support as I wrote this book. First and foremost are my family members—my husband, Edmund, siblings Kay and Bruce, and my children Lisa, Wade, and Shandra—as well as my friend Veda Jones. They served as patient proof readers, enthusiastic contributors, and provided encouragement during years of my working at a daunting task. Next, sincerest gratitude and appreciation go to the many servicemen, especially Frank Trautman and John Carrig, and their family members who spoke with, corresponded with, and broke bread with me, engendering my special admiration for their dedication to one another and their vital shared experience.

I am appreciative of the Knox College Alumni Office and the University of Chicago rare documents librarians for their invaluable assistance. I also want to thank Park University for awarding me a faculty research grant supporting early years of my investigation and my Honors students who transcribed personal correspondence for simpler access as I wrote. They also asked excellent questions. I'm grateful to my faculty peers who encouraged my work on this project and to Professor Dennis Okerstom specifically, who seemed always to know the correct moment to step into my office and ask, "How's it going?" Finally, I thank Sunbury Press for bringing my 15 years of research and writing to the public page.

ABOUT THE AUTHOR

VIRGINIA BRACKETT, Professor Emeritus of English, retired in 2016 from Park University where she received varied teaching and service awards, including Faculty of the Year, 2013, Exceptional Services to Student Veterans. She served as a discussion facilitator for the 2017 NEH-funded initiative for veterans and their families, Planting the Oar, and as a member of the Kansas City Veterans Writing Team, presents writing workshops for veterans and their families. Her fiction placed second in the fall 2018 Owl Canyon Hackathon and was a finalist in the 2019 William Penn Foundation Early Childhood Book Challenge. Citations for her 15 books include *The Facts on File Companion to 16th and 17th-Century British Poetry* named Booklist "Editor's Choice, Reference Sources, 2008"; *Restless Genius: The Story of Virginia Woolf* (2004), a recommended feminist book for youth by the Amelia Bloomer Project, 2005 (Feminist Task Force, American Library Association), PSLA (Pennsylvania State Library Association) YA Top Forty Nonfiction 2004 Titles, and "Writers of Imagination" series, Tristate Series of Note, 2005 and *A Home in the Heart: The Story of Sandra Cisneros* (2004), included in PSLA YA Top Forty Nonfiction 2004 Titles and Tristate Books of Note, 2005. Her articles have appeared in *War, Literature & the Arts; Selected Papers from the Eighteenth Annual Conference on Virginia Woolf; The Wildean; Mosaic; Arachne; Women & Language; Notes and Queries;* and *Absolutism and the Scientific Revolution 1600-1720.* Electronic books include *Angela and the Gray Mare* (children) and *Girl Murders*, a time-travel mystery, available at amazon.com.

Made in the USA
Monee, IL
17 February 2020

21887067R00180